GLOBAL FAMILIES

*To Br. Patrick Se-
One of the people
whose work continues
to inspire and motivate me.*

[signature: Meg Wilkes Karraker]

Meg Wilkes Karraker
University of St. Thomas

Volume Two in the Series
Families in the Twenty-First Century

General Editor
Susan J. Ferguson
Grinnell College

Boston   New York   San Francisco
Mexico City   Montreal   Toronto   London   Madrid   Munich   Paris
Hong Kong   Singapore   Tokyo   Cape Town   Sydney

Executive Editor: Jeff Lasser
Series Editorial Assistant: Lauren Houlihan
Senior Marketing Manager: Kelly M. May
Production Supervisor: Roberta Sherman
Editorial–Production Services and Electronic Composition: GGS Book Services
Photography Editor: Mark E. Jensen
Composition Buyer: Linda Cox
Manufacturing Buyer: Debbie Rossi
Cover Administrator: Elena Sidorova

For related titles and support materials, visit our online catalog at www.ablongman.com.

Between the time website information is gathered and then published, it is not unusual for some sites to have closed. Also, the transcription of URLs can result in typographical errors. The publisher would appreciate notification where these errors occur so that they may be corrected in subsequent editions.

ISBN-10: 0-205-50323-3

Library of Congress Cataloging-in-Publication Data
    Global families / by Meg Wilkes Karraker.
        p. cm.—(Families in the twenty-first century; 2)
    Includes bibliographical references and index.
    ISBN: 978-0-205-50323-0 (pbk.)
    1. Family—Study and teaching. I. Karraker, Meg Wilkes.

    HQ10.G52 2008
    306.8509—dc22   2007028569

Printed in the United States of America

10 9 8 7 6 5 4 3 2 1   11 10 09 08 07

Contents

FAMILIES IN THE TWENTY-FIRST CENTURY

The family is one of the most private and pervasive social institutions in U.S. society. At the same time, public discussions and debates about the institution of the family persist. Some scholars and public figures claim that the family is declining or dying, or that the contemporary family is morally deficient. Other scholars argue that the family is caught in the larger culture wars currently taking place in the United States. Regardless of one's perspective that the family is declining or caught in broader political struggles, family scholars are working to address important questions about the family, such as, what is the future of marriage? Is divorce harmful to individuals, to the institution of the family, or to society? Why are rates of family violence so high? Are we living in a post-dating culture? How does poverty and welfare policy affect families? How is child rearing changing now that so many parents work outside the home, and children spend time with other caretakers? How are families socially constructed in different societies, cultures, and time periods?

Most sociologists and family scholars agree that the family is a dynamic social institution that is continually changing as individuals and other social structures in society change. The family also is a social construction with complex and shifting age, gender, race, and social class meanings. As we begin the twenty-first century, many excellent studies are currently investigating the changing structures of the institution of the family and the lived experiences and meanings of families. *Families in the Twenty-First Century* is a series of short texts and research monographs that provides a forum for the best of this burgeoning scholarship. One goal of this series is to recognize the diversity of families that exist in the United States and globally. A second goal is for the series to better inform pedagogy and future family scholarship about this diversity of families. The series also seeks to connect family scholarship to a broader audience beyond the classroom, by informing the public and ensuring that family studies are central to contemporary policy debates and to social action. Each short text contains the most outstanding current scholarship on the family from a variety of disciplines, including sociology, demography, policy studies, social work, human development, and psychology. Moreover, each short text is authored by a leading family scholar or scholars who bring their unique disciplinary perspective to an understanding of contemporary families.

Families in the Twenty-First Century provides the most contemporary scholarship and up-to-date findings on the family. Each volume provides a brief overview of significant scholarship on that family topic, including critical current debates or areas of scholarly disagreement. In addition to providing an assessment of the latest findings related to their family topic, authors also examine the family utilizing an intersectional framework of race-ethnicity, social class, gender, and sexuality. Much of the research is interdisciplinary with a number of theoretical frameworks and methodological approaches presented. A particular strength of the series is that the short texts appeal to undergraduate students as well as to family scholars, but they also are written in a way that makes them accessible to a larger public of well-informed individuals.

About This Volume

To understand the institution of the family in the twenty-first century, we need to understand how globalization affects families across the world. *Global Families* investigates scholarship from sociology, economics, political science, history, anthropology, and even literature to assess the complex effects of globalization on contemporary families. The author, Meg Wilkes Karraker (University of St. Thomas) argues that this interdisciplinary approach is necessary because the literature on global families is just developing and somewhat fragmented. In this volume, Karraker begins with an overview of the concepts and theories related to globalization. Karraker also reviews several debates related to globalization and suggests the utility of feminist theory for understanding global families in this introductory chapter. After providing this background, Karraker examines specific topic areas that demonstrate the complex effects of globalization on families. These topics include demography, employment, violence, and culture. The last chapter looks at national and international policies that are attempting to address issues affecting global families. Throughout this volume, Karraker compassionately shows the consequences of globalization on families in both developing and developed countries.

A unique feature of this book is Karraker's use of original essays at the end of each chapter. These essays convey the issues presented in the chapters in a more specific and intimate matter. The authors of these essays, whether they are academics or a social service professional, provide additional perspectives, which enhance our understanding of global families.

Global Families is appropriate for use in any class concerned with family structure, social inequality, gender, and how globalization affects families in terms of employment, migration, and well being. This book is a valuable resource to teachers and students in beginning and advanced courses in sociology, family studies, women's studies, global studies, political science, social work, public policy, and other disciplines. It also finds an audience among any person interested in comparative family studies or those who work in various human services fields, including human development, social work, education, counseling, health services, and the government. This last statement is particularly true for social service employees who work with immigrant or refugee populations. This volume can help them to better understand the dramatic economic and social forces that transnational labor and migration have on families.

Future Volumes in the Series

Families and Social Class—Shirley A. Hill, University of Kansas

Family Policy—Janet Z. Giele, Brandeis University

Remarriages and Stepfamilies—Lawrence H. Ganong and Marilyn Coleman, University of Missouri

Families and Adoption—Nancy E. Riley and Kristin E. Van Vleet, Bowdoin College

Susan J. Ferguson
Series Editor

PREFACE

The series *Families in the Twenty-First Century*, edited by Susan Ferguson, was initiated in 2006 to illuminate critical issues facing contemporary families. The first book in that series, *Families in Poverty* by Karen Seccombe, offered a powerful synthesis of quantitative and qualitative data to reveal the scope, antecedents, and consequences of poverty for families in the United States.

Global Families is the second book in the *Twenty-First Century* series. Most family scholars are not yet familiar with the vernacular of globalization theory, so I ask the reader to bear with me as I explicate concepts and theories, methods and research from a diverse range of disciplines. Of necessity, *Global Families* draws on sociology, but also on economics and political science, as well as on anthropology, history, and even literature. The result is an interdisciplinary approach to a complex, but increasingly critical, issue facing societies today: the impact of globalization on families.

Global Families opens with an introduction to the field, situating an authentic global approach to families in the context of a long-standing comparative tradition. I offer a summary of the concepts, debates, and theories of globalization, along with a discussion of how globalization increases the potential for risk in a postmodern world. The first chapter also addresses the value of a feminist perspective for understanding the impacts of globalization on families. Each of the subsequent four chapters, 2 through 5, addresses a key area of families in global context: demography, employment, violence, and culture. The final chapter reviews some of the international and supranational policies which are "positioning families in global landscapes."

I am fortunate to be part of a network of academic and other professionals who have specialized expertise on global families and who communicate their knowledge in the most compelling, graceful, passionate prose. Each chapter ends with an original essay authored by one of these discerning scholars.

As Karen found writing on families in poverty, writing on globalization is a sobering business. However, as I wrote these chapters, I had before me the many images of the old and new immigrant families I encounter every day in Minneapolis/St. Paul (a globalizing city if ever there was one!). I also had in mind colleagues, students, and friends whose own family experiences with globalization inspire in me a sense of respect and admiration for their resilient valor. To Ani, Awa, Bao, Barbara, Boonmae, Dina, Henry, Jim, Jonathan, Lashere, Leah, Liam, Pedro, Putt, Richard, Thanos, Xia, Xong, and many others of Armenia, Cambodia, Croatia, Cyprus, Egypt, Germany, Ireland, Israel, Italy, Puerto Rico, Sierra Leone, Somalia, Thailand, Vietnam, and so many other societies around the world: I pray this book honors your global family stories.

ACKNOWLEDGMENTS

The call to participate in this promising series came from Susan Ferguson of Grinnell College. My first thanks goes to Susan, General Editor, who offered me constructive criticism that sustained the preparation of this manuscript. Susan, as well as Jeffrey S. Lasser, Executive Editor at Allyn and Bacon, saw the potential of a manuscript that went beyond the usual comparative perspective on families to a work that breaks new ground. I also prize the editorial and marketing assistance extended by Sara Holliday, Lauren Houlihan, and Kelly May.

For over a decade, my colleagues in the International Education Program at the University of St. Thomas have enriched my experience with global families. I am grateful for the exceptional support of that office over the years: funds to participate in international seminars, grants to research teaching and learning abroad, symposia and workshops (often accompanied by dinner), as well as opportunities to take sociology "on the road" and across the sea.

Likewise, in the Luann Dummer Center for Women at the University of St. Thomas, I have an enthusiastic community which has encouraged my development as a global scholar. A few years ago, the Luann Dummer Center provided me with a curriculum development grant which served in part as the seed from which this book sprouted. Also, the Center has served as a sounding board for my scholarship on this and other topics. I continue to be grateful for the support of my colleagues in the Center.

In Sue Hammons (Professor of Sociology, Abraham Baldwin College), Janet Grochowski (Professor Emerita, University of St. Thomas), and Buff Smith (Assistant Professor of Sociology and Criminal Justice, University of St. Thomas), I continue to benefit from colleagues who have extended themselves as critical, enthusiastic readers and the most supportive friends. Nicolas Carby-Denning (University of Chicago), Morten Ender (U.S. Military Academy), Amelia Wilkes Karraker (University of Chicago), Susan Smith-Cunnien (University of St. Thomas), and Lee Smithey (Swarthmore College) kindly suggested resources. Reference librarian Jan Orf, administrative assistants Martin C. Doyle, Lorrie B. Larson, and Ellen F. Uhrich, and student assistants Heather M. Martin and Kyra M. Shaw (all of the University of St. Thomas) provided able reference, technical, and clerical assistance. Mark E. Jensen, also of the University of St. Thomas, extended his valuable professional expertise as photography editor. Mark, Amelia, Miriam, and Gretel (all of Pratt Street) patiently assisted in checking citations and references, read the occasional passage, and repeatedly indulged me in "just five minutes more . . ."

Finally, I am blessed to be enmeshed in a loving, if geographically dispersed, family. My parents, Mary Gold Mitchell Wilkes and Herbert W Wilkes, Jr., introduced me to global travel before I could walk. My favorite global travel partner, Mark H. Karraker, is always ready for another trip. Finally, I recognize Amelia Wilkes Karraker and Miriam Wilkes Karraker, two young women whose respectful interest in societies and cultures and whose efforts to build relationships across borders inspires me and gives me hope for this world on a day with even the saddest global headlines.

While any errors are my own, I extend my sincere gratitude to all named above for their support in this work.

—MWK

ABOUT THE AUTHOR

Dr. Meg Wilkes Karraker is professor and chair of Sociology and Criminal Justice and director of Family Studies at the University of St. Thomas in St. Paul, Minnesota, U.S.A. She earned the Doctor of Philosophy at the University of Minnesota, following a Master of Science at North Carolina State University and a Bachelor of Arts at Clemson University, all in sociology, with supporting course work in anthropology, education, history, international development, psychology, and women's studies.

Dr. Karraker's interests in the impacts of globalization on families are rooted in her own life experience, growing up in a military family and spending the majority of her childhood and adolescence in Germany with travels through Europe and the former Soviet Union. In addition to research and teaching interests in family sociology, Karraker has long-standing interests in the impacts of social structure on quality of life. She teaches undergraduate courses on family, as well as adolescence, gender in global context, sociological theory, and social problems (in Italy).

A recent recipient of her University's Aquinas Scholars Honors Program Teacher of the Year Award, Dr. Karraker is President-elect of Alpha Kappa Delta, the international sociology honor society. With Janet R. Grochowski, she is the coauthor of *Families with Futures: A Survey of Family Studies for the Twenty-First Century* (Lawrence A. Ehrlbaum, 2006).

Dr. Karraker lives in Minneapolis, Minnesota, with her immediate family, Mark H. Karraker, middle-school student Miriam Wilkes Karraker, Gretel the sheltie, and a fine circle of friends. A second daughter, Amelia Wilkes Karraker is a graduate student in Madison, Wisconsin. Besides cooking, gardening, and enjoying music and theater in the Twin Cities, she would rather be no other place than sipping a glass of wine on a terrazzo in Assisi, while meditating on the Umbrian plain.

1

INTRODUCTION: FAMILIES IN GLOBAL CONTEXT

❦

IN 1960, THE SIX-YEAR-OLD DAUGHTER of a career officer in the United States army watched as dirty, shabbily dressed children about her age pulled discarded items from the garbage cans surrounding the apartment building where she lived in Nuremberg, West Germany. She observed the same children, who appeared to be unsupervised by any adults, stash some of the retrieved items away and, to her revulsion, eat bits of food they found in the cans.

More than four decades later, the same woman, now a college professor in her fifties, stood in the Piazza di Santa Marie Trastevere in Rome, Italy, fending off two very persistent Roma (more familiarly known by the derogatory term *gypsy*) boys begging for money. A colleague who works with children in Rome later told her that the marks she noticed on the children's faces and hands were cigarette burns inflicted by the children's parents. In the transient, nationless communities of the Roma, despised by much of the Italian society in which they live for the moment, when the children return home with less than the amount they were expected to beg (or steal) for the day, they are severely punished (Moffett 2000).

What societal circumstances put families in positions in which their most vulnerable members scavenge for basic necessities in the refuse of others? Under what kind of social conditions must children approach strangers with pitiful appeals for money or suffer the consequences?

I know other, more heartening, stories of families inhabiting global milieus. Some of my students at the University of St. Thomas come to study at our campus from across the globe. Some (but not all) of them come from families that have been displaced, either geographically or economically, or that have fled countries like Cambodia and Vietnam, Croatia and the former East Germany, Sierra Leone and Somalia. Some have spent time along the way living in resettlement camps or joining other diaspora communities. Some of these students represent the first generation in their family to speak English or to complete high school, let alone to earn a college degree. I cherish the stories of their many successes and happiness as they share news of their career achievements and postgraduate plans, but also of their continued connections with their extended kin and the new families they form as they move into adulthood.

The world is an international place today. A visit to a public high school, a trip to a shopping mall, or a stroll down many streets in even a Midwestern city in the United States reveals how diverse American society is becoming. A recent walk across my own campus (a private, Catholic college in St. Paul, Minnesota—often noted as one of the "whitest" states in the nation), sounded like a convocation at the United Nations, with a scattering of voices speaking not only American English, but also Arabic, Armenian, Hmong, Karekare (a language of Nigeria), Somali, Spanish, Russian, and English with an Irish lilt.

In the twenty-first century, economic, political, cultural, and other social forces trespass national, regional, and other borders in ways unanticipated even a few decades ago. Legal and illegal migration between nations stretches social structures so families may call multiple countries or even continents "home." Transnational commerce and differences in life chances between the most- and least-advantaged societies create wide discrepancies in the supply of and demand for human labor, including the care work of families and households. Families continue to inherit the legacies of colonialism and armed conflict. Worldwide revolutions in mass media and consumerism raise the specter of cultural homogenization and challenge traditional family norms and values. All the while, programs and policies intended to guide economic, political, cultural, and other institutional performance are increasingly not just international, but transnational.

What, then, is the quality of family life in a world in which national borders are increasingly permeable and global forces directly affect families in the most profound ways? In *Global Families,* I examine the extent to which globalization impinges on the family through demographic transitions, transnational employment, international violence, worldwide cultures, and supranational policies that transcend borders.

Family, Change, and Global Context

For all the variation in cultures and societies across the globe, families provide a certain measure of universal experience for their members. The classic articulation of these functional consequences of the family for society was offered by Murdock (1949) in the middle of the twentieth century. From his functional analysis of the institution of family across societies, Murdock concluded that every society contains family units organized around common residence, economic cooperation, and sexual reproduction. The family thus structured, Murdock argued, meets critical needs for both family members and societies, including the care and socialization of infants and children.

Murdock's (1949) functional analysis can be criticized on a number of fronts. First, his traditional definition of family as two adults in a sexual relationship is narrow and fails to capture the rich variety in the intimate bonds which function as family. Second, some societies vary in the centrality of the family in meeting critical social needs. In some societies, the family shares with religion, government, education, and other institutions the social organization of households, the production and distribution of goods and services, the regulation of sexualities, and the socialization and care of children and other family members.

In *Global Families*, I favor an inclusive definition of family, one that captures family diversity. Thus, "family" refers to a small group organized around kinship, often, but not always, involving marriage between one man and one woman. Families are a primary means of socialization for society. However, families also can provide emotional and physical care for their members, including the youngest members of society, newborns and children, but also elders, the disabled, the infirm, and other potential dependents. Families may also include more extended networks of what Stack (1974) called fictive kin.

As offered in Karraker and Grochowski's *Families with Futures: A Survey of Family Studies for the Twenty-First Century* (2006), *Global Families* favors a definition of family that stretches beyond a shared household and bonds formed by marriage, blood, or adoption to comprise intimate relationships among individuals who play significant roles of support in one another's lives. While this definition may be messier than traditional definitions, such a dynamic definition of family enables scholars to encompass the kind of relationships increasingly found not only within but also across societies.

Although social scientists debate the definition of the family and the precise functions the institution of the family fills in society, virtually everyone agrees that the family is in transition. Further, social scientists recognize that the velocity of social change around the globe in the postmodern era is shaping the family as an institution in revolutionary ways. With the tremendous variation in structure and function exhibited by families worldwide, societies in the twenty-first century are undergoing what Giddens (2001:17) has termed a "global revolution in family and personal life."

Silverstein and Auerbach (2005) have identified some major trends families faced in the twentieth century:

1. A movement from homogeneity to diversity
2. A movement from stability to change
3. A movement from gendered parenting to transgendered families
4. A movement from male dominance to greater egalitarianism

Although Silverstein and Auerbach (2005) apply these trends primarily to families in the United States, the same five trends can be said to apply to families in many parts of the world today. Throughout the world, diversity in family forms is expanding to include new patterns of cohabitation and childbearing, as well as extended family forms and lesbigay families formed by gay, lesbian, bisexual, or transgendered (GLBT) couples. Unmarried cohabitation is supplanting marriage, even with the presence of children, in many parts of the world. Extended kin relations are less central in many societies, perhaps dangerously so in places where centralized governments have reduced or never supported social safety nets for the increasing numbers of people living alone or living longer. Last, "[q]ueerness is now global" (Cruz-Malavé 2002:1): The globalization of gay and lesbian politics and the increasing visibility of queer sexualities and cultures worldwide (Adam, Duyvendak, and Krouwel 1999a; Binnie 2004) challenges the old assumption of a married man and woman and their biological offspring as the elemental family unit.

Changes, such as later age at first marriage, separation, and divorce, indicate not only elasticity within individual families, but also less predictability in family structures within and across societies. In part, the viewpoint of families as shifting from stability to change—sometimes conceptualized as one of the culture wars because of the highly charged, political nature of the debate (Berger and Berger 1983)—reflects greater realism in popular views of families. But romance about the family dies hard.

Skolnick and Skolnick (2001) argue that four myths contribute to a romantic view of the family as a safe, secure haven for children and adults: (1) the myth of the universal nuclear family, (2) the myth of family harmony, (3) the myth of parental determinism, and (4) the myth of a stable, harmonious past. Such myths have been discounted by historian Stephanie Coontz in her series of best-selling books *The Way We Never Were* (1992), *The Way We Really Are* (1997), and *Marriage,*

A History: How Love Conquered Marriage (2005). Social historians, among them Phillipe Aries (1960) in *L'Enfant et Lavie Familiale sous l'Ancien Régime* (published in the United States under the title *Centuries of Childhood: A History of Family Life*), have revealed that childhood and family life in Western Europe has often been anything but blissful and innocent. In case any doubt remains, news accounts of families across the world, disrupted and rendered ineffective by famine, natural disaster, war, and social crises, as well as those that willfully exploit and oppress their own members, leave only the most naïve to adhere to the popular image of the traditional family as integrated units that function successfully as in some mythical, simpler time. In the essay at the end of Chapter 6, Marsha A. Freeman argues that one of the most important tasks of supranational organizations is to hold societies accountable for the well-being of families and their members. Doing so requires seeing, to use Coontz's (1997) phrase, "the way we really are."

As parenting relationships in some parts of the world shift from traditional gender and sexual roles to include dual-work couples and those led by GLBT parents, greater role sharing and even degendered parenting characterize an increasing proportion of families. Parallel changes in the education, employment, and other roles of women and new movements for children's rights proceed apace with the erosion of patriarchy, the ideological framework that has characterized all human societies throughout history to at least some (and usually to a major) degree.

Silverstein and Auerbach (2005) write primarily of changes facing American families at the end of the twentieth century. True, traditional family structures may be relatively less changed in the more remote regions of the planet (Gielen 1993); however, as discussed in Chapter 5 (and, poignantly, in the essay by Cawo M. Abdi at the end of that chapter) in most areas of the world, the diffusion of Western culture sometimes has had dramatic and often vehemently contested effects on indigenous family institutions. All families are affected by modernization when populations migrate from rural to urban areas (as discussed in Chapter 2 and revealed in Margaret L. Kvasnicka's essay on women seeking a home in a refuge for immigrant women in St. Paul, Minnesota) and when employment patterns become more complex (as discussed in Chapter 3 and illustrated by Joanna Dreby's essay on the life of a mother engaged in transnational employment). Those changes often result in more centralized governmental control and greater detachment from localized means of production, as well as greater absorption (again, often highly contested) of Western values and norms and alienation from local groups and relationships which traditionally guided family life (Giddens, Duneier, and Appelbaum 2006).

The changes facing families today are not only national but are also global, encompassing social forces that transcend national and even regional or continental borders. These forces have the potential to enhance and empower or exploit and oppress families and their members, as well as whole societies. As described in the United Nations Human Development Report, *Globalization with a Human Face* (1999b:1):

> Global markets, global technology, global ideas and global solidarity can enrich the lives of people everywhere. . . . [G]lobalization has swung open the door to opportunities. . . . But markets can go too far and squeeze the non-market activities so vital for human development. . . . Globalization is also increasing human insecurity as the spread of global crime, disease and financial volatility outpaces actions to tackle them.

In *Global Families*, I explore a series of issues through which globalization can enrich, but also too often can squeeze families, while increasing families' risk in the face of national, international, and transnational policies to assist families and their members.

From Comparative to Global Perspectives on Families

Interest in the effects of globalization on families is a relatively late development among family scholars, but family scholarship has a long-standing tradition of comparative study across space and time in anthropology, history, sociology, and other social sciences. Family and kinship structures were keystones in Murdock's (1949, 1982) Cross-cultural Survey and development of his Human Relations Area Files. Also, the work of the late Tamara Haraven (1977; 1982; 2000) and others further reveals the value of the study of historical forces to family sociology, especially in areas of study such as life course.

The Comparative Tradition

Goode's (1963) *World Revolution and Family Patterns* serves as a model of scholarly effort on world families, a tradition continued through Bryceson and Vuorela's (2002) *The Transnational Family,* Adams and Trost's (2005) *Handbook of World Families,* and others. In the latter part of the twentieth century, textbooks like Hutter's *The Changing Family: Comparative Perspectives* (1981), Leeder's *The Family in Global Perspective: A Gendered Journey* (2004), Roopnarine and Gielen's *Families in Global Perspectives* (2005), and, most recently, Ingoldsby and Smith's *Families in Global and Multicultural Perspective* (2006) are witness to the value of comparative approaches in family studies.

Likewise, special issues on international perspectives on families in the *Journal of Marriage and the Family* (2004), as well as the establishment of dedicated journals, such as *International Family Studies* and the *Journal of Comparative Family Studies,* and specialized divisions in professional associations (e.g., the International

Section, one of eleven sections of the *National Council on Family Relations*) affirm that international approaches have become institutionalized in the social scientific study of families.

Recent volumes, such as Scott, Treas, and Richards' *The Blackwell Companion to the Sociology of Families* (2004), have included chapters with titles such as "Families in a Global World," yet the focus remains on North American and European families. Other works, like Kamerman and Kahn's *Family Change and Family Policies in Great Britain, Canada, New Zealand, and the United States* (1997), are typical of much of the comparative writing on families. Only more recently have volumes, such as Robila's *Families in Eastern Europe* (2004), examined families in non-Western regions of the world. Still, many nationalities, especially those in Africa and Southeast Asia, remain less frequently represented in the literature.

Part of the reason for the inattention to non-Western families lies in the nationality of family scholars and their institutions. Adams (2004:1077) notes that productive family scholars are plentiful in Western societies, as well as India, Japan, and Taiwan, along with a "scattering of professionals throughout the Middle East, sub-Saharan Africa, Russia, China, and Latin America." However, family scholars in other regions of the world are considerably less abundant. Adams suggests that the reasons for this underrepresentation relate to communication, money, and values. Family scholars may be active and even publishing in their own venues in underrepresented societies, but their work does not enter into the larger stream of family scholarship if those scholars are not in communication with outside, especially Western, scholars. Also, research—from research design and collection through data analysis and dissemination—is expensive and thus limited by local or regional fiscal constraints. Finally, research may be restricted in more subtle ways by conservative political, religious, or social values that constrain analysis of families and family problems in many parts of the world.

Not surprisingly then, family sociology gives the appearance of having a decidedly Western bias. Further, Edgar (2004) charges that study of the family has increasingly come to emphasize individualism and free-market liberalism, as represented by personal psychology and concern with the actualization of the self, characteristic of Western societies. According to Edgar (2004:7), even scholars such as Beck (1998; 2001) and Giddens (1992), whose work represents postmodern and often global concerns, are "too dismissive of the still important collective contexts in which the risks of biography are mastered."

Adams (2004) also notes that, in addition to national and regional gaps in research on families, research is sparse on certain categories of families. Although some families, such as those of the very wealthy and those living in rural areas offering challenges of accessibility, our knowledge also is limited concerning the families of poor urbanites and other oppressed groups, as well as the families of refugees and other nomads. Such biases reflect not only Western viewpoints, but also often white privilege, effectively serving to silence the voices of families on the margins. Regrettably, this costs family scholars understanding of the influence of legal, religious, and other social structural forces and economic and other status inequalities on families and their members.

Although, admittedly, scholarship on non-Western societies is scarce, cross-cultural, historical, and other comparative studies enhance our understanding of the macrosocial forces that shape the institution of families across societies. Such studies deepen our understanding of both that which is unique about some families within specific societies and that which is common about families across societies. In other words, comparative research promises to reveal both variations between and contrasts within cultures, while providing insights into familial and societal influences on individuals. A truly global approach can compliment the strong comparative tradition in family studies.

Toward a Global Perspective

Even though the institution is undergoing dramatic change, the family remains a central intercessory force in social life. The family is vital to the operation of society and critical to the formation of human capital, cultural capital, and social capital. However, comparative studies or even a cross-cultural or cross-national approach do not do justice to the need for a critical synthesis of family scholarship that addresses the effects of globalization on family systems. The study of transnational circumstances in which family background, networks, and values shape life chances can reveal the significance of family in times and places of rapid social and even global change. *Global Families* begins to remedy a gap in scholarly literature by focusing on the effects of global processes on families across societies.

Global perspectives on families are many-layered. On the one hand, the families which are the subject of this book are *transnational*. A definition of transnational families is premised in transnationalism as "a social process in which . . . social fields cross geographic, cultural, and political borders" (Schiller, Basch, and Blanc-Szanton 1992a:ix). Transnational families span borders, as those family members act, decide, feel, and express identities across social networks that traverse two (or more) societies, often simultaneously.

At another, broader level, families are *global*; that is, every family on earth is more or less touched by global economic and political realities, and also by the globalization of culture and other social systems. In the essay which follows this chapter, "Globalization and Family Down Under," Janet Grochowski, Professor Emerita of Family Studies, offers an illustration of the particular ways in which globalization manifests itself in a specific society. Using data from the Centre for

Social Research at the Australian National University, Grochowski describes Australia as a society with a uniquely global history, both embracing and challenged by the global forces acting on Australian families. Grochowski discusses how Australians' attitudes toward family diversity are linked to these complex attitudes toward globalization.

Globalization as an Analytical Framework

An understanding of these transnational and global families requires an understanding of globalization. Because globalization is a relatively new paradigm for family scholars, in the following section I introduce the definitions, debates, and theoretical principles surrounding globalization. In this section, I also link globalization to other sociological theories familiar to family scholars, including postmodernism and feminist perspectives.

The issues surrounding globalization are not unfamiliar to sociologists grounded in classical traditions in the discipline. Concern for the consequences of large scale, societal change on the quality of social life has long been a major theme in sociology. For example, Durkheim (1897/1951) noted the extent to which rapid social changes, such as those caused by either sudden disaster or unexpected prosperity, compromise social solidarity and contribute to social instability. *Anomia*[1] is the resulting sense that familiar customs and standards can no longer be relied on to give meaning to and control of everyday life (Karraker [Wilkes] 1975).

Other theoretical concepts also provide a backdrop for examination of social change on a worldwide scale. Classic modernization theorists (e.g., Rostow 1961) view traditional norms and values as inhibiting or repressing social change. From this perspective, families in a society in the earliest stages of demographic transition (a concept discussed in Chapter 2), one with a high birth rate, have difficulty putting resources aside for the future. When coupled with high infant and other mortality rates, members of such societies may hold a fatalistic outlook and accept hardship, while resisting conservation of resources, including "saving for a rainy day." (In those societies, the "rainy day" is outside the window and, to be sure, will be there again tomorrow.) To modernize, a society must surrender traditional ways of life in favor of modern culture, institutions, and technologies, which in turn favor economic and social investment and which are premised on values favoring optimism, a Western work ethic, and, most of all, capitalism.

---

[1]While many contemporary writers use the term *anomie* (most prominent among them Merton [1968]), Durkheim (1897/1951) and some more recent scholars, including Srole (who developed the Srole Anomia Scale [1956]), Mizruchi (1960), Miller and Butler (1966), Karraker [Wilkes] (1975), Fischer and Srole (1978), Bilsen and de Witte (2001), Rippi (2003), and others have preferred the term *anomia* to refer to this persistent sense of interpersonal alienation and normlessness.

As demonstrated in the dramatic economic growth in some East Asian nations, including some former European colonies, political stability, centralized planning, and social programming may be critical for modernization (Giddens, Duneier, and Appelbaum 2006). However, the processes of modernization are abetted when wealthy nations, often through such supranational organizations as the International Monetary Fund and the World Bank, finance programs aimed at economic and social development in less developed nations. Often, ostensibly, economic policies are linked to policies targeting families through population control. Thus, nations moving toward modernization reduce the rate of their population growth, enabling them to invest in economic development while institutionalizing values and norms common to developed (and capitalist) societies. What follows is a push toward the high standard of living and high levels of mass consumption characteristic of developed, high income societies, but perhaps at the cost of turmoil in family relationships (Rostow 1961).

Social change theorists (e.g., Chase-Dunn 1998), including those in agreement with Wallerstein's (1996) world system paradigm, emphasize the global interdependence of economic systems. They view world populations as divided into capitalists—those who own and control the means of production and the distribution of goods and services—and others who do not. From this perspective, goods and labor operate in world markets shaped by economic and political competition (and sometimes cooperation) among the most powerful nations. These processes result in a three-tiered system: (1) core nations, which reap the greatest benefits; (2) peripheral nations, mostly agricultural, which are exploited to the advantage of the core nations, and (3) semiperipheral, semiindustrialized, nations which sit at a point of wealth between the core and the periphery.

The result is a worldwide system of dependency, in which nations are linked in exploitative global commodity chains of labor, production, and consumption. In Chapter 3, I describe one such global chain which occurs when women from peripheral countries leave their own families to care for families in core countries. Thus, global capitalism creates economic and political systems through which the most powerful nations colonize weaker nations in order to secure the raw materials (including slave and wage labor) to monopolize industrial production and markets. In the twentieth century, colonization was replaced by multinational and transnational corporations which still, and often with the collaboration of powerful economic and political interests, exploit resources and labor in poor countries. Thereafter, local economies in poor countries cannot compete in such a global market, and so poor countries are maintained in a state of economic and political dependency on the wealthier countries. As described in Chapter 4, colonialism and global political conflict have important, often tragic, consequences for the sexual, marital, and other social orders that shape family life.

The effects of rapid social change on a global scale are evident at both macro and micro levels, both in institutions and in everyday life (Ray 2006). As Giddens (1991:32) opines:

> [C]hanges in intimate aspects of personal life . . . are directly tied to the establishment of social connections of very wide scope. . . . [F]or the first time in human history, self and society are interrelated in a global milieu.

Global Families articulates the far-reaching effects of globalization on that most primary aspect of social and personal life, family. However, the vernacular of globalization theory has not yet permeated family sociology or family studies. Hence, in the following section I define globalization as a critical concept for family scholars. I also delineate the debate among those who remain skeptical about the place of globalization on the world stage, those who embrace globalization as a critical paradigm, and those who recognize the significance of global forces, yet acknowledge the extent to which regional, national, and even local forces continue to shape social life. Finally, I set globalization theory firmly in the orbit of other sociological theories, particularly when accompanied with consideration of the place of risk in a postmodern world and a feminist perspective on family and society.

Globalization Defined

Globalization conventionally refers to the development of economic, political, and cultural systems which extend worldwide. These systems and the consequent relationships result in a world system which in turn can be seen as constituting a single social order (Giddens, Duneier, and Appelbaum 2006). Such a global social order is autonomous and independent of any single nation or region (Appadurai 1996; Bauman 1998).

Globalization theorists often emphasize one of three frames: economic, political, or cultural. Table 1.1 summarizes these three dimensions of globalization theory. For example, Sklair (2002) takes a neo-Marxist economic approach, focusing on transnational capitalism, including transnational corporations, the formation of a transnational capitalist class, and a worldwide culture of consumption. Political theorists, such as Rosenau (2003), see globalization as advancing both "distant proximities" (a sense of that which is remote is also nearby) and "fragmentation" (a situation in which the world is simultaneously globalizing, centralizing, and integrating at the same time it is localizing, decentralizing, and fragmenting). Political theorists see these seemingly contradictory processes as facilitated by new microelectronic technologies, the erosion of territoriality, and increasing subgroup formation across historic political boundaries (Ritzer 2007). Some cultural theorists underscore

Table 1.1 Economic, Political, and Cultural Dimensions of Globalization

Dimension	Key Concepts and Generalizations
Economic	Transnational capitalism, including transnational corporations, transnational class structure, and the culture–ideology of consumption is contributing to emerging global socialism (Sklair 2002).
	Capitalist imperialism will be replaced by global empire (Hardt and Negri 2000; 2004).
Political	The world is increasingly decentralizing, fragmenting, and localizing while simultaneously centralizing, integrating, and globalizing (Rosenau 2003).
Cultural	
Differentialism	Lasting differences among cultures are little affected by globalization (Huntington 1996).
Convergence	Globalization is leading to increasing homogeneity among world cultures through greater emphasis on efficiency, calculability, predictability, control, and rationality (Nedervee Pieterse 2004; Ritzer 2004a).
Hybridization	Globalization and creolization contribute to cultural hybridization (Appadurai 1996).

cultural differentialism, arguing that globalization has little effect on the deep differences that exist within and between societies. Other cultural theorists highlight cultural convergence, the idea that globalization is resulting in an increasing cultural similarity among societies, as exemplified by Ritzer's (2004b) "McDonaldization" thesis. Still other cultural theorists (e.g., Nederveen Pieterse 2004) see not differentialism or convergence, but cultural hybridization. For example, Appadurai (1996) believes that globalization is leading to cultural amalgamation and the generation of new cultures composed of a creative mixture of cultures in contact with one another.

Across economic, political, and cultural dimensions, globalization results in the "widening, deepening, and speeding up of worldwide connectedness in all aspects of contemporary social life" (Held, et al. 1999:2). Globalization speaks to the extent to which local events take on global significance across broadening geography and expanding chronology with increasingly dense networks and relationships beyond national borders. From an almost micro social perspective, globalization presumes a replacement of local affinities and associations with global connections and networks, often disseminated and perhaps promoted by a widening system of global communications. Tomlinson (1999:2) describes this as a "rapidly developing and ever-densening network of interconnections and interdependences [that] characterize modern social life." Where Giddens sees an increasing collision between fundamentalism and cosmopolitanism, Tomlinson predicts the evolution of what he calls a global cosmopolitan society.

Thus, globalization involves the motion and absorption of goods and capital, politics and power, information and technologies worldwide. But globalization also involves the transmission of pollution, crime, and other social problems across and beyond national, regional, and other spatial borders. Environmental hazards generated in one part of the world certainly show no respect for national sovereignty. Trafficking in drugs, guns, and human beings (as described in Jennifer Blank's essay at the end of Chapter 4) is profitable, precisely because material and human commodities are so easy to transport and market without regard for the same national borders. Further, the persistence of widespread violence in some African, Asian, Central and South American, and Middle Eastern countries must be seen, at least in part, as grounded in transnational and increasingly worldwide systems of economic despair, political enmity, religious antagonisms, and cultural collisions in a global world.

The "Globalization Debate"

Some scholars debate the novelty of globalization as a force in historic social change. They note that economic interdependence, as well as international migration, trade, conquest, and other global phenomenon, have existed in other periods, shaping the histories of such divergent locations as Buenos Aires and Bombay, Cairo and Chicago, Mogadishu and Moscow, Shanghai and Sydney. Even beyond that, the concept, processes, consequences, and social and familial implications of globalization are contested. Three positions on the significance of globalization in today's world are articulated by the skeptics, the hyperglobalists, and the transformationists (see Table 1.2).

Skeptics of globalization (e.g., Boyer and Drache 1996; Hirst and Thompson 1992) view globalization as a counterfeit concept that exaggerates the power of international economies, while obscuring the control still exercised by regional and national governments. Skeptics see not a globally integrated system, but increasing internationalization in the form of contacts among national economies. They see internationalization as accompanied by persistent inequality between developed

Table 1.2   Three Positions in the *Globalization Debate*

Position	On Globalization	Representative Scholars
Skeptics	Globalization is a counterfeit concept which exaggerates the importance of international economics and obscures the importance of national governmental controls and regionalization.	Boyer and Drache; Hirst and Thompson; Huntington
Hyperglobalists	Escalating global capitalism increasingly affects other aspects of social life, creating a more borderless, transnational, and denationalized world. National economies and governments are subordinated and diffused by hybridization.	Appadurai; Greider; Hardt and Negri; Nedervee Pieterse; Ohmae
Transformationists	The world is becoming interconnected to an unprecedented degree across not only economic and political, but also cultural and other social systems. This global society is more uncertain, risky, and stratified.	Giddens; Ritzer; Rosenau

Sources: Appadurai 1996; Boyer and Drache 1996; Castells 2000; Cochrane and Pain 2000; Giddens 2000; Greider 1997; Hardt and Negri 2000, 2004; Held, et al. 1999; Hirst and Thompson 1992; Huntington 1996; Nedervee Pieterse 2004; Ohmae 1995; Ritzer 1993, 1995, 1996, 2004b, 2005b; Rosenau 1997.

and developing nations, as well as increasing regionalization that results in fragmented ethnic and cultural blocs, especially in opposition to Westernization (Castells 2004; Held, et al. 1999). A skeptical approach to globalization and families suggests that families face challenges from a myriad of sources, internal and external to societies, globalization being but one of those challenges.

To the contrary, hyperglobalists (e.g., Greider 1997; Ohmae 1995) contend that escalating global capitalism in economic marketplaces increasingly affects other aspects of social life. Hyperglobalists observe that systems of production and distribution, finance and trade are more and more transnational, borderless, and, in essence, denationalized than ever before in human history. Hyperglobalists see a dramatically globalized economy, accompanied by widespread subordination of national economies and governments. Further, they observe that political, cultural, and other institutional systems are likewise globally diffused and hybridized into immense global systems (Cochrane and Pain 2000; Held, et al. 1999). To hyperglobalists, globalization is placing families and their members at increasing risk, through migration, employment, violence, media and culture, and other changes occurring at an accelerating rate across national borders.

The third party in the globalization debate, transformationalists (e.g., Giddens 2000; Rosenau 1997) recognize an increasingly interconnected, but more uncertain, world. Like hyperglobalists, global transformationalists see globalization as a historically unprecedented set of economic, political, and social forces shaping societies and the world through a wide range of cultural, demographic, ecological, military, technological, and other social patterns. However, rather than confirming the advent of a single, unified world society, transformationalists point to increasing global stratification, as some societies and their members reap the benefits of globalization, while others become increasingly marginalized on the world stage (Held, et al. 1999). Transformationalists view families as encountering global forces, but with some measure of resistance.

Critics of the forces of globalization, such as Fifty Years Is Enough: U.S. Network for Global Economic Justice (2006), paint a very grim picture. They see evidence of nations, communities, families, and individuals subsumed under an increasingly oppressive, even malevolent, global cloud. In contrast, Bhagwati (2004:30) takes a more sanguine view of globalization. He sees critics of globalization as "alarmist" and offers a "defense of globalization" in a book of that title. He acknowledges the "perils of gung-ho international financial capitalism," but believes that the hazards of globalization are exaggerated. He also sees antiglobalization sentiments as masking anticapitalist, anticorporate, and anti-American (or at least anti-Western) prejudices.

Bhagwati (2004) agrees with critics of globalization that, across the world, the wealthiest nations are more integrated in a worldwide economy, obstacles to global trade have never been lower, and information technologies make increasingly rapid worldwide movement of capital and services ever more possible. Bhagwati (2004:68) recognizes that, according to the International Labor Organization, 100 million to 200 million children under fifteen years of age are working—almost 95 percent of these in poor countries, half of them in Asia. However, he finds that globalization has generally increased family wealth in poor countries and has decreased the incentive for parents to put their children to work and increased the inducement for children to be in school.

Certainly, the association between globalization and other social conditions is not unilateral. Globalization presses forward through such social, economic, and political developments as the lowering of trade barriers in the Western hemisphere and the collapse of the Soviet Union. These changes create new markets for goods and services and may help to reduce poverty in places like China and India, thus making the world a more stable place, which, in turn, reduces families' exposure to war and other armed conflicts. Globalization also benefits some families through lower prices on luxury goods and services, from the latest flat-screen television to strawberries enjoyed during a Minnesota winter. And the competition fostered by global markets may increase the purchasing power of low-income families, while extending a check on inflation and boosting returns in the stock market.

But the evidence is persuasive that globalization of market forces facilitates exploitation of the most vulnerable members of society on an even larger scale than previously possible. As companies automate, downsize, outsource, and relocate off-shore, wage growth stagnates and health and retirement costs and risks are shifted to workers (Obama 2006). Bhagwati does not include in his analysis the problem of transnational movements of children to work in other countries, often under the poorest conditions. He also does not address the situation of child prostitution. According to Bhagwati (2004:72) those "are products of globalization only in the sense that there are profits to be had in movements across borders." As the author of *Global Families,* I disagree. Human trafficking is the very epitome of the worst side of globalization: the convergence of economic, political, cultural, and other forces in ways that transcend any national or even international social systems.

Even some supporters of globalization find the argument specious that increased global competition will reduce structural inequalities in society, for example, by ensuring that prejudice and discrimination will be too competitively costly for firms (Bhagwati 2004). Case in point: The supply of women willing to work for exploitative wages inadequate to support themselves and their dependents still far exceeds the supply of positions at the bottom of the employment ladder (i.e., those with the lowest wages, the least security, and the most dangerous working conditions). Capitalist employers operating in global markets seeking the best return on investment can effectively outbid employers in women's home countries, thus maximizing profits by minimizing labor costs. The broad consequences of these risky global practices are disproportionately borne by the least advantaged families, in the least advantaged societies.

Globalization Theory

As discussed earlier, the concept of globalization has usually been approached from the perspective of economics, politics, or culture. But these three dimensions do not encompass the entire theoretical scope of globalization. In explaining family opportunities and outcomes in the context of globalization, family scholars face a significant challenge in moving beyond the economic, political, and culture based theories that have, to date, dominated the field. At the same time, family scholars can reexamine and sometimes repackage theories which have informed family sociology and family studies to better explain the effects of globalization on families.

Family studies, in general, and family sociology, in particular, have made great strides in theoretical development in the four decades since publication of Christensen's *Handbook of Marriage and the Family* in 1964. That elegant, classic volume included review essays on only four theoretical schools: the institutional approach (Sirjamaki 1964), the structural functional approach (Pitts 1964), the interactional and situational approach (Stryker 1964), and the developmental approach (Hill and Rodgers 1964).

A half century later, Karraker and Grochowski's (2006) *Families with Futures* included seven theoretical perspectives:

1. Exchange theory
2. Symbolic interaction theory
3. Family developmental theory
4. Family systems theory
5. Conflict theory
6. Structural functional theory
7. Family ecology theory

Even more family theories might be added to that list, either as distinct theories in their own right or as important extensions of or variations on other theories. For example, Ingoldsby, Smith, and Miller (2004) and White and Klein (2002) consider life course theory a strand of family developmental theory. Others (e.g., Allen 1989) argue that life course is a distinct theory. (For detailed elaboration on each of these theories, consult Karraker and Grochowski [2006], White [2005], or White and Klein [2002].)

The study of globalization and families would benefit from the kind of interdisciplinary empirical and theoretical scholarship advocated by Karraker and Grochowski (2006) and Scott, Treas, and Richards (2004). Already, some scholars (e.g., Giele 2004; Giele and Holst 2004) are using life course and family systems theories, as well as exchange and symbolic interaction theory, to understand the effects of new global divisions of labor between men and women on patterns in family life across societies. Structural functional theory still offers an opportunity to consider the manifest and latent functions and dysfunctions embodied in now-global economic, political, cultural, and other changes shaping the family. Conflict theory exposes the systems of exploitation and oppression reflected in social arrangements for men, women, and children in families both within and between societies. By including the world system in understanding the family as located in human-built, social–cultural, and natural physical–biological environments, family ecology theory (e.g., Bubloz and Sontag 1993) can detect opportunities, as well as constraints, for families operating in global societies. By extension, an ecological approach implies that global policymakers should consider the effect on families of supranational legislation and other social initiatives, perhaps even composing global family impact statements.

Each of these middle range theories (see Merton 1968) may prove useful for analyzing certain aspects of families in global context. Also, family scholars are exploiting theories beyond those on which family scholars usually draw. For example, Ward (1990) has examined the "global assembly lines" that disproportionately exploit women (and compromise their families) through the lens of world systems theory. Ward describes the "assembly lines" as occurring in semi-periphery or periphery countries, while research, management, and profit are controlled by core or developed countries. Postmodernism and feminist theory (both of which are described later in this chapter) may offer even greater promise for articulating the consequences of globalization, including risk, across family systems and through intersections of class, gender, race/ethnicity, natality, and other dimensions of social opportunity.

At the same time, as suggested by global transformationists, family theory that does not take into account globalization theory falls short of the potential to explain the challenges and opportunities experienced by families in an increasingly global world. To fully utilize globalization theory, family theorists must forego the assumption that "nation" equals "society" (Beck and Beck-Gernsheim 2004:501) and that family location is nation-bound. Instead, family sociologists must push the "territorial frontiers" that presumed that a family's culture and biography was bound by national society. Family sociologists must acknowledge that families may move among "local and international, indigenous and foreign" networks (Beck and Beck-Gernsheim 2004:501).

Further, any examination of the effect of globalization on families should be sensitive to the potential for *glocalization*. Ritzer (2007:268) defines *glocalization* as the "interpenetration of the global and the local resulting in unique outcomes." The concept of glocalization recognizes the significant, creative potential of individuals and local groups not only to resist the homogenizing forces of globalization, but also to fashion an increasingly pluralistic world (Robertson 1995). Chapter 5 includes a discussion of ways in which some families, including parents and their children, "push back" against globalization, and, thus, epitomize glocalization.

Glocalization also involves increases in ethnic group and other more local cultural solidarities that transcend national borders, that is, new tribalism, or what Edgar (2004) refers to as project-identity social movements. Examples of such movements are Islamic fundamentalism and the ethnic/national rebellions in the former Soviet Union and the Balkans. Other such identity movements are aimed at building a certain civic ethic (e.g., to demand more responsive government, to take action against globalization). Joseph's (2002) work articulating the global/glocal intersections of political economy and other aspects of queer life is also an example of such an approach. Still other identity movements are smaller and seem to offer a sort of functional equivalent for individuals seeking more familylike connections to others. Thus, families and their members are linked not only to national and transnational systems, but also to more local and glocal identity systems.

Risk in a Global Postmodern World

Another concept, *risk*, further illuminates the challenges posed by globalization for families in a postmodern world. In postmodern theory, risk refers to uncertainty and insecurity in economic, political, and other spheres of life. In postmodern theory, the term also connotes a heightened level of personal responsibility for individual achievement, personal outcomes, and quality of life, as one experiences life less and less enmeshed in localized, communal family, neighborhood, or community, or even in the predictable features of class, gender, ethnicity or race, religion, or tribe or nation. Quintessentially, such risk is the story of globalization.

Beck describes globality in precisely such a sense: national, regional, and other spatial boundaries are increasingly illusory. Through globalization, national boundaries are interwoven and destabilized by transnational actors in financial, government, religious, cultural, and other institutions. From this perspective, denationalization (the decline of the nation–state) and the development of transnational organizations, and even transnational states such as the European Union, can be seen as part of a "second modernity" (Beck 2000). But with this increasing (post) modernity comes a loss of tradition and the certainty that accompanies the familiar. Further, globalization implies that individually determined senses of self and identity may be chosen and created without reference to customary relationships, including families. In such a postmodern, self-reflexive social order, everything, even sense of self and relationships, is subject to constant revision and refabrication as new information and new social forms are constantly being received and evaluated (Giddens 1991).

Thus, globalization heightens social risk, jeopardy outside the formerly comfortable boundaries of nation, society, culture, kinship, and family. For example, in the case of increasingly global job markets, workers and their families face greater uncertainty as jobs are outsourced and families are dislocated when some members migrate for employment while others remain behind. And such changes come not once, but over and over again, many times in a lifetime.

Furthermore, no region or nation, regardless of economic or political advantage, is totally immune from the risks associated with postmodern life, as evidenced by the events associated with the bombings of the Pentagon and the World Trade Center in the United States on September 11, 2001, and the bombings in the mass transit systems in London on July 7, 2005, as well as recent natural disasters in the southeastern United States. But the positive and negative effects of globalization are unequally distributed. For some families, globalization can enhance mobility and freedom to create security, meaning, and opportunity. Bauman (1998) writes of privileged elites who are able to move easily across global borders and, likewise, of those who are not able to do so. He differentiates between tourists (those who move about the globe because they can and want to do so) and vagabonds (those who move about the globe because they find their location hostile or intolerable).

Poverty and other inequalities attract uneven quantities of risk. The most severe consequences of risk disproportionately fall to poor nations, continents, and the Southern hemisphere. Not only does globalization not eliminate scarcity and want, but the pervasiveness of global media (as discussed in Chapter 5) that can transmit generous images of affluence serves to worsen the sense of absolute or relative deprivation of the word's most needy (George 1999). The risks that accompany globalization exacerbate class and other divisions in society (Beck 1992), and the risks associated with global inequalities apply to individuals, as well as to nations, continents, and hemispheres (Ritzer 2004a). Families experience risks and disadvantages associated with large-scale, global social change in disproportionate measures to their privilege and material and other resources.

Thus, a theme of "runaway risk," and the accompanying anxiety and fear created by globalization, runs through postmodernism (e.g., Giddens 2000). Some

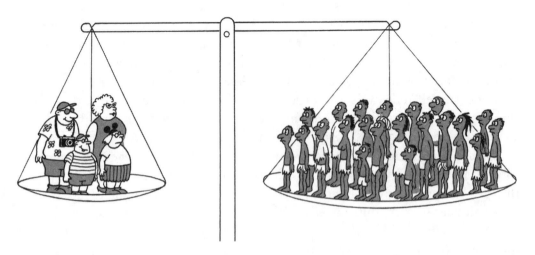

Globalization by Stan Eales
Source: © cartoonstock.com

postmodernists (e.g., Beck 1992) see risk as a fundamental, defining characteristic of modern society. Long a staple in the economic analysis of labor markets, the application of risk to family life is a recent development, exemplified in Furlong and Cartmel's (1997) and Nayak's (2003) analyses of adolescence in working class families in Great Britain and other western societies. Also, Don Browning (2003), Professor Emeritus of Divinity and Alexander Campbell Professor of Religious Ethics and the Social Sciences at the University of Chicago, depicts postmodern marriages and families at serious risk in a global world. First, the positive changes found in modernizing societies around the world (e.g., higher family income, better health, longer life expectancy) are unevenly distributed. Second, some of the changes moving across the global landscape, including expanding educational and employment roles for women, smaller families, more egalitarian gender roles in marriage, and less involvement of extended kin are creating crises regarding care of family members.

For Silverstein and Auerbach (2005:34), the postmodern family represents "a deconstruction or transformation of at least one aspect of the traditional family." A family no longer requires two parents, male and female, sharing a household with their biological offspring. An accurate construction of family must include single mothers by choice, lesbigay couples, families which are constructed using new reproductive technologies (e.g., in vitro fertilization, surrogate mothers, sperm donors), and transnational families living across borders, such as those described in Chapter 3. The uncertainties associated with these new diversities of family form and function—adaptive as they may be—represent yet another potential source of risk, fear, and anxiety for families in postmodern societies, especially when they are not acknowledged or affirmed by the dominant society. Thus, such risk is heightened by the absence or withdrawal of the state as a provider of social safety nets. Such postmodern families challenge traditional gender, sexual, and other ideologies and can benefit from feminist analysis.

Globalization Through a Feminist Lens

Globalization and the risks associated with postmodern life on a worldwide scale are not gender neutral. In fact, Marchand and Runyan (2000) and Naples and Desai (2002) suggest that resistance to globalization is often, by necessity, gendered because women and their families disproportionately bear the consequences of demographic transitions, transnational employment, international violence, and worldwide culture shifts. A gender lens offers a distinctive opportunity to understand global restructuring, encompassing the effects of globalization on the lives of women and their families and the place of gendered ideologies in globalization.

The transnational commodification of care work and mate selection and the global networks that characterize not only reproductive labor, but also such intimacies as sexual exchanges, are "prime manifestation[s] of the complex gendered dynamics of contemporary globalization" (Hawkesworth 2006:2). For example, Sarker and De (2002) demonstrate how globalization is nuanced by gender in South and Southeast Asia in employment, sexuality, identity, and other areas of social life, as well as in various aspects of destabilization and resistance associated with globalization. Safa (2002) reveals how patriarchy continues to structure inequality in the global labor force, using the example of women in the Dominican Republic who continue to toil under patriarchy and a male breadwinner model reinvigorated by globalization. These women encounter pernicious sexism and face occupational discrimination and the unwillingness of labor unions and other social organizations to consider critical women's and family concerns, such as maternity leave.

In a concise but comprehensive articulation of contemporary feminist theories, Lengermann and Niebrugge (2007a) frame basic theoretical questions, describe contemporary feminist theories, and offer insights into where feminist theories can take sociological theory. To begin, they define feminist theory as "a generalized, wide-ranging system of ideas about social and human experience developed from a woman-centered perspective" (p. 185). Feminist theory takes women's experience as the starting point for sociological study and attempts to view society from the point of view of women.

Lengermann and Niebrugge (2007b) describe four varieties of feminist theory: (1) gender difference, (2) gender inequality, (3) gender oppression, and (4) structural oppression (see Table 1.3). Each of these varieties holds promise for the understanding of the effects of globalization on families. For example, Iwao's (2001) work on the "battle of the sexes" among young Japanese suggests that, in spite of dramatic modernization in that nation, men and women continue to experience modern life in profoundly different ways—perhaps because of their respectively different phenomenological locations, as suggested by gender difference theories. Gender inequality theories, such as that by feminist economists Barker and Feiner (2004), are already enabling us to understand the persistence of gender inequality in the transnational workforce.

Most gender oppression theorists would say societies fall far short of Jackson's (2001:81) contention that, "[m]en's social dominance was doomed from the beginning. Gender inequality could not adapt successfully to modern economic and political institutions." More typically, scholars such as Bose (2006b) and Ollenburger and Moore (1998) draw on feminist theories of structural oppression to lay bare the intersections of patriarchy, capitalism, and colonization, while recognizing that gender intersects with class, ethnicity, natality, race, and sexual orientation. Thus, feminist theorists working in the area of globalization and family can extend and

Table 1.3   Four Varieties of Feminist Theory

Feminist Theory	What About the Women?	Why Is Women's Situation as It Is? (Variations Within Theory)
Gender Difference	Women's position in and experience of most social life differs from men's experience.	Biological Cultural Institutional Interactionist Phenomenology
Gender Inequality	Women's position in social life is both different from and unequal to men's position.	Liberal feminism
Gender Oppression	Women are oppressed. Women are not just unequal to men, but also are subordinated, shaped, exploited, and abused by men.	Psychoanalytic feminism Radical feminism
Structural Oppression	Women's experiences of difference, inequality, and oppression vary by position within capitalism, patriarchy, and racism.	Socialist feminism Intersectionality

Source: From P. A. Lengermann and G. Niebrugge. 2007a. Adapted with permission from G. Ritzer, *Contemporary Sociological Theory and Its Classical Roots*, 2nd ed., pp. 185–214. New York: McGraw-Hill.

expand Collins's (1990) classic formulation of Black feminist thought as representing the intersectionality of race, class, and gender, and, more recently, sexual orientation, to consider the global issues of colonialism, immigration, and nationality. Some scholars (e.g., Eisenstein [2004] *Against Empire: Feminisms, Racism, and the West*) are beginning to accept the challenge.

Lengermann and Niebrugge (2007b) argue that postmodernism and feminism have much in common. Both postmodernism and feminism are concerned with whose formulations of knowledge matters. Both postmodernism and feminism aim to use the method of deconstruction to unpack the place of gender in postmodern society. And both are concerned with resisting the inclination of theory to become a means of categorizing and, therefore, oppressing, disenfranchised members of society. At the same time, Lengermann and Niebrugge are suspicious of postmodernism's fixed place in the privileged academy, as opposed to venues that would facilitate inclusion and liberation of marginalized groups. Likewise, postmodernism's emphasis on individualization and de-emphasis on broadly conceived social structural constraints rankles with feminist concerns of identifying systemic sources of inequalities.

As the title of Turpin and Lorentzen's (1996) book *The Gendered New World Order* suggests, globalization may be arranging the planet in novel ways, but gender remains a primary determinant of those arrangements. Feminist theory is increasingly important in family studies (Baber and Allen 1992) and some scholars (e.g., Haney and Pollard 2003) are revising existing family theories around feminist frameworks in order to better understand the effects of globalization on families.

In *Global Families,* I apply concepts from globalization theory (globalization and glocalization), postmodernism (risk), and feminism (gender difference, inequality, oppression, and intersecting structures) to explain the complex systems through which globalization affects families. Feminist theory portends to explore the social sources of gender and other intersection inequalities. In asking where are the women, feminist theory has much to offer the global analysis of family in examination of areas associated with both public and private spheres. Finally, feminist perspectives can inspire those who wish to transform society. For example, in seeking ways to address that global scourge, HIV/AIDS, Bill Gates, chair of Microsoft Corporation and cochair of the $62 billion Bill and Melinda Gates Foundation, said at the opening of the 16th International AIDS Conference in Toronto: "We need to put the power to prevent HIV in the hands of women" (Picard 2006:A1). Gates recognizes that needed social change in lowering the rates of HIV/AIDS would not come about without empowering women in their relationships, families, and society.

Global Families: Plan of the Book

Global Families answers a call extended by Robertson (1990:15) to "redirect theory and research toward explicit recognition of globalization." But family scholars must avoid having "'globalization' . . . become an intellectual 'play zone'—a site for the expression of residual social–theoretical interests, interpretative indulgence, or the display of world-ideological preferences" (p. 16). That challenge is never far from my mind, as I synthesize scholarship around such intellectually and socially charged issues as HIV/AIDS, global care chains, sex trafficking, globalized media, and supranational policies aimed at the family.

However, to continue to avoid globalization as an organizing principle in family studies would be a grievous error. Globalization has consequences not only for entire societies and regions, but also very significantly for human development and for families. Such analysis requires consideration of demographics, employment, violence, and culture, as well as the role of the state and international political bodies in shaping family-centered issues worldwide. I have organized the following chapters in *Global Families* around these five important themes, critical to the study of family life.

Chapter 2, *Global Change and Demographic Shifts: Family Characteristics and Societal Transformation,* places global families against the backdrop of dramatic changes in population characteristics. Declining fertility, variable mortality, and especially sweeping migration are shaping the structure and function of contemporary families in fundamental ways. A particular case, that of AIDS orphans, illustrates the broad effect of global demographic shifts on family life.

Chapter 3, *Transnational Employment: Work–Family Linkages Across Borders,* summarizes the literature on families and international labor force participation, with a particular focus on domestic labor migrants and the effect of transnational employment on family care work. The concept of global care chains is used as an example of the complex means through which global labor and family are woven together.

The effects of globalization on families may occur in the context of international violence against families and their members. Chapter 4, *International Violence: Family Legacies of Oppression and War,* reveals the extent to which colonialism and armed conflict shape families and family life in profound ways. The chapter reveals potentials for not only risk, but also resiliency, in the face of international violence. Sexual domination, in the forms of rape, sexual slavery, and sex trafficking, is offered as a system through which families are reshaped by global economies in a criminal context.

Chapter 5, *Families and Worldwide Culture Systems: Effects of Media and Consumption on Norms and Values,* explores the effect of globalization on the cultures in which families are embedded. The chapter examines the controversy surrounding globalization and cultural homogeneity, as well as the effect of mass media, including television and computer-assisted technologies, and consumerism on families. The chapter concludes with an examination of globalization and family values.

The concluding chapter, *Positioning Families in Global Landscapes: Families, Policies, and Futures,* notes the persistence of global disparities among families and the issue of human rights as family rights. Two decades after the International Year of the Family, social scientists are positioned to view social policies regarding the family from a global perspective. Returning to earlier themes by way of critical appraisal, *Global Families* concludes by asking if we are entering a postfamily global society, a society in which globalization severely compromises the ability of the institution and individual families to fulfill their obligations to society and their members.

Finally, each chapter closes with an essay authored by an authority in the field.

- Chapter 1: "Globalization and Family Down Under," by Janet R. Grochowski, Ph.D., Emerita Professor of Family Studies
- Chapter 2: "Immigrant Women, New Neighbors, Global Families," by Margaret L. Kvasnicka, CSJ, Director of Sarah's . . . An Oasis for Women
- Chapter 3: "A Migrant Mother's Story: Paula Rodriguez," by Joanna Dreby, doctoral student in sociology at the City University of New York Graduate Center
- Chapter 4: "Sex Trafficking: A 'Family Business,'" by Jennifer Blank, M.A., criminologist
- Chapter 5: "Contested Norms and Values in Transnational Families," by Cawo M. Abdi, Ph.D., sociologist
- Chapter 6: "The Global Human Rights of Families," by Marsha Freeman, Ph.D., director of the International Women's Rights Action Watch and Senior Fellow in the Law School Institutes at the University of Minnesota

These essays serve as cases to illustrate and extend key issues raised in *Global Families*.

Summary

In spite of a long tradition of cross-cultural and international scholarship, family studies have yet to realize an authentically global perspective on families. *Global Families* calls for inclusion of globalization as a critical tool for analyzing families and the family institution in the twenty-first century.

Globalization is the development of economic, political, cultural, and other relationships beyond national and regional spatial borders, and the social consequences of globalization are evident at macro and micro levels. But globalization is something of a contested concept. Skeptics see globalization as a false concept that exaggerates and obscures the power of international economies controlled by regional and national governments. Hyperglobalists see increasingly borderless, global economies accompanied by diffusion and hybridization of political, cultural, and other institutional systems. Still others see globalization as a historically unprecedented set of economic, political, and social forces transforming societies and the world through a range of cultural, demographic, ecological, military, and technological patterns and increasing worldwide stratification.

Although an increasing number of middle range theories drawn from family studies are being used to examine the family globally, any global analysis must resist the tendency toward Western bias and must take into account worldwide economic, political, cultural, and other institutional influences. In additional to globalization and glocalization, both postmodernism, with an emphasis on risk analysis, and feminism are among the most promising complements for the analysis of the effects of globalization on families.

Global Families reveals the complex effects of demographic transitions, transnational labor, international violence, and culture transcending borders on families. The migration of family members from their extended kin and community shapes marriage, parenting, and other family structures and provides opportunities for economic, political, or cultural liberation. Global care chains have the potential to affect the youngest, eldest, and most vulnerable members of society, while institutionalizing discrepancies between the most- and least-developed societies during situations such as the HIV/AIDS epidemic in sub-Saharan Africa. Wars and sexual domination introduce yet more global hazards into societies, while revealing both the depth of oppression and exploitation and the potential for human and family resiliency. Global developments may challenge the cultural integrity of individual cultures, but offer untold opportunities for communication and exchange. Finally, *Global Families* considers the effects of supranational organizations, such as the United Nations, as well as other national and international political bodies, on families in a global world.

Globalization and Family Down Under
By Janet R. Grochowski, Ph.D.

Australia has the distinction of being both a society founded through global processes and one that today embraces globalization. The original human inhabitants of this island continent arrived 30,000 to 50,000 years ago, but the earliest recorded European mariners did not reach "Terra Australis Incognito" (unknown southern land) until 1606. Approximately 54 European merchant ships from various countries visited this new land prior to 1770, when English explorer Captain James Cook claimed the entire east coast of Australia for England, naming it New South Wales. An English-inhabited colony was founded in 1788, when English ships carried 1,350 settlers to the territory. Shortly thereafter, the first penal colony was established in Sydney, starting a flow of convicts from the United Kingdom to Australia that did not end until 1968 (Australian Government 2006a).

The penal colonies were populated primarily by convicts, marines, and the families of the marines. Efforts were made in the 1820s and 1830s to address a shortage of single women:

> [t]he sex imbalance in the old convict colonies was rekindled during the gold rushes and exaggerated for much of the rest of the nineteenth century by the attraction for young men of rural and outback Australia where there was little prospect of employment for young women, though prospects of marriage were good for the bold or the desperate (Kingston and Byron 2006:1).

This serious imbalance diminished during the late twentieth and into the twenty-first centuries. Today the current sex ratio is 1.02 males to 1.00 females for Australians 15 to 64 years of age (Central Intelligence Agency 2006).

The fate of the first immigrants, Aboriginals, also left lasting imprints. Although 1818 is marked today as the official date of the founding of Australia as a British colony, for many Aboriginals that date symbolizes not celebration, but grief. Beginning in 1788, contact with British immigrants often resulted in economic marginalization, a loss of political autonomy, and death by disease for the Aboriginals. By the 1940s, most Aboriginals were "missionized" and assimilated into rural Australian society as low-paid laborers with limited rights, and many Aborigine children were taken from their natural parents and given to foster parents (Moses 2004). As recently as July 2000, Australia faced harsh criticism over its historical (e.g., removal of Aboriginal children from their homes) and current (e.g., discrimination related to arrests) treatment of Aboriginals (Doole 2000).

Despite these problems and concerns, the establishment of The Commonwealth in 1901 found Australia increasingly recognized as a desirable destination for voluntary immigrants, especially those flooding out of continental Europe after World Wars I and II. Between 1948 and 1975, two million European immigrants chose Australia as their new home, a home that, while welcoming a European cultural mix, resisted non-white immigration into a distinctive Australian lifestyle. The 1972 election of the Labor Party ended the "White Australia Policy," and adoption of a nondiscriminatory immigration policy helped usher in the National Agenda for a Multicultural Australia in 1989 (Inglis 2004). Today, a growing proportion of Australia's over 20 million people is from Asia, with the most significant growth occurring in Asian-born immigrants who make up 24 percent of the foreign-born population in Australia (2004:2). Yet, the cold realities of racism and xenophobia surface in corners of Australian society. For example, in the early years of the twenty-first century, Human Rights Watch (2001) faulted Australia with xenophobia as revealed in its "punitive asylum policy" and harsh measures, including mandatory detention of all asylum seekers and other noncitizens arriving illegally (2001:7).

In 2002, a United Nations' Commission on Human Rights report on racism in Australia offered ten recommendations suggesting ways to enhance Australia's multiculturalism policy. These recommendations focused on further reducing discrimination toward Aboriginals and stressed that the Australian government should review its policy of multiculturalism (Glele-Ahanhanzo 2002). Just three years later, research indicated that Australia, in fact, had reduced discrimination and enhanced multiculturalism. Smith (2005) found the Australian character of a "fair go" is a vital aspect of Australian culture and the belief that people are to be treated fairly and equally has been strengthened. Still, Smith and others acknowledge that, while progress is being made through a Declaration and Program of Action, much work remains to insure that all Australians enjoy the full benefits of living in a multicultural society.

Culture is "an ensemble of [attitudes and] practices . . . that together form a way of being for a given community" (Heaven and Tubridy 2006:152). Although Australian society continues to struggle with discrimination, this land of immigrants increasingly recognizes a need to embrace diversity, as well as a distinctive Australian flare for life. Australian culture today is embodied in peoples whose national attitudes and behaviors reveal how economics, politics, cultures, and families are linked to the global community beyond. These globally receptive attitudes are reflected in the Australian Survey of Social Attitudes (AuSSA), a national survey first conducted in 2003 by the Centre for Social Research at the Australian National University. Assessments of the findings from this survey are published in the *Australian Social Attitudes: The First Report* (Wilson, et al. 2005).

Globalization is complex and dynamic, but often wrongly reduced to a one-dimensional process. Some analysts (e.g., Marsh, Meagher, and Wilson 2005) suggest that Australians are closed toward globalization. Still others argue that this assessment overgeneralizes and neglects to consider the complex realities of Australian attitudes toward globalization. Those scholars propose a more dynamic understanding of globalization and social responses, based on a four-fold classification of globalization (James 2006; Nairn and James 2005).

First, embodied globalization tracks the movements of people. Although Australians maintain firm opposition to trafficking in human beings, Australian attitudes toward legal immigration have shifted. Between 1996 and 2003, Australians expressed an increased positive attitude toward immigration. In 2003, 69 percent of respondents thought that "immigrants are generally good for the economy" and 74 percent believed that "immigrants make Australia open to new ideas and cultures" (James 2006:3). James suggests that future research needs to ask Australians about their attitudes toward tourism and the movement of family, friends, and themselves around the world. This shift in attitudes toward embodied globalization surfaces in Australian families whose members travel extensively.

Second, object-extended globalization centers on the movement of objects such as traded commodities around the world. James (2006) suggests that, as in other societies, Australians desire more global choices, but also wish to protect their economy. As Australian families negotiate the benefits and costs of engaging in the global marketplace, they are both receptive to and cautious about global consumption.

Third, agency-extended globalization reflects the global shifts in locations of companies and corporations. Australian families recognize the wisdom of reclaiming control of their natural resources, rather than shipping off so much of their raw mineral wealth, thus avoiding becoming what world systems theorists would call semi-peripheral nations.

Fourth, disembodied-extended globalization includes the many information and communication technologies typical of the global networks of computers and other digital devices. Access to the World Wide Web is highly valued in Australian families, and 70 percent of the respondents to the AuSSA reported having Internet access (Denmark 2005). The Internet and instant wireless communications make families living in the outback less remote and connect families and friends on a global scale. Again, as in many societies, telecommunications are embraced enthusiastically, yet technology remains the least regulated of the four forms of globalization.

The AuSSA also reveals Australians' increasingly pluralistic attitudes toward family structure in terms of what constitutes a family. For many Australians, having a child or children appears more important in defining family than the religious or even civil status of marriage. Ninety-two percent of 18–34-year-old Australian adults viewed single-parent households as families. Sixty-two percent of this same demographic agree that gay and lesbian couples with children also are families (Evans and Gray 2005:19). These findings of the AuSSA have important repercussions for Australian educational, governmental, and social agencies, including the development and delivery of Australian family policy and services.

While embracing family diversity in the face of globalization, Australian society is intent on actively appreciating families through national initiatives aimed at building local communities and strengthening families (Scott 2000). Many Australians do not see families as islands unto themselves, but rather as elements in larger ecological systems composed of families, communities, and the global environment.

Such a dynamic understanding of globalization provides a richer analysis of the impacts of globalization on societies and families. Contrary to an interpretation that Australians are closed to globalization, many Australian families appear to hold balanced and increasingly positive appreciation of living in a global world, even encouraging their children to be global learners (Australian Government 2006b). This emerging shift in Australian cultural attitudes is consistent with continued exploration of innovative family structures and community approaches to strengthening families, as well as additional review of multicultural needs and policies. The winds of globalization demand that a society like Australia honestly reflects on its responsibilities in the world and project the type of global community it desires to be, while embracing change, diversity, and challenge.

Janet R. Grochowski, Ph.D., is Professor Emerita, University of St. Thomas, St. Paul, Minnesota. Over her 29 years developing curricula and teaching undergraduate courses in health studies and family studies, globalization emerged as a central theme. Since 1990, her academic and scholarly interests and professional travel have included a focus on Australia and the South Pacific region.

Critical Thinking Questions:

1. How does a global perspective on families differ from a cross-cultural or comparative perspective on families?
2. What is there about globalization that may place families at risk? What may enhance the quality of family life?
3. How can postmodernism or a feminist lens enrich a global approach to families?
4. Grochowski discusses Australian family and society in a global context. In a similar fashion, place families in another society, other than your own, in such a global context.

2

Global Change and Demographic Shifts: Family Characteristics and Societal Transformation

The statistics are staggering. Worldwide, 40 million people live with the human immune deficiency virus (HIV), which causes acquired immune deficiency syndrome (AIDS). In 2006 alone, 4.3 million new cases of HIV/AIDS were reported ("Global AIDS Epidemic Continues to Grow" 2006). The World Health Organization estimates that the number of AIDS orphans—children under 15 years of age who have lost both parents to HIV/AIDS—will reach 41 million by the year 2010 (World Health Organization 2003).

The HIV/AIDS pandemic illustrates the effects of an overwhelming health crisis on families in societies across the globe. Many of the people infected with the virus are in their most productive years, often having just begun new families. The burden of care for family members infected with HIV/AIDS, coping with the loss of family members, and the increasing number of children orphaned by HIV/AIDS stresses families and societies to the extent that, at times of uncertain or dwindling resources, extended families and the communities in which those suffering with

HIV/AIDS live may be reluctant or unable to commit scarce resources to feed, shelter, or educate orphans. In some regions of Africa, families are increasingly headed by grandparents and even adolescents (United Nations 2003).

The impact of globalization on families may originate in economic, political, cultural, technological, or other spheres. However, perhaps in no other area of family life is the effect of globalization more evident than in changes in population characteristics. Morbidity and mortality, fertility, and migration serve as powerful driving forces through which global economic, political, and other patterns influence marriage, parenting (including adoption), and other family structures, often in very gendered ways. Still, the paucity of demographic data in some areas, such as those concerning the death, birth, and migration patterns of GLBT individuals, limits our understanding of the effects of demographic forces on the full range of diverse family forms in a global society.

I begin Chapter 2 with a brief presentation on the significance of demographic transition and the place of population dynamics in families' lives, followed by a summary of what we know about the global morbidity and mortality, fertility, and migration of families today. I apply a gender lens to migration and examine the phenomena of migration for marriage and transnational adoption. I close the chapter with a discussion of the ways in which demographics in general and migration in particular are contested, particularly across generations, as well as the ways in which our full understanding of global immigration is hampered by a limited definition of family. Finally, an essay by Margaret L. Kvasnicka, a Sister of St. Joseph and director of a refuge for immigrant and refugee women in St. Paul, Minnesota, demonstrates the potential for personal and family resiliency even under the most trying circumstances.

Demographic Transition and Family Dynamics

Demographers examine changing patterns of population growth and decline through the nexus among death rates, birth rates, and migration rates. The net sum of changes in these three rates provides an estimation of a population's growth rate. Although individual and family actions compose the data that result in population growth and decline, demographic transitions both reflect and shape families' competition for such scarce resources as food and shelter, even employment, as well as the supply of members eligible for one to marry and available to care for dependent members. In other words, demographic characteristics can reveal much about the global directions of social change.

Briefly, the theory of demographic transition explains how premodern societies, with high mortality rates and high fertility rates, shift to modern societies with low fertility and low mortality rates. In early stages of demographic transition, death rates decline due to control over infectious diseases, as well as improved standards of living around nutrition, sanitation, and childbirth. Demographic transition holds that, as societies modernize, cultural patterns involving labor shift, and women and their partners acquire both the desire and the means to control human reproduction effectively. Children become more expensive in terms of both direct and indirect costs. Hence, cultural changes weaken the value of larger family sizes, but increase the value placed on each child. The ensuing declines in fertility rates and mortality rates produce slower population growth (Kirk 1996).

As depicted in Table 2.1, total world population more than doubled, from 2.5 billion to 6.1 billion, in the last quarter of the twentieth century. Although the world population growth rate has slowed, the total world population is still projected to reach 9.1 billion by the year 2050. The most dramatic increases in population growth are projected to occur in Africa, which will grow from 224 million in 1950 to almost 2 billion in 2050, and in the least developed regions of the world, which will grow from slightly more than 200 million in 1950 to 1.7 billion in 2050.

Morbidity and Mortality

As stated earlier, as a society moves through the stages of demographic transition, the rates of disease and death from such factors as infection and childbirth decline. Profound shifts in morbidity and mortality provide families with greater certainty that adults, as well as the next generation, will be around to provide economic support, protection, socialization, and care for family members.

But infectious and parasitic diseases remain one of the prime causes of death, especially of children, in the developing world today. The maternal mortality rate (deaths of mothers per 100,000 live births) ranges from a low of 2 in Greece and 6 in Australia and Canada to a high of 2,100 in Sierra Leone and 2,300 in Rwanda. Yet, in one of the most developed countries in the world today, the United States, as a result of the wide variation in access to and quality of prenatal, childbirth, and maternal health care, the maternal mortality rate in the United States is 12 (Seager 2003:104–111).

I opened this chapter with a synopsis of the crisis facing families as a result of the HIV/AIDS pandemic. Family scholars are well-advised to be concerned about the implications of this scourge on families. As with so many other global concerns, the Southern hemisphere bears a grossly disproportionate share of the pandemic. Seventy percent of the earth's inhabitants infected with HIV live in sub-Saharan Africa. Most of those infected will die of complications associated with this disease (Project on Global Working Families 2006; Seager 2003:48).

Table 2.1 World Population, 1950–2050

Year	1950	1975	2000	2025	2050
			Thousands		
World Total	2,519,470	4,073,740	6,085,572	7,905,239	9,075,903
Continents					
Africa	224,068	415,824	812,466	1,344,491	1,936,952
Asia	1,396,254	2,395,218	3,675,799	4,728,131	5,217,202
Europe	547,405	675,548	728,463	707,235	653,323
Latin America and the Caribbean	167,321	322,449	522,929	696,541	782,903
Northern America	171,615	243,931	314,968	388,032	437,950
Oceania	12,807	21,284	30,949	40,809	47,572
Regions					
More developed	812,772	1,047,196	1,193,354	1,248,954	1,236,200
Less developed	1,706,698	3,026,543	4,892,218	6,656,285	7,839,702
Least developed	200,789	355,870	673,524	1,167,461	1,735,368

Source: Compiled from United Nations 2005c: Panel 1, Basic Data.

That quintessential feature of globalization, geographic mobility (even short-term mobility), is a significant risk factor in the transmission of HIV. Population movement increases dissemination of the virus, while setting in motion risky sexual behaviors such as frequent casual sexual relations with multiple partners among individuals (mostly men, but also women) who move frequently from place to place for reasons related to employment, war, and other actions (Legarde, et al. 2003).

In most societies, women's lower social and sexual status places them at particular risk of HIV infection by their male partners. A series of factors, characteristic of patriarchal social systems, further increases the frequency of women's exposure and decreases women's ability to reduce the likelihood of transmission. These factors include:

- Men's entitlement to sexual access to women
- Women's limited power to negotiate safe sex practices
- Coerced or violent sexual contact
- Polygyny (one man with multiple wives)

As a result, over half of all cases of HIV infection are borne by women. In some countries, the prevalence of HIV infection among pregnant women has fallen (e.g., to 11 percent in Uganda), but in other countries (e.g., Botswana) almost half of all women seeking prenatal care still test positive for HIV (Seager 2003:48). Undoubtedly, these gendered effects reflect differences in national health policies and public health programs, as well as variations in the social norms regarding women's status, power, and autonomy. However, as the traditional caretakers for their families, when unmarried women, wives, and mothers become ill, they are often bereft of someone to care for them. When women become ill and die, they leave entire households and family systems without a primary caregiver.

To reduce their perception of the risk of HIV infection, African and Asian, but also European and other men, seek young girls, presuming them to be infection-free. However, the practice does little to reduce men's actual level of exposure, because young girls are sold as "virgins" multiple times. Such practices do result in higher demands for young girls in the sex trade and, consequently, in girls being infected at earlier ages. According to the World Health Organization (2003), on average, females contract HIV five to ten years younger than do males.

Morbidity and mortality from diseases like HIV/AIDS impact family systems in critical ways. First, adults' ability to provide for their families as income earners is compromised. Second, family systems are strained as the balance between well and infected members shifts. In particular, extended family systems are taxed as parents die, leaving behind orphaned children. Third, children may be forced from school in order to seek employment or to care for other family members (World Health

Organization 2003). Further, in male-dominated societies, with the death of husbands and fathers, children, women, the elderly, and other surviving vulnerable family members are left more exposed to sexual and economic exploitation.

Browning has described AIDS in Africa as a study in how globalization threatens marriage and the family. Browning begins with Kilbride and Kilbride's (1990) analysis of how modernization and globalization have compromised "Africanity," the high value placed in East African societies on procreation, children, and parenting as a way of "realizing the divine in human life" (Browning 2003:181). While this traditional system operated in a system that endorsed polygyny, a double sexual standard, and higher status for men, Africanity was a system embedded in local community. Browning believes that the increased emphasis on male participation in a wage market (often involving long periods of time away from wives) and the continued discrimination against women in the same system, as well as the geographic mobility and urbanization that has accompanied modernization, have weakened extended family ties, bringing "the East African family system to the verge of chaos" (Browning 2003:181).

Browning's argument is persuasive. Economic and social systems such as those found in globalizing Africa are ripe for the widespread transmission of HIV/AIDS. HIV/AIDS decimates families by fostering child abandonment and fatherlessness, contributing to a rising prevalence of children raising themselves on the street, and increasing the overdependence on grandparents as surrogate parents. The pandemic threatens not only individual families and entire social systems, but potentially destabilizes the entire world as family disintegration, poverty, and other deprivations erode the very fabric of society, making society vulnerable to internal and external violence and oppression. In the words of then U.S. Secretary of State Colin Powell, speaking in recognition of World AIDS Day in 2003 (Bureau of International Information Programs 2003):

> Each death represents a personal tragedy—the loss of a mother, father, sister, brother, son, daughter, loved one. Each death also is an irreparable loss to our international community.
>
> Left to ravage, the disease decimates a society's most productive members. It sickens those between the ages of 15 and 24, those who take care of the very young and the very old. It destroys those who teach and trade, support their families, and otherwise contribute to their nation's development. AIDS saps global growth. Unchecked, AIDS can lay waste to whole countries and destabilize entire regions of the world.

Biological and social risks of AIDS are inextricably woven together (Gdadebo, Rayman-Read, and Heymann 2003), and the magnitude of the pandemic and its effects on individuals, families, societies, and whole regions is almost unfathomable. However, innovative research programs and intervention strategies offer some hope. For example, a recent partnership between the Harvard University School of Public Health and the government of Botswana aims to better understand work-place, home, and community experiences that affect those infected with HIV or car-ing for others who are living with HIV/AIDS. The program administers social and medical interventions in the workplace, where most adults spend their time. Such research-guided programs could dramatically improve the quality of family life, including the care and survival of not just those living with HIV/AIDS, but also those orphaned by AIDS and caring for those with health and other problems asso-ciated with the virus (Project on Global Working Families 2006).

Declining Fertility

Morbidity and mortality are critical parts of the engine that moves demographic transition. Fertility is another. As societies move through the first to the second stage of demographic transition, human fertility levels remain high long past the time death rates begin to fall. Cultural supports for high fertility can persist beyond the time when infant mortality begins to fall and life expectancy begins to rise.

Across the globe, fertility is on a steady decline and family sizes are shrinking. Many European nations now find themselves with fertility rates well below human replacement level, thus creating grave problems for labor supply and economic consumption. Mean household size has fallen to 2.8 in developed regions of the world, while, even in the developing world, mean household size has fallen dramatically: to 3.7 in East Asia, to 4.1 in the Caribbean, to 4.9 in Southeast Asia, and to 5.7 in North Africa. Across the world, families are shifting from large, extended families to smaller, nuclear families and single-person households (United Nations Programme on the Family 2003a).

However, statistical means regarding national fertility rates can mask variations within countries, such as lower fertility rates in urban areas of India, while rates remain high in rural areas in the same country (Singh 2004). However, as presented in Table 2.2, over the last two decades of the twentieth century, the percentage of coun-tries with total fertility of 4.5 or higher children per woman fell from about 60 percent to about 40 percent. During the same time, the proportion of countries with total fertility of 2.5 or fewer children per woman rose from one-sixth to one-third. These changes have been observed in not only the most developed countries, but also in the least developed countries. Although sub-Saharan Africa, Arab Southwest Asia, and Melanesia are exceptions to this general decline, Caldwell (2001:93) observes that "the range of populations involved in the decline was unpredicted and unprece-dented." Further, the decline in worldwide fertility of the last years of the century accelerated faster than previous projections (Bulato 2001).

Table 2.2 Declines and Projected Declines in Fertility Rates, 1950–2050

	5-Year Period	1950–1955	1975–1980	2000–2005	2025–2030	2045–2050
		Number of Children per Woman				
World Total		5.02	3.92	2.65	2.23	2.05
Continents						
Africa		6.72	6.60	4.97	3.69	2.52
Asia		5.89	4.18	2.47	2.02	1.91
Europe		2.66	1.97	1.40	1.65	1.83
Latin America and the Caribbean		6.69	6.75	5.47	3.61	2.60
Northern America		3.47	1.78	1.99	1.83	1.85
Oceania		3.87	2.81	2.32	2.05	1.92
Regions						
More developed		2.84	1.91	1.56	1.72	1.84
Less developed		6.17	4.65	2.90	2.31	2.07
Least developed		6.64	6.44	5.02	3.50	2.57

Note: 2045–2050 is the last period for which current projections are available.
Source: Compiled from United Nations 2005c: Panel 2, Detailed Data.

Declining worldwide fertility is both a cause and a consequence of major changes in values and norms regarding, among other social factors, women's roles, as well as national and international population control efforts. That shift in family structure, coupled with the general pattern of demographic aging, is due not only to declining fertility rates, but also to increasing age at first marriage, increasing divorce rates, and increasing longevity.

The reduced population growth in certain European countries with low and declining birth rates over the past quarter century is occurring in spite of accompanying declines in death rates. But to what extent can demographic transitions be said to be impacted by globalization? Global patterns of migration, and the consequent geographic shifts in families' locations, structures, and cultures, give some indication of the effects of globalization on worldwide demographics. The worldwide fertility decline can be viewed in similar global terms. Bulato (2001) offers seven theoretical approaches to understanding the effects of global fertility transitions on families:

1. Demographic
2. Historical

3. Sociological
4. Psychological
5. Economic
6. Gender
7. Policy

Demographic theories associate declining fertility rates with declining mortality rates. Historical theories emphasize socioeconomic development and the availability of effective contraception, as well as ideologies regarding population explosion. Sociological theories attribute worldwide fertility decline to mortality reduction, declines in the demand for children, and increases in the ability to regulate fertility. Psychological theories stress the individual's readiness, willingness, and ability to moderate fertility. Economic theories for this decline rely on microeconomic factors originating in the family, along with human capital theory, including the cost of raising children and opportunity costs, particularly regarding maternal employment. Gender perspectives consider the indirect influences of family and gender systems, such as women's autonomy in more or less rigidly stratified societies. Finally, policy perspectives seek to reveal the place of population policy, including family planning programs, in influencing access to contraception and attitudes favorable to contraceptive use.

Rather than a single theory, a combination of theoretical approaches provides the best fit in terms of explaining societal shifts in fertility. In fact, a recent study conducted by the Organization for Economic Cooperation and Development (d'Addio and d'Ercole 2005) confirmed that cross-country variations in fertility rates are related to macro- and microsocial drivers such as labor markets and social and fiscal policies, as well as to individual characteristics. For example, demographic transition can be mediated by historical events such as wars, which can, in turn, yield dramatic imbalances in the gender ratio (at least in the short run). Families may produce a bumper crop of babies in anticipation of or immediately following periods of extended separation due to migrant employment, military deployment, or other circumstances. Or, as discussed earlier, the extent of the lag between declining death rates and declining fertility rates can be shaped by psychological factors, including perceptions of the risk of infant mortality or adult death from disease or violence.

While dramatic, long-term changes in population rates are usually associated with social development, including the indirect effects of changes in women's educational and employment opportunities, spectacular reductions in fertility rates have been achieved in relatively short periods of time by coordinated, often aggressive, family planning policies. Some government interventions, such as China's one-child policy, have had demonstrable effects not only on fertility rates, but also on sex ratios (Sheng 2004; Yi 2002). That country's population policies have been accompanied by increases in the selective abortion of female fetuses and in female infanticide, demonstrating that changes in the mean preferred number of children can be complicated by traditional gender structures, including male preference. The consequences of the gender imbalances produced by China's policy are only now beginning to be felt, especially in urban areas, as the one-child generation enters adulthood and becomes eligible for marriage.

Sociologists have another immediate opportunity to study the impact of sweeping social policies surrounding fertility. Births in Germany dropped 4 percent from 2004 to 2005, to 690,000, the lowest number since World War II ("Germany Beefs Up Benefits to Bolster the Nation's Birth Rate" 2007). However, effective January 1, 2007, Germany's "Eltengeld" program allows a worker who leaves employment after the birth of a child to receive up to two-thirds of her or his net wage, up to $2,375 per month for a year following the birth. Similar incentives, such as those found in France (Moore 2006), already appear to be having an impact on fertility rates across Western Europe.

The next few years may demonstrate the demographic intersections of psychological and social factors at a particular point in demographic history. As the policies which have been described above play out across China, the European Union, and other Western societies, we may see continued and even increasing shifts in the demand by highly developed, postmodern economies for immigrant workers and their families. Such demographic shifts will continue to both shape and reflect gender relations, most likely in an egalitarian direction.

However, the attainment of equilibrium in fertility and mortality is complex and may not involve couples' explicit calculations of death and birth rates. As societies develop, children contribute less economically. Children in more developed societies spend less time in work and more time in education. Essentially, children in more developed societies are more directly costly than children in less developed societies. But children in more developed societies are also indirectly costly because they compromise adults' economic and other opportunities, including maternal employment and earnings and family savings.

Accompanying these fertility changes during periods of economic development, societies shift from expectations that families will be larger, multigenerational households emphasizing communal values, to smaller, conjugal households emphasizing individualistic values. High fertility is often supported by religious institutions and close community associations. But, as societies modernize, both state-sanctioned norms and more informal social controls encourage individual decision-making regarding fertility and, consequently, smaller family size. Diffusion of information serves to provide individuals and couples with access to cultural ideas and practices that shape fertility patterns. Bulato (2001) summarizes these social changes which intersect to create population declines:

- Mortality reduction, including maternal and infant mortality
- Reduced economic contributions from children
- Opportunity costs of bearing children
- Family transformation
- Vanishing cultural supports for childbearing
- Marriage delay
- Cultural diffusion surrounding fertility practices
- Improved access to effective fertility regulation

Fertility shifts have been dramatically affected by the last of these factors: the availability and distribution of effective contraceptive technology. With social development comes improved technology and access to effective, safe fertility regulation, including contraception and abortion. Today, the percentage of married women using some form of modern contraception is highest in the developed world (e.g., 78 percent in Germany, 79 percent in Switzerland) and lowest in the developing world (e.g., 1 percent in Burundi, Chad, and Mauritania) (Seager 2003:104–111).

The factors implied in the eight explanations do not operate in mutually exclusive ways, however. For example, Bulato (2001) notes that government family planning programs are often associated with societal development. Also, sociohistorical crises can interrupt the usual demographic patterns, at least on a temporary basis. Caldwell (2004) found this to be the case during both the English civil war of the seventeenth century and the fall of communism in Eastern Europe in the late twentieth century. At times such as those, deferred marriage and declining marital fertility may also reflect uncertainty about the future during new socioeconomic and legal times.

Coale (1973) argued that three factors must occur in order for fertility rates to decline in a society. First, fertility must be within the realm of possible rational choice. Second, reduced fertility must be perceived as an advantage to the individual (or couple or society). Third, effective techniques—contraception and/or abortion—must be available for fertility control. Likewise, delayed marriage in more developed societies reduces the potential years of partnered fertility, particularly in societies in which nonmarital fertility is negatively sanctioned.

Italian society provides an interesting illustration of the dramatic changes in fertility patterns facing a society hurtling into the postmodern era. As described in Table 2.3, while the crude death rate in Italy has been essentially unchanged, the total fertility rate is approaching half the rate in 1950. Between 1950 and 2000, the population in Italy grew 10,611,000, due primarily to a net migration rate

Table 2.3   Factors in Population Growth for Italy, 1950–2000

Year	1950	1975	2000
Total fertility rate	2.32	1.89	1.28
Crude death rate	9.9	9.8	10.0
Net migration rate	n/a	n/a	2.1
Population growth rate	0.64	0.36	0.13
Population (thousands)	47,104	55,441	57,715

Source: Compiled from United Nations 2005c: Panel 2, Detailed Data.

higher than that in the rest of Europe (albeit comparable to other more developed countries). Population growth in Italy, with an exceptionally low birth rate and a relatively stable growth rate, is due, not to shifts in the death or birth rates, but instead is in large part to the influx of migrants—legal as well as illegal—into that country. Otherwise, contemporary Italy has all the family characteristics of a society with a declining rate of population growth:

- Increasing age at first marriage
- Increasing percentage of cohabiting unmarried couples
- Increasing separation and divorce rates
- Increasing percentage of single-parent families
- Increasing percentage of blended families
- Declining birth rates
- Increasing birth rates outside of marriage

Although some (e.g., Comunian 2005:226) choose to describe these changes in Italian society as an "institutional crisis," many of the changes are rooted in gender liberation, specifically the greater equality between men's and women's roles, as well as increasing legal protection of the rights of women and children.

In turn, decreasing family size shapes marital dynamics, including decline in polygyny and arranged marriage and increasing frequency of cohabitation and forms of nonmarital pairing (Adams 2004). Both macrosocial forces (e.g., economic and legal changes and improved educational and employment opportunities for women) and what Jelin (2004:33) calls "sociocultural factors linked to individuation" (e.g., modern values such as personal autonomy and free choice of marriage partners based on romantic love) influence marriage, divorce, and remarriage patterns during periods of declining fertility. In fact, the very meaning of marriage as a "divine match," a holy sacramental union, appears to wane with macrosocial changes in societal development and fertility (Singh 2004). As a consequence, families in many parts of the world, even the least developed, are shifting from being economic producers who consume to a more fragile collection of individuals who are economically bound primarily as consumers (Adams 2004; Vincent 2000).

Other changes in structural arrangements of families reflect religious, national, and cultural differences, as well as economic constraints. For example, Italy's divorce rate of 12.5 percent (1 divorce for every 8 marriages) lags far behind the 44 percent divorce rates of Sweden and England. Also, although young adults in Italy are delaying marriage, they are often doing so while continuing to live in the same household with their family of origin, rather than alone or in cohabitating arrangements. In other words, Italians continue to value attachments to their families of origin, even as they may be less likely to form new families of their own (Comunian 2005:227).

Finally, lower fertility also results in "grayer" demographics. Declining fertility rates, coupled with increasing life expectancy, have increased the proportion of older persons (60 years and older) within overall populations and decreased the support ratio (the number of working people relative to the number of retired people). By the year 2050, the numbers of older persons will more than triple, from 606 million to 2 billion worldwide. In developed regions, the population of those older than 60 is predicted to increase from 20 percent to 33 percent; in developing regions, the population of those older than 60 is predicted to increase from 8 percent to 20 percent. The effects of demographic aging are seen in families, with challenges to intergenerational solidarity and care giving, as well as housing, social security systems, and health costs (United Nations Programme on the Family 2003a).

Population Control as an International Policy Concern

Ideological concerns regarding population are a key part of understanding fertility transition in a global perspective. Caldwell (2001:102) discusses how, beginning in the 1940s, simultaneously, but in contrast with deeply rooted pronatalist traditions in the developed west, Western ideologies grew around beliefs "that the deliberate control of fertility in poor, high-growth countries was desirable, even the path of virtue." By the middle of the twentieth century such outlets as *New York Times* had published editorials endorsing worldwide population control, the World Council of Churches had adopted a policy position favoring the same, and the American Public Health Association formally advocated the inclusion of family-planning services as part of health services. By the late 1960s *The Population Bomb* (Ehrlich 1968) had encapsulated the belief that fertility decisions and outcomes were of consequence, not only to individuals and their families, but also to nations and the entire planet.

As a result, governments in developed societies are more likely to view their fertility rates as being too low, whereas governments in the south are increasingly more likely to view their fertility rates as too high (Seager 2003). In the developed world, population control ideology has provided couples, and especially women, with a belief system to support delaying childbearing, limiting family size, and even, for a few, ruling out marriage or childbearing altogether. Economic prosperity as well as social movements (e.g., the civil rights movement, women's movements) provided corollary inducements for such dramatic social changes as extending the time spent in formal schooling, women's employment, and delayed marriage. However, ironically, at least in the United States, but also in some other developed Western societies, a population double standard exists. Although women of economic, racial, and other privilege may be celebrated for their fertility and celebrated for taking heroic means to resolve infertility, poor women, women of color, and immigrant women, especially those receiving some form of public assistance, are stereotyped (e.g., as "welfare queens") and denigrated for having children.

Rosero-Bixby (2001) argues that government-led family planning programs hold a critical place in fertility decline. These programs can stimulate consideration of previously taboo subjects (like birth control) and can create a critical mass in the population. In turn, these processes can increase demand for family planning services and technology and, eventually, stimulate supply of those services and technology. Rosero-Bixby distinguishes between two rationales shaping global family planning programs—one macrolevel rationale and another microlevel rationale consistent with social activism, such as that led by Margaret Sanger in the early twentieth century in the United States. The macrolevel rationale may be favored by centralized government officials in their efforts to stem the rate of population growth and associated economic and social problems related to environmental degradation, economic development, social unrest, and rural-to-urban migration. The microlevel rationale may be favored by health practitioners and social workers concerned about women's reproductive health, sexuality, and rights, often across national borders. By the 1994 International Conference on Population and Development, family planning policy shifted demonstrably from macro- to microlevel rationale. This shift has had implications for political and social support, funding, effectiveness, and persistence of global initiatives directed at population control.

These national population ideologies can shape access to reproductive health systems, not only domestically, but also abroad. Annually, major donors for overseas population programs give more than 10 million U.S. dollars to overseas population programs, primarily in Southern countries. Most of this funding (63 percent) is in the form of direct assistance from developed countries, with another 20 percent in the form of loans from the World Bank. A smaller, but significant, amount of funding (11 percent) comes from private foundations and nongovernmental organizations (NGOs). Six of the seven biggest donors among private foundations and NGOs are from the United States. Those donors include the Bill and Melinda Gates Foundation, the Ford Foundation, the Packard Foundation, the Population Council, the MacArthur Foundation, and the Rockefeller Foundation. Marie Stopes International, a foundation based in the United Kingdom, is the second biggest donor among private foundations and NGOs (Seager 2003:42–43).

As a result of improved contraceptive technology and increased access to safe abortion, virtually certain birth control with little or no risk is available to most women in Western societies. Beginning in the 1960s, the birth control pill and intrauterine contraceptive devices, as well as sterilization (of males as well as females) for family planning and safer, easier suction abortion techniques made birth control increasingly widely available and practiced in the most developed countries (Caldwell 2001). Birth control methods with higher user and technical failure rates, methods with more side effects, methods involving coital partner cooperation, and methods available only through medical sources have lower rates of adoption, continuation, and success in preventing pregnancy than other methods.

Yet, forty years of research has repeatedly confirmed that individuals in the least developed societies are less likely than individuals in the most developed societies to practice effective birth control—and are unlikely to even contemplate restricting family size—because they do not have access to family planning services. In the least developed nations of the world, methods of contraception are often unavailable and abortion is rare and not used to limit family size (Balfour, Evans, Notestein, and Taeuber 1950; Caldwell 2001).

While unplanned children are not the same as unwanted children, when women are unable to control the number and timing of their births, their children and their families bear substantial direct and indirect costs. Quantity and quality of physical and social resources, as well as parental time and energy, may be strained. Further, a woman's childbearing patterns, including the number and spacing of children, are directly related to her ability to maintain employment and pursue economic advancement and independence, as well as her own and her children's health and well-being.

Fertility in a Global, Postmodern World

In some ways, fertility preferences in a global, postmodern world can be perplexing. Bachrach (2001) suggests that certain values, attitudes, and orientations associated with the postmodern individual are likewise associated with changes in fertility preferences. She identifies these ideals as self-realization, personal freedom (in lifestyle and relationships), quality of life valued over material well-being, questioning traditional authority, and tolerating and respecting diversity. Further, she connects these traits with a declining reliance on institutions that support high fertility. The postmodern individual relies less on traditional, authoritarian religious systems and communal, patriarchal family systems. Thus, a postmodern culture emphasizing self-actualization may act to decrease fertility. Individuals may prefer to postpone or avoid childbearing altogether, in order to pursue personal objectives related to work and leisure (Bachrach 2001).

However, in societies such as Finland and Sweden with a high percentage of the population espousing postmodern views, preferred fertility rates continue to surpass actual fertility rates. Fertility preferences may be slow to change, or childbearing and childrearing may be a source of personal fulfillment in a postmodern world (Bachrach 2001). These postmodern value orientations may well be global phenomena associated with transnational contact via educational programs, mass media, international social policies, or other means.

Sweeping Migration

In addition to mortality and fertility, demographic transition depends on migration. Three percent (175 million) of the world's population live outside their country of birth, and the United Nations estimates that 20 million people worldwide are refugees. Migration and refugee status is linked not only to economic aspirations, but also to discrimination, violence, and even natural disasters across the globe. Cultural, ethnic, racial, and religious differences and lack of integration into the host country place significant stress on relationships among parents, children, elders, and other family members. Migration by men, both internal and seasonal, contributes to higher numbers of female-headed households worldwide. Meanwhile, sex trafficking and sexual exploitation of women and children and associated international crime continues to increase (United Nations Programme on the Family 2003a).

Like morbidity and mortality, as well as fertility, transnational migration plays a key part in determining the demographic complexion of a society. Table 2.4 shows that the net effect of migration favors immigration into more developed regions (North America and Europe, as well as Oceania) and emigration from less and least developed regions (Latin America and the Caribbean, as well as Africa and Asia).

Historically, immigration has been a one-way path of no return. Immigrant individuals and families departed the home country with little or no expectation of ever returning to the society and loved ones left behind. Of the emigration of the Irish to America, Peter McCorry, Irish nationalist and weekly newspaper editor for the Irish community in New York City in the late 1860s and early 1870s, wrote in 1870:

> They had passed the bitter ordeal of leave-taking with friends and relations; they
> had looked for the last time on the graves of parents and children, gazed tenderly

Table 2.4 Net Migration Rates, 1995–2000

Continents	
Africa	−0.4
Asia	−0.4
Europe	1.5
Latin American and the Caribbean	−1.7
Northern America	4.5
Oceania	3.0
Regions	
More developed	2.2
Less developed	−0.6
Least developed	−0.5

Source: Compiled from United Nations 2005c: Panel 1, Basic Data.

and affectionately on the well-remembered spots of their childhood, with feelings which no pen has ever yet or ever shall be able to describe. Some had left fathers and mothers, and sisters and brothers; some had left wives and young families, dependent on the mercies of a cold and callous world, who sustained themselves with the thought that, with God's help, before long, they would be able to send the first remittance to cheer the desolate homes they had left forever. (McCorry 1984:154)

Miyoshi (1993:748) describes the experience of migrants who, upon arriving in the new country, are "cut off from their own homes . . . [and who] disappear into huge urban slums without the protection of a traditional . . . mutual dependence system."

Organizations like the International Organization for Migration (2006), an intergovernmental organization founded in 1951, are "committed to the principle that human and orderly migration benefits migrants and society." Today, family reunification is a primary goal of the immigration policies of most nations. As demonstrated in Table 2.5, by far the most frequent class of immigrants admitted to the United States is immediate relatives of United States citizens. In fact, two-thirds of immigrants into the United States in 2004 were children, spouses, siblings, or grandparents being reunited with kin. An estimated 2 million people—husbands, wives, children, and siblings of legal, permanent residents of the United States—qualify for admission, but remain on waiting lists to become legal, permanent residents. A backlog in processing applications, plus the immigrant visa quotas set by the

Immigrants from Europe arriving in Haifa, Israel by Robert Capa
Robert Capa/Magnum Photos

Table 2.5   Immigrants Admitted to the United States by Class of Admission, 1990–2004

Class of Admission	Number	Percentage
Immediate relatives of U.S. citizens	406,074	43.0%
Family-sponsored	214,355	22.7%
Employment-based	155,330	16.4%
Refugees and asylum seekers	71,230	7.5%
IRCA*	128	0.0%
Other immigrants	99,025	10.5%
Total immigrants	946,142	100.1%

*The Immigration Reform and Control Act of 1986 virtually completed the amnesty process before 2000.

Source: Adapted from U.S. Census Bureau 2006: Table 6. Immigrants Admitted by Class of Admission, 1990–2004.

U.S. Congress, ensure that only a small number of family members are admitted to legal, permanent residence status each year (Hopfensperger 2006:A1). According to State Department statistics, the lag time is as much as 22 years for siblings from the Philippines who applied in 1984 (Hopfensperger 2006:A21). Such delays create significant hardships for families, who are unable to reunite, and who, therefore, may be forced to live alone or as single parents, while waiting for family reunification.

For example, to meet the growing demand for foreign nurses in the United States, particularly in the elder care sector, the Immigration and Naturalization Service had created a special pool of 50,000 visas restricted to foreign nurses and their families. The last of those special visas was issued in December 2006. Such a system has been criticized for creating a "brain drain" in the Philippines and other countries, which send skilled workers to developed societies like the United States. The termination of that special immigration program leaves nurses who immigrated ahead of their families with no assurance that they will be reunited in the near future, if ever (Hopfensperger 2006).

Although policies of first preference in granting visas for family-sponsored immigration favor unmarried daughters and sons of current United States citizens, marriage to an American citizen has long been a model for immigration into the United States. Time-series analysis has revealed that an increase in marriages to United States citizens often accompanies a change in the law guiding qualifications for immigrant visas (Jasso 1997). However, immigration procured through marriage has potentially troubling consequences for the families thus established. Immigration-motivated marriages may be more fragile and less stable than marriages contracted under other circumstances.

Independent of immigration policies and practices, the challenges and cultural contradictions of immigration can affect an array of family dynamics, including parenting styles, intergenerational care giving, and gender relations. For example, research has found that Jamaican men who immigrated to New York are likely to continue to espouse the traditional gender double standard, whereas their wives, who remained behind, rejected such a standard (Roopnarine and Shin 2003). Booth, Crouter, and Landale's (1997) synthesis of the research on immigration and the family demonstrates that immigration policies themselves have a direct impact on the ability of families to adjust and adapt to transnational life. Transnational families who are unable to be reunited may have great difficulty synchronizing members' life courses and family timetables and managing parenting and intergenerational care giving (Leung and Lee 2005).

Consideration of the impact of migration is not complete without consideration of migration's role in assimilation. Occupational segregation and concentration in urban ghettos, as well as the settlement house and immigrant language, education, and civic programs, have played critical roles in the "Americanization" of new immigrants to the United States. Hutter (1986–1987) describes the significance of patterns of "chain migration" in which family and friends from the home country migrate in successive waves while extending networks of mutual assistance in the old and the new country, thus assisting in adaptation to the new society. However, under the best of circumstances, immigration and assimilation may severely disrupt family order as the family negotiates differences between the adopted society and the home society. This can lead some couples to seek professional help in dealing with the social class, culture, and especially gender contradictions caused by the immigrant experience (Inclan 2003). Not surprisingly then, immigrant families are overrepresented in the social service system (Roopnarine and Shin 2003).

Such a pure assimilation approach to immigration studies has fallen into disfavor among immigration scholars. A more recent segmented assimilation approach (see Portes and Zhou 1993) emphasizes the variations in adaptation among different types of immigrants (i.e., highly skilled professionals, executives, and managers; undocumented and low skilled workers; refugees and asylum seekers). A segmented assimilation approach emphasizes the divergent resources and consequent risks that these different immigrants and their families bring with them into the host country. These resources are financial and human capital, such as social class from the home country; political capital, such as legal status upon entry into the destination country; and social capital, such as social networks, family structure, and family cohesion (Landale 1997; Rumbaut 1997). From this perspective, the most advantaged immigrants may arrive in the host country with an abundance of resources and quite well-suited to family life in the new society.

Hutter (1986–1987) argues that the ultimate ability of an immigrant group to establish itself in the host country has been highly dependent on the group's ability to reestablish and normalize family life in the host country. For example, he has described the resettlement of groups such as the Hutterites from rural Russia to relatively isolated rural communities in the United States in the late nineteenth century. Due to their isolation, Hutterites were able to maintain idiosyncratic patterns of family life, including early marriage, strict expectations of endogamy (marriage within extended kinship groups), very high fertility, and virtually universal remarriage after widowhood in the context of a cooperative, patriarchal social structure.

In contrast to earlier perspectives on assimilation and integration, cultural diversity is increasingly a theme of contemporary immigration. Immigrants often bring with them new forms of household and family formation which challenge conventional family structure. These new forms may include different traditions regarding age and other criteria of marriage and childbearing, greater emphasis on cohabitation, various blended family systems, as well as a higher or lower propensity for divorce and other forms of marital dissolution.

For example, Shaw (2004) found that Caribbean and South Asia families immigrating to Great Britain challenged that society in dramatic ways. But variations in family forms are evident even within immigrant groups. Transnational Caribbean families emphasize strong extended kin and socioeconomic relations with family remaining in the Caribbean. Transnational South Asian families are characterized by larger, three-generational households, comprised of sons who marry and bring their wives and subsequent children into the parental household. Yet, even there, significant variation exists among South Asian families, as between Mirpuri Muslims (who originate in Kashmir) and Jullundri Sikhs (the majority of Indian Punjab migrants living in Great Britain). The former were still adhering to patterns of close consanguineous marriages (especially to first cousins) and expressed preference for extended three-generational households. The latter were more likely to reject arranged marriage in favor of assisted or self-initiated marriage partner choice and neolocal residence, once the couple had married (Shaw 2004).

Immigration has always been a large part of globalization.[1] Yet, during certain periods, nations like the United States have enacted severely restrictive immigration legislation, such as the Chinese Exclusion Act of 1882 and Immigration Acts of 1921, 1924, and 1929 that placed severe restrictions on immigration from certain European countries. Bose (2006a:569) writes of these policies as representing a:

> retreat from globalization; a national acquiescence to racism, prejudice, and intolerance; and an affront to the basic fabric of a nation built by the labor of many immigrant nationalities.

Today, courts, the media, and public opinion in France, the Netherlands, the United Kingdom, and elsewhere contest the desire of immigrants to retain aspects of their home culture. For example, a tribunal court in Leeds, England, refused to overturn a school decision in which a teaching assistant in West Yorkshire, England, was dismissed for her refusal to remove her veil (Wainwright 2006). In the Netherlands, the Dutch cabinet has offered a statement that "burqas disturb public order, citizens, and safety" (BBC News 2006).

Host society ambivalence to immigrants and their families is hardly new. Today, in the face of concerns about "the other" as parasitic threats to national identity, resources, and (increasingly since the bombings on the World Trade Center in New York City on September 11, 2001) national security, immigrants and subsequent generations of their families may have a more difficult time securing distinction as productive contributors to a society and as diverse peoples who can enrich the host culture. The dominant societal perspective on immigration shapes policy, practice, rules and regulations involving controls, restrictions,

---

[1]For a brief history of immigration in the United States in the nineteenth century, see Karen Seccombe's *Families in Poverty* (2007), the first book in the *Families in the 21st Century* series.

rights, and privileges, including access of migrant families to economic, educational, legal, medical, and other social resources and, ultimately, the ease of their transition to the new society.

But the postmodern immigrant experience also increasingly involves lives lived across borders with ties maintained to home. Schiller, Basch, and Blanc-Szanton (1992a:ix) have defined transnationalism as a particular immigrant experience, a social process through which "transmigrants develop and maintain multiple relations—familial, economic, social, organizational, religious, and political—that span borders." From this perspective, immigrant families retain, extend, and preserve relationships, act and decide, and experience concerns and identities, even traveling back and forth across two or more societies over extended periods of time (Schiller, Basch, and Blanc-Szanton 1992a; Silverstein and Auerbach 2005).

Contemporary migration may well be linked to capitalist economic and other systems on a global scale, but migration also is grounded in the everyday experiences of the migrants themselves. In the twenty-first century, transnational migration defies and spans the usual concepts of culture and society, nation and tribe, race and ethnicity in a world shaped by globalization. Thus, Schiller, Basch, and Blanc-Szanton (1992b:11) describe the identities of transnational migrants as "complex," "multiple," and "fluid," and as variable from individual to individual. In the following sections, I elaborate upon some of the effects of immigration on families, including gender, marriage, transnational adoption, and parent–child relationships. In Chapter 3, I address the particular implications for families of migration across national borders by those seeking employment.

Gender and Migration

Historically, men have greatly outnumbered women as migrants. However, today women constitute a growing proportion of migrants worldwide and even outnumber men as migrants from some areas, such as the Philippines and Sri Lanka (Seager 2003). This has led some researchers (e.g., Anthias and Lazaridis 2000:1) to refer to the "feminization" of international migration.

Both the existence of a large informal economy in which irregular employment is common (with the accompanying issue of undocumented workers whose legal status rests in the hands of their employers) and an increase in female employment among local women support increasing demand for women's migration into the destination country. Thus, the feminization of migration correlates with the following in the destination country:

- A concentration of women in the service sector, particularly as domestic maids in the homes of women employed outside the home
- Poor welfare provisions

- Poor state facilities for child care
- A demand for women as sex workers, often recruited for these dangerous and vulnerable positions through sex trafficking (See Chapter 4)

Still, migrant women have been almost invisible in migration studies. Anthias and Lazaridis (2000:11) note the extent to which the sexism explicit in migration "intersects with different forms of 'othering' and racialization" through the "cross-cuttings of gender, ethnicity, and class." For example, these authors describe how policies originating in the European Union make little reference to migrant women, leading them to be critical of welfare systems, such as those found in Italy, which fail to provide basic support for migrant women and their families. An absence of training and infrastructures for employed migrant mothers ensures that these women will be permanently relegated to domestic work or illegal sex work or, if reunited with their husbands, to continued subordination within their own families. These gendered effects have consequences not only for the female migrant but also for the longer-term quality of life for her family.

Bologna, in the Emilia-Romagna region of Italy, seems to be an exception. In that city, migrant women from the Philippines, Somalia, Eritrea, and Ethiopia significantly outnumber migrant men, and the Bologna city council seems to have made a concerted effort to take gender into account when providing services to migrants. The Bologna city council aims:

> to document the presence of migrant people bearing in mind the differences between men and women and between different nationalities. If we were to have aggregate statistics under the "blanket" of the word *extracomunitari*, without specifying anything about sex or nationality, we would not face these issues properly and in their complexity in the Bolognese area. (Bernardotti, Capecchi, and Pinto [1994:2], as quoted in Orsini-Jones and Gattulo [2000:132–133])

In fact, the very decision to migrate may be mediated by gender. Toro-Morn (1995) studied working-class and better-educated middle-class Puerto Rican women who immigrated to Chicago after their husbands. Although working-class women reported migrating to care for their children, husbands, and families, middle-class women reported migrating for professional reasons. Even though working-class husbands supported their wives' employment as a temporary accommodation to life in the United States, the accommodation did not change the traditional division of labor in the household. In contrast, the middle-class women in Toro-Morn's study developed strategies that gave equal standing to career goals and family. Toro-Morn's research demonstrates how migrant women experience the dual worlds of productive work in the social economy, including experiencing reproductive work in their families in ways different from men, as well as how gendered migration experiences intersect with social class.

Personal and group networks shape the content, direction, and timing of migration, provide housing and social needs, and enable the migrant to assemble a support system to assuage the privation and isolation of separation from family and home. Chell-Robinson (2000) describes a series of concentric spheres with close relatives at the center, followed by more distant relatives, friends, and others from one's home country on whom one may depend for support. In this last category, she includes migrant traffickers, religious organizations, and the national governments. The closer a relationship is to the core of the sphere, the greater the degree of obligation among the individuals involved. These relationships can assist the migrant woman in building a sense of identity in her new location. However, ironically, Chell-Robinson finds that the very existence of these spheres of obligation, for example, the requirement to send money home, can impede the migrant woman's achieving independence in the host society.

Finally, migration, even when to a country promising greater economic, political, religious, or other opportunity, carries with it significant gendered risk in terms of safety and security. While the discontent among young male immigrants in the impoverished housing projects of the suburbs of Paris has received a great deal of attention in the news media, the plight of girls and women has received very little. According to Fadela Amara, founder of *Ni Putes Ni Soumises* (Neither a Whore nor a Submissive), women and girls are "double victims" in France's immigrant society. Not only do females experience racist and sexist discrimination in employment and social opportunity, but some Muslim females also suffer from sexual harassment and violence, including domestic violence, rape, and gang rape, in their own families and communities (Faramarz 2005:A20).

The incidence of domestic violence among refugee and immigrant women in the United States is extensive and likely consistent with incidences of domestic violence in other populations (Alvi, Schwartz, DeKeserdy, and Bachaus 2002; Immigrant Law Center 2003; Minnesota Advocates for Human Rights 2004). However, refugee and immigrant women face significant obstacles in securing safety for themselves and their children and in prosecuting their abusers. I discuss domestic violence among immigrant populations in greater detail in Chapter 4.

Marriage Migrants

Sometimes lost in the discussion of immigration as movements of large groups of people across national borders for economic, political, religious, or other opportunity is the reality that some immigration occurs because individuals wish to form or build new families. While certainly not disconnected from the other macrosocial rationales for immigration, marriage and adoption are both a continuing part of global migration.

Immigration for purposes of marriage is not a new phenomenon. However, the number of marriages in which the spouses are of different nationalities is increasing dramatically. With over 250 marriage bureaus and catalogs operating in the United States alone, an estimated 150,000 women are advertised each year as available for marriage across national borders (Seager 2003:56). For example, in Germany in 1995, the proportion of marriages in which one partner was *Ausländerinnen oder Ausländer betreiligt* (i.e., holder of a foreign passport) was only one in 25. However, just four years later, by 1999, the proportion of such marriages in Germany had risen to one in six. In the United States, a quarter of men and more than four out of ten women who enter the United States do so as marriage migrants (Beck-Gernsheim 2001:79).

The transnational business of agents and agencies that match men from developed societies to women from struggling ones is the subject of considerable, often sensational, attention in the media. Research on the husband's side of the equation (for example, those who use international services for second marriages and families) is sparse. However, Beck-Gernsheim, Butler, and Puigvert's (2001) analysis of advertisements for marriage placed in newspapers by professional marriage agencies suggests that transnational marriages are most favored by men with serious social shortcomings and, at their worst, are arrangements characterized by gendered oppression, abuse, and violence. Thus, transnational marriages may best be described as grounded in the interactions among disparate worldwide socioeconomic dependencies, international labor migration patterns, and universal gender inequalities.

Williams (1991) cautions that the popular view of marriage between American men and women from other countries is clouded by sometimes unfounded stereotypes. Yet three factors—economic inequality, national inequality, and gender inequality—are problematic in many migrant marriages. In such marriages, the economic disparity between the husband, who is usually of higher status, and the wife is often significant. Also, the women in these marriages often come from countries that are politically unstable or economically stagnant, thus complicating their unsteadiness in the world. Further, the agencies that broker such marriages seem to cater to traditional gender expectations, depicting the women as "loyal, home-loving," "demure," and "all heart and soul for the man and the family." In combination, these conditions set the stage for a husband to exert power over a wife, or even violence against a wife who disappoints (Beck-Gernsheim 2001:70–71).

In Japan, the largest group of international marriages (75 percent) is between Japanese men and foreign women, usually of Philippine, Korean, Chinese, or Thai origin. Piper's (2000) study of international marriage between Japanese men and

Southeast Asian women views such marriages as part of a global, gendered, political economy. She (2000:212) describes the marriages among participants in her study as "marriages of convenience," with the women leaving relatively low-status or low-paying positions with little opportunity for advancement for immigration and work in the Japanese entertainment industry.

The number of foreign women entering Japan increased dramatically in the last decades of the twentieth century (Herbert 1996), and the largest number of immigrants to Japan are young Filipina and Thai women (Muroi and Sasaki 1997). The women in Piper's study originally immigrated to Japan as autonomous, yet vulnerable, parties, relegated to work in the flourishing sex and entertainment industries. Such systems reveal a need not only for the lowest skilled labor in countries like Japan, but also for a system of patriarchal gendered realities. In Southeast Asia, the hospitality or tourism industry provides sex tours for men traveling alone or with other men[2] from Japan or other developed societies with the expressed intention of purchasing the services of prostitutes. The women employed in this industry work at low wages in hazardous circumstances that compromise their health and well-being. The shift from prostitution by indigenous Japanese women to prostitution by immigrant women from other Southeast Asian countries is a by-product of an increase in more legitimate employment opportunities for Japanese women.

Although some of the women who immigrate to Japan or other developed Southeast Asian countries are employed as domestic and childcare workers and in other low-status occupations, the burgeoning sex industry offers strong competition for women seeking better employment than they could secure in their home countries. The transnational sex trade also provides an opportunity for marriage migrants in some countries to meet their future husbands. In fact, the majority of the participants in Piper's study met their future husbands at their place of work, which was a bar or a club. Piper notes also that the circumstances under which these husbands met their future wives contributed to the husbands' subsequent treatment of the wives as property and domestic slaves. One of Piper's respondents said, "Many men do not marry to have a wife, but . . . they 'buy' these women to be their slaves" (2000:217).

Further, these foreign-born wives face additional discrimination, not only from their past status in sex work, but also in a stratification system in which race and social class place them even closer to the bottom of the stratification system in Japanese society. Upon marriage, the women's short duration in Japan, their lack of understanding of the culture, and their isolation often lead to harsh circumstances, including living with drunkenness and violence, but with few resources to leave.

---

[2]Chant (1997) estimates that of foreign visitors to the Philippines in 1990, in some regions, eight out of ten of the tourists were male, four out of ten were men traveling alone, and one out of three were men traveling with male friends. Only one out of eight were traveling with a spouse.

A neglected part of the research on marriage migration is immigrant men who return to their country of origin to select and marry a woman from their home country. Viet Kieu are Vietnamese living abroad. According to Thai (2002), Vietnamese men who have immigrated to the United States are increasingly returning to Vietnam to seek brides. Further, such marriages are often between two of the least marriageable in society: a highly educated woman and a man with a low-wage job. These marriages are often arranged, or at the very least suggested by a close friend or family member, and, in contrast to the transnational marriages described above, these individuals rarely meet on their own (e.g., at bars or clubs), but rather are likely to be introduced by kin.

Further research is needed regarding the stability of migrant marriages and the quality of satisfaction in such marriages. Research suggests that couples such as those in Thai's study, composed of more traditional husbands and more liberated wives, are often ill-prepared for disparities in their understandings of marital gender relations. Yet, at least some manage to process a complicated calculus of exchange in this regard. In the words of one Viet Kieu man:

> I know many men . . . who go to Vietnam to marry beautiful young women. . . . Those women . . . will leave their husbands when they get the chance. They can use their beauty to find other men. . . . [T]he educated women, they know it's important to marry and stay married forever . . . Educated women must protect their family's reputation in Vietnam by having a happy marriage, not have it end in divorce. (Thai 2002:251)

Thai sees such a "marriage squeeze" as directly related to global processes. High male mortality during the Vietnam War and high male emigration during the subsequent years created an acutely skewed ratio of women to men in Vietnam. Likewise, male emigration created a parallel tilted ratio of men to women in Vietnamese communities abroad. Globalization expanded the market for Vietnamese capital, goods, and labor, while opening opportunities for more personal exchanges of emotions and marriage partners. But even though goods and capital tend to flow in two directions, the divide between the First World economy of the West and the Third World economy of Vietnam makes it impossible for women in Vietnam to go abroad to look for grooms, but very easy for Viet Kieu men to go to Vietnam for brides. Just as global corporations and factories moved to Vietnam to partake of its large supply of labor, Viet Kieu men go there to choose among its large selection of potential brides.

Global transfers apply not only to populations, but also to culture and values. Thai (2002) concludes that globalization may appear to offer Vietnamese women an avenue to escape patriarchal norms by marrying abroad. However, to the extent

For Better or for Worse by Lynn Johnston

that highly educated women marry men with more traditional marriage values, these women may find themselves disappointed. The high value placed on marriage in Vietnamese culture—and the fact that these marriages are transnational ones—enables these nontraditional couples to transcend the usually strong norms regarding the marriage gradient in Vietnamese culture.

Transnational Adoption

As in the case of marriage migrants, global demographic analysis rarely takes adoption into account. However, transnational adoption offers an opportunity to reveal the intersections among not only gender, race, and ethnicity, but also culture, nationality, and family, as they are woven together through immigration and identity.

Today, the United States is the largest receiving country in the world for international adoptions. The U.S. State Department issued more than 22,000 visas for incoming to-be-adopted children during 2005 (Hamwi 2006:17). However, the number of foreign adoptions by Americans appears to be dropping, as other countries have begun to institute policies requiring efforts be made to place children in adopted families in-country before children can be adopted by someone from another country. According to the U.S. Bureau of Consular Affairs, in 2005, adoptions from China fell 18 percent and adoptions from Russia fell 22 percent from the previous year (Ode 2007:A13).

The U.S. State Department does not track the number of such visas for American children to be adopted in another country. However, the latter number is annually likely less than 300, primarily black and biracial children, whose birth mothers seek a society in which their children will experience less racial prejudice. However, beginning in 2007, with the United States scheduled to ratify the Hague Convention on International Adoption, the State Department will begin monitoring the outplacement of American children (Hamwi 2006:17). When ratified, the Hague Convention will prohibit ratifying countries from approving adoptions from countries which have not ratified. In that case, adoption of children from countries like Guatemala to the United States will no longer be possible (Ode 2007).

Although the literature on transnational adoption does not sit on a particularly strong foundation, at least one author, Dorow (2006) has attempted a critical analysis of this oft-romanticized aspect of what can surely be considered another form of global family. Her study focuses on one of the most common forms of international adoption today—the situation of Americans who adopt children from other countries, especially infant girls from China. Her research reveals the sociohistorical context and inequalities that make possible this particular global exchange (Dorow 2006). Adoptable Chinese daughters reflect China's fertility and other social policies, including the "one-child policy" and strong male preference. Also, China represents a logical extension of gender and racial ideologies and hierarchies present in the United States, ideologies which discount African American children, while declaring Asian children to be "model minorities," and girls to be easier to assimilate.

Migration for marriage and transnational adoption constitutes small but significant pieces of the global demographic puzzle. Another piece of that puzzle, GLBT families, remain almost totally ignored in considerations of global demographics, including migration.

Gay, Lesbian, Bisexual, and Transgendered Families in Global Demography

Several scholars (e.g., Adam, Duyvendak, and Krouwel 1999b) argue that the modern capitalist world system has reorganized public and private spheres of social life, diversifying family and kinship codes in unprecedented ways. The resulting changes in traditional family structures has resulted in greater personal autonomy (albeit not without significant resistance) in family formation, including more frequent cohabitation outside of marriage, young adults returning to the family of origin, and long-term committed partnerships between GLBT individuals. Adam (1995:13–14) speaks of these emerging new relationships and institutions as "oases of refuge and intimacy" in a globalizing world.

But, just as social movement theory has largely neglected the organization of GLBT communities (Duyvendak 1995), the demographic literature on global changes shaping the family has given short shrift to global patterns of morbidity and mortality, family formation and fertility, and emigration and immigration among GLBT populations and their families. Novel methods, which include the voices of immigrants and others, are required to advance our understanding of demographics in a global world. The paucity of research and theory on demographic shifts among GLBT populations is, at the very least, inopportune for scholars wishing to secure a full understanding of global change. Continued exclusion of consideration of GLBT populations in demographic analyses seriously compromises a full understanding of family characteristics and societal transformation. Adams, Duyvendak, and Krouwel (1999b) posit that the reasons for the inattention to immigration dynamics in GLBT populations are both social and epistemological. First, the concept of being "gay" or "lesbian" is contested, not only among but also within societies. Second, same-sex association does not always involve construction of either a personal identity or an identifiable shared community. Third, a variety of social conditions continue to limit the formation of social movements around GLBT issues, thereby hindering the very study of those communities.

Adams, Duyvendak, and Krouwel argue that, in a postmodern, global world:

> national traditions shape discourses through which homosexually interested people come to understand themselves and their "rightful" place in the societies in which they live. . . . any sense of commonality that might be evoked by the widespread adoption of such terms as "gay," "lesbian," or "bisexual" must be tempered by the diversity within and among national cultures (1999b:8–9).

Thus, globalization studies have the potential to extend scholarship, not only to be more inclusive of groups previously invisible, but also to expand the power of demographic theories to explain a wider range of social phenomena and to recognize the diversity within those phenomena.

Immigration, Assimilation, and Families

Foner (1997:961) has written of the immigrant family:

> The family . . . is a place where there is a dynamic interplay between structure, culture, and agency. New immigrant family patterns are shaped by cultural meanings and social practices immigrants bring with them from their home countries, as well as social, economic, and cultural forces in the [adopted country]. . . . Immigrants live out much of their lives in the context of families.

The literature on immigration, particularly in the last decades of the twentieth century, makes clear the critical role families play in the adaptation and adjustment and in alleviating the cultural and social hardships associated with immigration.

(See Bodnar 1987; Foner 1997; Meissner, Hormats, Walker, and Ogata 1993.) For the immigrant child, youth, or adult, including marriage migrants and adoptees, the family is *home*, potentially a place of refuge and haven, a place where the individual is linked to larger identities through socialization, stories, and even names. Families' adaptations and adjustments to the new society is a function of the stage of the family life cycle, as well as factors such as poverty, discrimination and prejudice, physical well-being, and mental health. Even aside from the traditional emphasis on family reunification in immigration policy, families are clearly critical to understanding the processes through which individuals, communities, and societies engage immigration.

Social reformers such as Jane Addams (1910), founder of the American social welfare movement, appreciated the complimentary roles of immigrant parents and their children, and the particular role of children and youth as agents in their parents' assimilation, in turn-of-the-twentieth century Chicago. But Rumbaut (1997) reminds us that the family also constrains the immigrant, potentially binding the individual to traditions and customs ill-fitted to the new society and creating conflicts across genders and generations. The potential for these schisms in the new society to compromise family cohesion and solidarity and to lead even to family conflict and disruption has long been a source of concern. More recent research (e.g., Purkayastha 2005) has emphasized how the very process of assimilation is layered even beyond generational factors with considerations of gender, race, and ethnicity.

In two subsequent chapters, Chapter 3 and Chapter 5, I discussion the challenges transnationalism presents for parenting and global cultural systems across intergenerational relationships. A compelling body of research has documented the extent to which social–structural factors, such as residential segregation, life in ghettos, inferior education, and racial discrimination in employment, as well as serial migration and changes in lifestyle in the destination country, can corrode the ties that bind immigrant parents and their children (Waters 1994). Further, immigrant parents may find themselves working long hours in distant locations from their homes. Coupled with greater isolation from kin and community than in the home country, immigrant parents may thus find themselves less able to supervise their children in the new society. Those factors may all compromise parental authority for immigrant families (Landale 1997).

Still, in many ways, immigrants and their families endure and even triumph. In the United States, even though immigrants and their second-generation family members tend to be poorer and have lower incomes, lower status occupations, and lower levels of education than members of the general population, immigrants and even second-generation immigrants are less likely to be divorced and children are more likely to live with both parents than other Americans. Thus, the persistence and resilience of family ties serve as critical economic, cultural, and social capital for their immigrant families (Rumbaut 1997).

In the essay that closes this chapter, Margaret Kvasnicka, CSJ, describes the lives of immigrant and refugee women finding a home and relationships at Sarah's Place . . . an Oasis for Women. These women struggle to secure legal immigration status for themselves, while acquiring the language, education, and employment skills necessary to support themselves and their families. Their words provide first-person testimony to both the hardships and the achievements of women and their families seeking refuge and asylum. Such narratives provide scholars and students with an authentic sense of the action of demographic forces such as immigration on families.

Summary

The United Nations Programme on the Family has identified three major demographic trends that have dramatic effects on families across the globe: (1) the HIV/AIDS pandemic, (2) declining fertility (demographic aging), and (3) the rise in immigration. These three trends are, in turn, fueling a series of changes in family structure (United Nations Programme on the Family 2003a). Demography—mortality, fertility, and migration and the processes of demographic transition—offer a first glimpse into the impact of global changes on families. Infectious and parasitic diseases remain prime causes of death and disease in the developing world. The case of HIV/AIDS, which infects over 40 million worldwide, again demonstrates the gendered nature of social and family life. HIV/AIDS dramatically impacts the family through eroding the capacity of adults to provide for their families, by straining caregiving systems, by forcing children to leave educational pursuits, and by leaving family members vulnerable to sexual and economic exploitation.

World fertility, even in the least developed parts of the world, shows steady decline due to a complex of factors related to shifting norms and values around mortality, direct and indirect costs associated with children and childbearing, improved methods of and access to birth control, delayed marriage, and cultural diffusion regarding fertility practices. Population control today has a global dimension, both in terms of nations' satisfaction with their own fertility rates and the involvement of international organizations in shaping population policy. Like other factors related to globalization, changes in fertility patterns seem to be associated with postmodern influences on culture and society.

Obviously, migration is a key component of global demography. Historically a one-way path, migration today is more complicated than ever before, with family members emigrating and immigrating in different streams. While traditional perspectives on immigration viewed the family as a cornerstone of assimilation, more contemporary views see greater diversity in immigrant experiences. Yet, even in the best of circumstances, migration can be a significant stress for families, as a gendered process, a process that may include marriage migrants and transnational adoption, and a process with implications for the parent–child relationship.

Some immigrant families and their members flourish, even in the face of adversity, as demonstrated by the stories of the women of Sarah's Place in the essay which follows this chapter. Yet the study of globalization and demography is limited by inattention to death, birth, and migration among certain populations, including gays, lesbians, bisexuals, and transgender individuals.

Immigrant Women, New Neighbors, Global Families
By Margaret L. Kvasnicka, CSJ

Mantras at Sarah's . . . an Oasis for Women:

You come to Sarah's in order to leave.
Sarah's will always be your home.
You can do it!
You are a good woman.
May peacemaking prevail on Earth today!

Mission:

Sarah's provides hospitality for women seeking home, community, and safety on a temporary basis.

Vision:

Sarah's fosters the self-empowerment of women in community through life skill development, advocacy, and referral services.

Ada and Malena[1]

The phone rang late in the evening of December 23, 2006, and a young mother's voice came through clearly. "Sister, my children are on the plane!" Ada's voice carried an excited lilt I had not heard before. "They will get to Minneapolis–St. Paul International Airport at 1:30 P.M. tomorrow, Christmas Eve! I paid the extra fee to make sure they were placed in first class so they will be really safe!" And then a stream of memories poured through the

---

Note: Kvasnicka adapted this essay from a longer work she authored. She retains the right to use the original work or any portion of the work.

[1]Names and nations have been changed to protect individuals where necessary.

phone line. "You know how hard I worked in this country and in my own country with my husband, waiting and praying for this day to come. Now it is finally here, and it is Christmas! All that paperwork and waiting, and paying fees and then there was more paperwork. It was never done. You know that I haven't seen them for more than three years, and now they are coming!" Ada is a refugee[2] from an African nation.

Almost five years earlier on September 11, 2002, I accompanied Malena, also a refugee, to the same airport to welcome her three adolescent children to the United States. "I won't be crying," she said to me. "I know that God loves me because my children are coming. My children are coming! I won't be crying today. God loves me." Assuring her I would be crying for both of us, I continued to listen to her joy. "I have worked so hard. I wandered through many countries to get here, and I have waited ten years to see my children again." Over the years, Malena faced serious health issues, including cancer, but through the supportive network of the Sisters of St. Joseph[3], she recovered her health each time, while managing other personal and family challenges in a new country.

Sarah's . . . an Oasis for Women: A Ministry of the Sisters of St. Joseph of Carondelet

Two women from two different nations in Africa came to the United States with refugee status. Each found home, safety, and community for a period of time at Sarah's . . . an Oasis for Women, a ministry of the Sisters of St. Joseph of Carondelet in St. Paul, Minnesota. Each woman fled her home nation for her own safety and that of her family. Each came to the United States, eventually arriving in Minnesota, a federally designated refugee resettlement area. At Sarah's, these two women found the self-empowerment they needed to restart their lives in a strange and new country.

Ten years ago, a convent of the Sisters of St. Joseph of Carondelet in St. Paul became available when the work of another ministry was completed. Thus, in mid-1996, Sarah's . . . an Oasis for Women opened its doors to women who were homeless, needing safety, and willing to share a community experience with other women. This new ministry would welcome any woman in any kind of life transition, to live communally with sisters.

Homelessness among immigrant and refugee women in Minnesota is severe, and a majority of those served today at Sarah's are women new to the United States. In ten years, this home for women with a capacity for 30 residents has served 500 women from nearly 50 nations, while always including one or more sisters in residence and on staff. Sarah's is one expression of the overall ministry commitment of the Sisters of St. Joseph's to direct service among those most in need and to advocate for systemic change where there is

---

[2]As defined by the U.S. Refugee Act of 1980 and the United Nations, a refugee is a person who leaves her country of origin because she has dire fear of persecution for her race, religion, nationality, membership in a particular social group, or political opinion (Minnesota Advocates for Human Rights 1995).

[3]The Congregation of St. Joseph (CSJ) is a congregation of Catholic women founded in LePuy en Veley, France, around 1650. The community is dedicated to "the practice of all the spiritual and corporal works of mercy of which woman is capable and which will most benefit the dear neighbor" (Primitive Constitutions). The Sisters of St. Joseph of Carondelet have United States mainland provinces in Albany, Los Angeles, St. Louis, St. Paul, and vice-provinces in Hawaii, Peru, and Japan, and are part of the U.S. Federation of Sisters of St. Joseph (Congregation of Sisters of St. Joseph 2003).

structural injustice affecting the lives of people across the globe. Sarah's was named for Sarah of the Old Testament, the elderly biblical woman who faced the impossible in her life with humor and hospitality.

By now, Ada and Malena have probably met each other through one of Sarah's reunion events, perhaps while shopping at St. Paul Halal Grocery near University Avenue in St. Paul, or at the new Midtown Global Market on Lake Street in Minneapolis. Or, because they both profess Orthodox Evangelical Christianity, perhaps they have found each other at church on Wednesday, Saturday, or Sunday. With the safety and support of a home setting, they found educational, employment, health, language, legal, and social services. Each learned English in a St. Paul English Language Learner (ELL) program while she lived at Sarah's. They found jobs and began to plan for their own living space. They repaid loans and sent funds to their families back home, all the while acquiring the skills to live in the United States. They learned that women can not only live together, but can heal themselves and each other in community. The security of *home* at Sarah's empowered them to do what they needed to do to reclaim their lives.

Through shared lives and household responsibilities, and through stories, laughter, and tears, lifelong relationships and connections are established in this place many women call "their mother's home." All at Sarah's learn to treasure the power of hospitality, meal preparation, and even cleaning—across nations, cultures, and family practices—as ways of creating and practicing community, security, and home with other women. Ada has written, "I have learned so much at Sarah's that enables me to live with people of diverse backgrounds and cultures. It is at Sarah's that I discovered my love for *injera* (an African flat bread). The household jobs at Sarah's are essential for they offer responsibility as well as accountability. Sarah's is like a mother who gives responsibility to her children. We learn how to do all this work in preparation for our own homes. What a home this is!"

Beauty and Healing: Women Among Women

Located in a residential neighborhood with access to public transportation, Sarah's is carefully managed, with beauty evident in its grounds and throughout its household. The house is set back on the property, which adds natural beauty to the neighborhood and provides a sense of physical space and welcome. Split-level construction somewhat disguises the size of the 30-bedroom home. The interior of the house features public spaces for community gatherings, a learning center equipped with computers and high speed Internet, laundry and storage space, a south exposure interfaith chapel and reflection space, parlors for visiting, and, of course, a kitchen and dining room.

Beauty and color, including art from around the world, frame every space in the house, inviting a new woman into a place of care, compassion, and peace, all bound together in the security and safety of home. At the entry of the house, a basket of flags representing nations of residents welcomes visitors and newcomers. Naima from Somalia walked through the hallway at her residency interview tearfully exclaiming, "This is a peace place. This is a peace place! It is so beautiful here. How can a home be so beautiful? Is it just for me? Can this be my home?"

From their initial interview forward, women learn that "Sarah's will always be your home." Wednesday dinners and annual reunions celebrate this mantra as present and former residents share times of homecoming and re-connection. "You come to Sarah's in order to leave" is another mantra learned all along the way. Everything about the experience in this household prepares a woman for an independent, contributing lifestyle in her own neighborhood, work, school, faith, and civic communities. While at Sarah's, she has her own bedroom and her own phone service. She has access to all the public spaces—resources like the learning center, food, and food storage—and use of the television sets in the house. She has a household job which changes every few months, sharing the responsibility of group living and preparing her to manage her own household, usually within a year of coming to Sarah's. She has the support, respect, and care of every woman in the household.

"We are sisters to each other in this place," says Everlyne, a woman of Kenya. "Our sisterhood as women from so many nations makes this a global home. We respect each other." This home for women among women is interfaith and intergenerational, as well as international. Solitude and community are offered to each and all.

Education and Learning: Drawing out the Potential Within

Every woman comes to Sarah's desperate and alone, homeless, most without English, nearly all without a penny, but determined to make a new life. Sarah's is about responding to a woman's homelessness and desperation, and Sarah's is also about supporting her determination.

Teaching and advocating is daily work of Sarah's. Education is the way that the mission and vision of Sarah's comes alive for each woman—learning new life skills such as managing a home or apartment (e.g., using a gas range and a vacuum cleaner) or navigating technology (e.g., voice mail and the Internet), while gaining confidence with public transportation, procuring banking, health, and language services, and, eventually for many, moving through high school to postsecondary education. One woman who is an asylum seeker has said:

> I came from having nothing, I was hopeless and desperate. Now I am a graduate of the College of St. Catherine. I am a nurse, and I am starting a new job. All of these accomplishments go back to Sarah's and the Sisters of St. Joseph. Yes, I am still having problems with immigration in this country, but I am supported here. I know I could not have survived alone, even though I try to be strong. I don't think I could have accomplished all of this without the support of living at Sarah's.

Selam moved from Sarah's more than four years ago and remains deeply connected with this community of women as she pursues asylum[4] in the United States. While at Sarah's she learned English in a local English language learner program, found full-time work,

---

[4]*Asylum* refers to legal permission to live in a country, given by the country's government, to people fleeing danger or persecution in their original homeland (Minnesota Advocates for Human Rights 1995).

regained her health, began and completed her Bachelor of Arts degree in nursing. She is now employed full-time in a skilled nursing facility.

> The problems we've faced sometimes make us feel like we are worthless. Sarah's women have become my family and my friends. Sometimes you don't know all that you have inside you. There should be somebody who can look through all of that with you and tell you, "You can do it." I am not alone here with all my immigration struggles.

Her asylum request denied, Selam is appealing that judgment and preparing for even more grueling and lengthy legal work. Words fail to tell the whole story of the sheer grit, faith, conviction, and struggles of this young woman seeking legal status and eventual citizenship in this country.

A number of the immigrant and refugee women completed their high school education while living at Sarah's. One of these women, an immigrant[5] named Keshauna, graduated with honors and has since become a United States citizen. She was so proud the day she arrived at Sarah's door with her citizenship document. "Come, be in a picture with me and my United States citizenship papers!" She, with her new husband, whom she was finally able to bring to this country, now lives and works in the Twin Cities. They are making plans for their future here while also knowing they are able to return home to their country and families of origin, should they choose. "I am so happy for all I learned at Sarah's and in this country. I want to go on to college for more education, and I know I will," she says.

For these women, education is self-empowerment and opens doors to opportunity, influence, and power in the world. Education can end poverty, assure health care, especially for women and children, allow peacemaking to prevail over violence, assure an earth for humanity's caretaking, and create communities of possibility among diverse life experiences.

Making a New Life

"Sarah's became a place to practice what I want to be and do in the rest of my life, and I found so many new friends," said Amey, as she prepared to move to Illinois after a time at Sarah's. From Ethiopia, Amey came to the United States through what is known as the diversity lottery, which allowed her to procure the documents needed to move here, including a Minnesota identification card, a work permit, and a social security card. "Ready for work," said she. But her English language skills were limited, and with no income or even relatives or other connections in this country, she was indeed documented but, desperate, alone, and determined. Several months later, with improved language and work skills, she was re-energized. With a community of new friends and skills in living, she was on her way to a new state and a new job, to further education, and the self-confidence matching her accomplishments.

---

[5]An immigrant is one who comes to a country intending to settle permanently and obtain citizenship (Minnesota Advocates for Human Rights 1995).

Another woman, Elena, said: "Here I am, Sister. Will you teach me how to write a check so I can give something to Sarah's?" The pride and delight on Elena's face was amazing to see as she came with pen and checkbook in hand! "Finally, I can give some money to Sarah's for all Sarah's has given to me." With a job comes the opportunity and expectation to contribute financially to Sarah's on a sliding fee basis according to income. Any adult woman in any kind of life transition, willing to set goals and do basic life planning, is welcome and becomes a contributing member of Sarah's.

Having and articulating life dreams, setting goals, and making a plan: All of this occurs routinely at Sarah's, through regular individual conferences with the director where goals are revised and new ones set, very often with the assistance of the staff of area agencies. When leave taking time arrives, a final visit with the director at Sarah's allows the woman to name and claim all her accomplishments. Often a woman sets new goals as she moves into more independent living where she will use her experience at Sarah's to establish new relationships and contribute to the larger community. This final consultation affirms and celebrates accomplishments and new hopes and dreams. Each woman is invited to continue her connections with Sarah's, while also becoming involved in her new neighborhood, faith, and civic communities. Each woman also is encouraged to make a financial contribution to Sarah's as she gets more settled, to deepen her own connection while enabling another woman to have an opportunity like she had while there. Two women stated:

> This truly is a home, a nurturing place, and a spring of hope for women. I found a social life here, and I really learned responsibility for myself and my home. I found love here. I got my health back, and my education. Now I am going to be a social worker and work in Minnesota. I am going to become a United States citizen.

> Confidence! I found my confidence in myself. I finished high school and now I am in college to become a nurse!

These women have recently moved from Sarah's into public housing. Each will do well because they possess the self-confidence that got them to this country and the courage that each derived in overcoming the hurdles of being alone and new and poor. Now in their twenties and early thirties, these empowered women have not only the impetus to live their individual dreams but also to make a difference in the lives of others.

Following Dreams

Eleanor Roosevelt once said, "The future belongs to those who believe in the beauty of their dreams" (Quotations Page 2007). A woman of Sudan, a mother, grandmother, sister, and aunt, a poet and business woman in her own nation, Maria tells parts of her story humbly and with great courage.

Maria came to the United States fleeing political oppression, war, and violence. She witnessed the murder of many family members, including her husband, and she now lives with HIV/AIDS. She, too, seeks asylum from the terror and torture she experienced and witnessed. She learns regularly of the illness and death of victimized family members and relatives, some now living with HIV/AIDS. Her daughters ask, "Can you ever return to us? Is it possible for us to come to America?" Maria's time at Sarah's allowed her to obtain good health care and support from HIV/AIDS communities while learning English. Now living in another state, she stays connected with Sarah's, but longs for higher education and employment, neither of which is possible for her without asylum. The long, legal process as an asylum seeker limited her accomplishments when she lived at Sarah's, but not her dreams or her hope. Yet, for Maria, "I know that Sarah's will always be my home. It was my first home in this new country and Sarah's is my mother here."

"I will become a doctor and return to my own people in Kenya," says Everlyne, a fourth-year nursing student at the College of St. Catherine. Everlyne is in the United States on an international student visa[6], which also allows her to work part-time on campus. She came to Sarah's when her living arrangements off campus became unsafe and says, "Sarah's became my life-saving moment. Sarah's has a plan that helps me achieve my dream, and I know I can!" Her dream includes going on to graduate school to become a physician and return to her native Kenya to work, especially among children, where HIV/AIDS is epidemic and healthcare is in great need. Systemic violence and oppression is worldwide, creating gaping needs for healthcare, education, and courageous work, including in the African nations that are home to most of Sarah's women. Those who know Everlyne's ability, energetic spirit, and determination know she will achieve her dream.

Sarah's is a global home that has become a place to learn the commonality and diversity of nations, people, and cultures. The experience of Sarah's allows those who live and work there to learn firsthand of the issues and systems that need change in order to create more just societies. Part of Sarah's work is to "watch over and watch out" for women and children of the world, and for potential laws that might affect their lives. The voices of Sarah's women are sent to inform those who make laws surrounding critical issues involving immigration. Letters to state legislators and to Congress on potential legislation that will impact the women's lives are sent regularly including real stories from the women. The experiences of Sarah's women are shared with policymakers through the Sisters of St. Joseph, a nongovernmental organization of the United Nations.

Sarah's: What provider of hope and home for women! What oasis for women in need of another chance! What community of women dedicated to "all of which woman is capable and which will most benefit every dear neighbor"! What would Sarah, symbol of three faith traditions, dream for women and the world? Meanwhile, the blessing at each community meal in the household of Sarah's includes another mantra, taken from the Peace Pole standing in the gardens near the front door of the house, "May peace-making prevail on Earth today."

Margaret L. Kvasnicka, CSJ, has been director at Sarah's . . . an Oasis for Women since 2002. Her professional experience has included education and religious education ministry in parishes, leadership in her province of The Sisters of St. Joseph of Carondelet, and work

---

[6]An international student is one issued a visa to study in this country for a given period of time (Minnesota Advocates for Human Rights 1995).

in adult spirituality and ritual, especially with women. She is a graduate of the College of St. Catherine and a current Trustee of the College. She holds graduate degrees from Loyola University of Chicago and the University of San Francisco. "It is a privilege to witness the self-empowerment of women among women in community. It is awesome to imagine the power and influence of these women to create a better, more whole world in their own circles, families, and larger communities. For each of them, their nations, and our world, we pray: May peacemaking prevail on Earth today!"

Critical Thinking Questions:

1. This chapter has examined three features of population growth: deaths, births, and migrations. Compare and contrast the ways in which each of these features impacts families in developed, developing, and the least developed parts of the world.
2. Families can easily be seen to be swept along in the general tide of demographic transition. In what ways can families be active agents in social demography? What forces inhibit families' abilities to do so?
3. The HIV/AIDS pandemic has been described as one of the most serious crises facing the world today. Why is this pandemic a critical issue for families?
4. Consider the inattention paid by researchers to GLBT populations and the accounts of women and their families at Sarah's . . . an Oasis for Women (described in the essay that follows this chapter). What cutting edge demographic trends do you predict will affect the quality of life for the world's families during your lifetime?

3

TRANSNATIONAL EMPLOYMENT: WORK–FAMILY LINKAGES ACROSS BORDERS

THROUGHOUT HISTORY, MEN AND WOMEN have migrated, with and without other family members, in order to leave behind economic hardship and uncertainty or to pursue economic opportunity and promise for themselves and their families. The flow of human beings and their labor, including the migration of domestic, childcare, and other workers, is today a global process.

Now, more than at any other time in human history, globalization involves hypermobility (Sassen 2002). Many of the most mobile populations are seeking employment across national borders, with significant consequences for their families and societies. Thus, global hypermobility is creating an unprecedented number of transnational families: "families that live some or most of the time separated from each other, yet hold together and create something that can be seen as a feeling of collective welfare and unity, namely 'familyhood,' even across national borders" (Bryceson and Vuorela 2002:3).

Family scholars must resist the urge to assume all transnational individuals or families are disadvantaged, exploited, oppressed, undocumented, or even (by what is becoming a somewhat pejorative term) migrant. Increasingly, well-educated, unattached workers can market their skills and position themselves anywhere in the world that has demand for their skills in engineering, medicine, technology, and other fields. These individuals and their cohorts, geographically separated from their families, are sometimes called "solos" or "generation-S" (Edgar 2004).

Families whose members relocate or move about because of their role in multi-national corporations or supranational political organizations may be transferring high levels of privilege, along with their greater educational, language, and other cultural and social capital, from one society to or across other spatial locations. Such transnational elites and their families are mobile cosmopolitans, often welcomed, even cultivated, by the host nation (Bryceson and Vuorela 2002).

A small body of research focuses on children in these privileged families. For example, Ender's (2002) edited volume on *Military Brats and Other Global Nomads* includes a study of career orientation among internationally mobile adolescents (Gerner and Perry 2002), a postmodern analysis of the adolescent experience among expatriates (Hylmö 2002), and research on development among children experiencing international relocation (Pearce 2002). The American foreign service establishment is evidently aware of the complications of transnational relocation on children and families, as witnessed by such guides as McCluskey's (1994) *Notes from a Traveling Childhood*, published by the Foreign Service Youth Foundation. However, beyond the study of children and adolescents, the lives of more privileged transnational families have received scant attention in the literature.

In contrast, less privileged migrants and members of their families are more likely to be viewed through a xenophobic lens by the adopted societies. They may be greeted with suspicion and portrayed as a potential burden, risk, or even danger to the country to which they have relocated. In this chapter, I focus not on the more privileged families, but on those less privileged for which globalization facilitates the transfer of certain economic and family roles, usually from less developed or developing societies to more developed societies, in the interest of economic improvement.

In Chapter 3, I describe the dynamic association between economic patterns and household labor, as men and, increasingly, women from developing countries take employment in more developed countries in search of higher income for themselves and their families. I present the implications of transnational employment both for gender roles and for family dynamics, including the impact of transnational labor on one type of care work, global care chains. Finally, even though some transnational workers are single or child-free, I offer a particular examination of the impact of migratory employment on transnational parenting. In doing so, I address the question: How does the delocation and potential fragmentation involved in transnational employment challenge conceptions of family across time and space?

Transnational Employment

Any discussion of transnational employment involving large transfers of labor must acknowledge the global basis of economic production today. Rosen's (2002) critical analysis of the globalization of the apparel industry in the United States is one such example. By analyzing United States trade policy following World War II, Rosen demonstrates how the role of protectionism and policies aimed at containing communism altered textile and apparel manufacturing and commerce, both in the United States and abroad. Rosen reveals how trade liberalization, including new trade agreements, tariff reductions, and unlimited import quotas, as well as the rise of transnational retail distributors (e.g., Wal-Mart), have created favorable conditions for American apparel producers to relocate to Mexico and Central America.

Jam Huyna Chi, Tailor and Cleaner by Mark E. Jensen
Mark E. Jensen/Minnesota Historical Society

Rosen (2002) and many others argue that such a neoliberal approach to transnational economics has not been to the benefit of workers. To the contrary, Rosen notes that the new global economic order has resulted in job displacement and wage loss on the domestic front and the expansion of low-wage retail jobs, both domestically and abroad. In effect, as I discussed in the first chapter, globalization has exacerbated the distances among the core, semiperipheral, and peripheral nations in the world system. According to a report by an economist from the Center for Economic and Policy Research in Washington, D.C., and an economist from the Center for Economic Performance at the London School of Economics, the earnings gap between immigrant and native-born workers increased between 1980 and 2000 in both Great Britain and the United States. For example, in the United States in 2000, male immigrants earned 18.4 percent less per hour than U.S.-born men, almost double the wage gap in 1980. The gap in earnings between immigrant and native-born women increased even more during the same period, from 3.4 percent in 1980 to 10.7 percent in 2000. Further, the magnitude of these gaps persists, even when controlling for age and education (Schmitt and Wadsworth 2006).

While labor migration is certainly not limited to women, transnational labor is increasingly a highly gendered phenomenon. Gender imbalances resulting from war and other conflicts are being exacerbated by the feminization of global employment (Economic and Social Commission for Asia and the Pacific 1998). The United Nations Economic and Social Commission for Asia and the Pacific estimates that Asian and Pacific women comprise 40 percent of industrial workers and 90 percent of workers in leading export industries, but at wages half the rate paid to men.

In a multimethod study of global and other macrosocial, as well as microsocial, influences on women's labor migration in Asia, Oishi (2005) found that more men emigrate from low-income countries (e.g., Bangladesh, India, Pakistan), whereas more women emigrate from high-income countries (e.g., Indonesia, the Philippines, Sri Lanka). Her results indicate that three factors interact to determine women's migration in developing countries in Asia: (1) emigration policies, (2) women's social autonomy, especially as related to women's education policy and nontraditional values about women's roles in the family and society, and (3) social legitimacy of emigration. In the developing countries she studied, the more women who emigrate, the greater the social acceptability of women's emigration.

Further, Apple (1987) and Tilly and Scott (1990) have suggested that more women migrate today without their young children than would have been possible in the past. Even this is related to globalization. The worldwide marketing of artificial infant formula enables women from developing countries to leave even their youngest children, an option much less possible when breast feeding (or wet nursing) was the only option for infant survival.

Therefore, gender holds a pivotal place in restructuring the global workplace. Ward (1990) has detailed the linkages between formal and informal work, as well as the part played by national and other governmental bodies, and the complex intersections among class, race, and sex on the "global assembly line." Ward employs a world system analysis (as described in Chapter 1) in which management and profit are centered in core, developed nations, while the actual labor is performed in semi-periphery or periphery, least developed or developing nations. The incentive behind this unequal economic system is diffusion of economic and political costs, access to markets, and diversity of product. Wealthier nations reap the profits, and their consumers reap the lower costs, whereas less privileged nations see growth in service sector economies and increased specialization in export industries.

But Ward (1990) does not see these workers as entirely passive victims of patriarchal control. She cites examples of women engaging in employment counter to dominant cultural norms, manipulating racist and sexist managers into extending feminine privileges, participation in informal activities, and unionizing. Ward demonstrates that men, families, and the transnational corporations themselves exert powerful control over women workers' lives, as women's wage labor often occurs in home-based or other informal sector work. Women's work is often unregulated in terms of hours, conditions, and compensation, and women's employment in these global industries falls below the low standard, even for men's wages in their home countries. Finally, the unionization that might increase women's wages and work conditions faces an uphill battle in these countries, often suppressed by military and security forces. Even in the case of crafts advertised as "hand made," the goods are most often made by women's and children's hands. In sum, women workers are exploitable and expendable, easily terminated during economic downturns.

Further, Salzinger (2003:2) contends that capitalistic enterprises do not "find" workers but rather "make" workers. "Transnational capital's dream of productive femininity" involves the manipulation of gender to construct different versions (sometimes assertive, at other times embattled, at still other times docile) of the ideal female assembly worker. Salzinger's contention is that this constructed ideal worker may be variable, but is always compliant, trainable, and acquiescent.

The "nannies, maids, and sex workers" of Ehrenreich and Hochschild's (2002) title represent such a case. These workers are disproportionately and increasingly women migrating from the Third World to the First World. This transnational labor movement:

> enables and even promotes the migration and trafficking of women as a strategy for
> survival. The same infrastructure designed to facilitate cross-border flows of capital,

information, and trade also makes possible a range of unintended cross-border flows, as growing numbers of traffickers, smugglers, and even governments now make money off the backs of women. . . . [W]omen infuse cash into the economies of deeply indebted countries and into the pockets of "entrepreneurs" who have seen other opportunities vanish (Sassen 2002:273).

Sassen refers to these complex interdependent networks of workers and traders as survival circuits. These new labor dynamics have originated in the northern hemisphere, but call ever greater numbers of migrants, especially women, from the southern hemisphere, willing or forced into labor in the factories, offices, or homes of the most affluent businesses or families, for the lowest compensation and under the least secure circumstances.

But globalization is about more than the flow of economic, political, and other capital across national borders. Globalization is about the fields, factories, homes, and other locations in which employment takes place, as well as the very quality of work processes and surrounding family and other social relationships.

Domestic Employment in Global Context

The legacies of slavery, with the violent emigration and subsequent forced employment in masters' households, should make even a national analysis of contemporary domestic work resonate with globalists. Beyond slavery, research has examined paid domestic work by indigenous female workers in the United States, with particular attention to the intersections of race and class, family and work. (See Dill's [1994] research on African American women's employment and Glenn's [1986] analysis of the lives of Japanese American women across three generations of domestic employment.)

The 1970s and 1980s saw a surge of interest by historians, sociologists, and other social scientists in the scholarly examination of housework. Lopata (1971), Oakley (1974), Strasser (1982), and others made visible work performed in the home, largely by women, as domestic labor. Later, in *The Second Shift* and *The Time Bind*, Hochschild (1989; 1997) and others took our understanding of housework beyond energy expended to accomplish tasks in the home to encompass the emotional labor which consumes so much domestic energy.

By the 1990s, Romero (1992) and others were systematically examining the lives of maids and other domestic employees. In *Maid in the U.S.A.*, Romero argued that domestic work has not been defined as employment, primarily because such labor takes place in a private home, a place associated with labor expended out of love for someone else's family members. In *Doméstica: Immigrant Women Cleaning and Caring in the Shadows of Affluence*, Hondagneu-Sotelo (2001:9) argued that "[p]aid domestic work is distinctive not in being the worst job of all, but in being regarded as something other than employment."

Some researchers have studied the lives of domestic workers in other Western countries. See, for example, Baken and Stasiulis's (1997) compendium on studies of foreign domestic workers in Canada. Most recently, and with increasing frequency, scholars have been investigating the social, political, and economic context of transnational, migrant domestic workers. For example, Gamburd (2000) has studied migrant Sri Lankan domestic workers, Constable (2002) has studied Filipina domestic workers in Hong Kong, and Parreñas (2001) has studied Filipina domestic workers around the world.

Women involved in transnational domestic employment become relatively invisible in the global economy, as they leave their own families and households in less developed or developing countries to travel to other more developed countries to work in the households of other, more affluent women. However, these women have a critical place in the expansion of global capitalism (Chang 2000). Dramatic improvements in the material quality of life in places such as Southern Europe (Greece, Italy, and Spain) have made it possible for families in those countries to hire live-in or hourly workers to execute their cooking, cleaning, childcare, and other domestic tasks. The same accelerating national quality of life makes First World countries attractive destinations for women seeking to earn higher wages than they could earn at home, even if it means leaving behind their own children, kin, and family responsibilities (Anderson 2000).

The status of migrant domestic workers—wherever they might live—depends not only on their day-to-day relations with their employers, but also on their interface with the policies of the country in which they reside. The security of a migrant worker's status in her adopted country is dependent on her maintaining employment in collaboration with immigration, employment, citizenship, and other policies administered by national governments, but mediated through her employer. Thus, the migrant domestic worker can find herself in a condition which enforces dependence on her employer and which can "institutionalize master/mistress–servant relations" (Anderson 2000:196).

National governments vary in how involved they become in recruiting and regulating domestic workers. For example, the United States has a market-driven, laissez-faire approach to the recruitment and regulation of immigrant domestic workers. On the other hand, some governments (e.g., Canada, Hong Kong) formally participate in establishing government regulated, contract labor programs that define the recruitment and working circumstances of migrant workers. These different strategies can determine, for example, the legal parameters of hour, wage, benefit, and other conditions of employment, as well as the consequences (including deportation) if the worker ceases to be employed, whether by decision of her employer or because the worker decides to leave an abusive or unjust work environment (Hondagneu-Sotelo 2001).

In an intriguing analysis of migrant domestic workforce issues in Italy in the last decades of the twentieth century, Andall (2004) found the dominant ideology shaping domestic–employer relations in that country up through the early 1970s was one which envisioned the domestic worker, not as an employee, but as an integral part of the family contributing to family well-being. Clearly, however, that point-of-view may have been romantically one-sided, expressing a rationalization for the vested interest of the status quo. By the 1970s, domestic workers were becoming less willing to reside in their employers' homes, increasingly preferring to work hourly and live away from their employers' households.

According to Andall (2004), virtually all (90 percent) of African and Asian migrant women to Italy in the early 1980s were employed in private household domestic service. However, by the mid-1980s, the Italian government no longer issued permits for persons wishing to enter Italy for domestic work. At the same time, the Italian government extended amnesty to certain undocumented immigrants. In 1990, another amnesty attempted to regularize large numbers of Filipinos and North Africans, most of whom, among females, were domestic workers. As a consequence, by early 1993, the majority of non-European Union, female workers granted employment permits in Italy were domestic workers.

Such policy shifts in increasingly affluent societies, especially those like Italy, with increasing labor force participation of indigenous women, seriously challenge demand for and the supply of potential live-in and even hourly domestic workers. For example, in 1996, the Italian government formalized policies through which illegal immigrants could be deported unless their employers testified that the worker had been in their hire for four months and agreed to pay social insurance contributions for the worker in advance. This policy resulted in documentation of and issuance of work permits to some of the estimated 25 percent of Italy's foreign population which was, at the time, undocumented and working illegally (Andall 2004).

Subsequent government policies in Italy and elsewhere have ensured that migrant women workers remain relegated to and dependent on national domestic labor market policies. But supranational organizations also shape domestic employment and care work—particularly in the lives of women—in dramatic ways. Organizations like the European Union, the International Monetary Fund, and the World Bank hold authority which can transcend that of any single national government. As such, these organizations have the potential to alter dramatically the progression of opportunities, especially for women and their families. For example, Zimmerman, Litt, and Bose (2006b) discuss the role of structural adjustment policies established by the International Monetary Fund with the intent of ensuring that Third World nations reduce their foreign debt balance. Such policies often require the debtor nation to reduce national deficits by curtailing public spending on such services as education and health. Curtailments in social welfare spending shift the onus for social welfare back to the family and into the laps of women. Under these kinds of structural adjustments, girls and women can be forced out of education and driven from the labor force, to assume education, health, and other caregiving functions for their families.

This describes the global political economy in which the most vulnerable workers can be said to be held hostage to their employers through state policies. However, the benefits to more affluent societies are enormous. Women are more able to accept substantial, meaningful employment outside the home. While someone else negotiates traditional female tasks of family life, couples need not struggle over domestic gender roles. Both men and women may be less mindful of the tensions between public and private spheres.

Immigrant women have streamed into the United States and other developed countries at times when the demand for their services has exploded. However, capitalism often carries forward both racist and patriarchal imperialist traditions. Immigrants are periodically met by waves of "racialized xenophobia" (Hondagneu-Sotelo 2001:18), which has resulted in various attempts to disenfranchise immigrants and their children through denial of education, health, and other basic social benefits and insistence on 'English-only' initiatives in civic institutions. Yet they bear these costs because of the promise of very real financial gain.

Thus, the two largest employment fields for immigrant women from the Third World newly arrived to a First World society are domestic labor in private households and prostitution (Anderson 2000). (I describe the latter in Chapter 4.) Globally, the demand for cheap, immigrant labor continues to grow. Worldwide, women are employed in some of the worst jobs available in terms of compensation and conditions, safety and security. The expected demand for cheap labor by women in countries like Canada, the United States, Northern and Western Europe, industrialized Asia, and the oil-rich Middle East will far exceed the expected supply coming from such predictable Third World regions as the Caribbean, Mexico, Central and South America, Indonesia, the Philippines, Sri Lanka, and Eastern Europe (Hondagneu-Sotelo 2001). Richmond (1994) has called the international division of reproductive labor a gendered version of global apartheid. Not only the poorest women, but also middle-class, highly-educated women, may choose transnational domestic employment at higher wage rates abroad. Gross inequalities among national economies create a type of 'talent drain' in counties which can ill afford to lose their best-educated women (Parreñas 2000).

Hondagneu-Sotelo (2001) speaks of these changes in the process of social reproduction as a "new world domestic order." Earlier scholars (e.g., Chaplin 1978;

Coser 1973) had inaccurately predicted that the commodification and fragmentation of household tasks and the introduction of new household technologies accompanying societal modernization and industrialization would lead to a decline in domestic service. However, the earlier scholars (Hondagneu-Sotelo [2001] notes that they are men) failed to predict the extent to which household tasks and the time spent on them could increase (e.g., see Vanek 1974) and standards accelerate (e.g., see Cowan 1983), thereby ensuring that housework tasks are never completed to satisfaction. Similarly, the commercialization of childcare in First World countries has exacerbated the stigma attached to having children cared for out of home, while ensuring that the labor force that fills that commercial need remains among the poorest compensated (Clarke-Stewart 1993; Wrigley 1995).

Implications of Transnational Employment for Family Dynamics

Transnational employment has potent consequences in the lives of the women and men who pursue work across national borders, as well as for the economies their labor helps to support. Labor migration quite often reduces the risk of poverty for immigrant families, especially for immigrants who can move beyond gateway cities, those border locations where other immigrants are concentrated, and into the broader society. For example, research by Crowley, Lichter, and Qian (2006) found much lower rates of poverty among Mexican immigrant families who lived outside the southwestern United States.

However, migration challenges families regarding finances, physical and mental health, language and culture, and legal and documentation issues (Dalla, et al. 2004; Vélez-Ibáñez 2004). Immigrant families which live an itinerant existence, such as Latino farm workers in the United States who move to follow agricultural seasons, are particularly vulnerable. Problems associated with transitory residence include securing reliable, quality educational experiences for the children in the family (Roeder and Millard 2000; Rothenberg 1998), as well as health and other services, to say nothing of social associations that are enhanced by living in a fixed location over time. Yet, a small body of research suggests that even the most disadvantaged migrant families exhibit a level of resiliency, as indicated by their overall life satisfaction, commitment to an ethic of hard work, and a sense of optimism regarding their opportunity for social mobility (however gradual), and an abiding sense of the centrality of family in their lives (Parra-Cardona, et al. 2006).

This kind of transnational employment also shapes family formation and family structure. Split household migration has been examined for Chinese (Glenn 1986), Italian (Foner 2000), Polish (Thomas and Znaniecki 1927), and other families migrating to the United States in the early part of the twentieth century, and more recently, for families immigrating from Mexico (Hondagneu-Sotelo 2001). An interesting, recent body of literature explores the impact of wives' migration from Taiwan to the United States, with husbands remaining in Taiwan, with husbands sending remittances to support their wives and children in the United States (Chee 2005). The research confirms that, at the most basic level, the quality of transnational family life is affected by practical considerations, such as having sufficient financial resources to afford the costs associated with maintaining contact, including transportation costs, such as airfare, and communication technologies, such as long-distance telephone calls.

Members of transnational families not only have multiple places of residence, but transnational families also have more complex issues of identity and loyalty than families whose members reside in one national space and who interact in closer time frames. Transnational families may experience prejudice and discrimination from members of the host society. They may be ghettoized, assigned to live and work in the least desirable areas. All the while, they may be pressured to hide or deny their religion, language, and other cultural heritage in order to assimilate.

Figure 3.1 represents a simple model for the association between households and capitalist economies. From families and households, firms derive a primary factor necessary for production, labor. In turn, this labor enables firms to produce

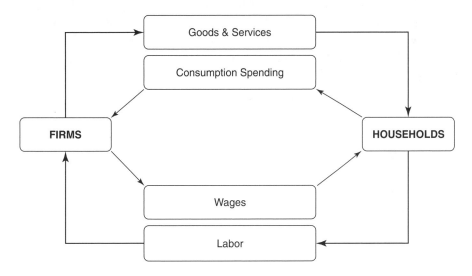

Figure 3.1 Household and Capitalist Economies

Source: Barber and Feiner 2004. Adapted with permission from D. K. Barber and S. F. Feiner, *Liberation Economics: Feminist Perspectives on Families, Work, and Globalization* Ann Arbor, MI: University of Michigan Press, 2004. Figure processed by Ellen F. Uhrich.

goods and services, for which households can spend the wages they receive in exchange for their labor. Thus, households and families are bound together in both the production and consumption phases of capitalist economics.

Globalization complicates the transfer of wages from labor (and other factors of production, including capital) and multiplies the locations of consumption spending by households. Wages earned by a family member in one location must be transmitted across time and space—often with considerable additional time and expense—to other family members in another location. For the transnational family, consumption spending occurs in at least two locations. Not only the family remaining behind, but also the family member having relocated for transnational employment, must engage in consumption spending in order to survive.

Further, this globalized pattern of exchanging wages for consumption spending places both the sender and the receiver in conditions of increased uncertainty and risk. Postal or other systems of remittance can be variable, unpredictable, and unregulated. If a mother working in Europe sends school clothes to her children living in Africa, how confident can she be that these remittances will reach them undamaged, or at all, in a timely manner? If her remittances or gifts do not reach her family, she has little or no recourse.

Transnational families must negotiate not only the procedures for establishing patterns of remittances involving transfers of monetary units as well as goods purchased in the adopted country and sent to family members in the home country, but also the expectations of rights and responsibilities by sender and receiver. Extensive kin obligations and lack of direct experience with wage and other financial norms, higher costs of living, and other economic realities in the adopted country create the potential for feelings of misunderstanding, mistrust, and even exploitation in families with even the best intentions.

Transnational Employment and Gender Roles

Women's greater participation in the transnational labor force cannot but help to change family dynamics, particularly in the area of gender roles. At least in Western industrial societies, women's increased participation in the labor force has been linked to new life patterns, including some shifts in the division of labor between men and women in the home. Women's participation in the labor force—whether domestic or transnational—yields for women the potential for increased economic, and often social, political, and cultural, capital.

Giele and Holst (2004) have described a series of evolutionary social changes—adaptive upgrading, technological innovation, and new patterns of use of time, space, information, material, and human resources—associated with women's increased labor force participation. As goal differentiation expands in the form of wider role options for men and women, they exercise more individualized self-determination, rather than lock-step conformity to traditional age, sex, and other social ascriptors. Meanwhile, in efforts to attend to macrosocial issues of inclusion and integration, societies must coordinate new rules and policies regarding gender equity around work and family. Finally, as society becomes more complex and specialized, social values are reconceptualized to facilitate better integration of economic productivity and caregiving functions.

Giele and Holst's (2004) theory draws heavily on Parsons' (1966) and Johnson's (1989) paradigms linking adaptive upgrading of resources and facilities, goal differentiation of roles within groups, integration and inclusion at the institutional level, and value generalization at the cultural level. This theory predicts that, as men's and women's gender patterns converge (with more women not only in the labor force but also in positions traditionally held by men), employment structures and national policies will evolve toward greater flexibility in order to facilitate women's employment. While women may experience overload as they try to manage their work–family roles, men's and women's breadwinning roles will become increasingly interdependent. Couples and corporations will create new strategies to facilitate evolving dual work and family roles (Giele and Holst 2004).

In such a social system, the new frontier for women—employment—will be accompanied by a new frontier for men—caregiving. Giele's (2004) research indicates that women and men already on these new frontiers differ from their more traditional peers on identity, goals and ambitions, social networks, and strategies for blending education, work, and family life. In particular, these modern work-oriented women and the new care-oriented men are more likely to seek to blend work and care roles. Giele's interviews with married dual-career mothers and homemakers confirm existing research on men who are full-time breadwinners and those who reject stereotypic male roles in Western Europe and the United States. The individuals who were the most innovative in restructuring gender roles had distinctive personal identities, received approval from family and peers, were women with career ambitions and men with intimacy ambitions, and were resourceful and inventive in developing practical means of accomplishing their desired life patterns.

Policies that support such changes in the traditional gender contract include permitting work to occur in more time- and space-flexible environments. Specific practices may invite part-time and flex-time work schedules, telecommuting, family leave and other provisions for time away from work, and early retirement, career shifts, re-entry, and other shifts in employment patterns. Giele and Holst (2004) acknowledge that these national differences do not just reflect national or regional variations in societal values, but also are the result of market forces, societal differences in work–family culture, and differences in social welfare establishments, as institutionalized in policies surrounding family income support, childcare, and gender.

Women's participation in the labor force does not inevitably result in egalitarian work and family policies at the national level. Some social democratic countries, such as Denmark, Finland, Norway, and Sweden, all with high female labor force participation, have institutionalized national policies that facilitate the blending of parental time with children and a gender-egalitarian division of labor. These policies address family leave, working-time regulations, early childhood education, and family care for both female and male workers. However, even today, most First World countries, including not only conservative countries of continental Europe like Belgium, France, Germany, and the Netherlands, but also, most notably, liberal countries with high female labor force participation, including the United Kingdom and the United States, have not implemented national policies which support egalitarian gender roles (Gornick and Meyers 2004).

Further, the trickle-down from women's employment to their greater status and power in the family and in the broader society can be slow. Cross-nationally, gender remains the strongest predictor of time spent in household labor (Kroska 2004), as well as the type of household tasks performed (Gupta 1999). Using data from the International Social Survey Program, Greenstein (2006) has documented that national context serves as a comparative reference in married women's determinations of fairness in the division of household labor. Women in nations with the highest levels of gender equity experience the greatest perception of unfairness when household labor is unequally distributed.

Even with the increasing participation of women in the transnational labor force, the majority (70 percent) of the world's poor remain women. Furthermore, the percentage of women in rural areas who are poor around the world is increasing. Almost two-thirds of the illiterate of the world are women. Almost two-thirds of girl children have no access to primary education. Fully one-third of families around the world are headed by women. Women and their dependents make up 80 percent of the world's refugees (Butron 2001:43–44).

All the while, women constitute one third of the world's paid labor force but work two-thirds of the hours for less than ten percent of the wages (Butron 2001). Sørenson (2004) has calculated an economic dependence score using the difference between the husband's and the wife's earnings divided by the couples' earnings together. Even though dependency variations across and even within developed societies are conspicuous[1], the most equitable economic relations between spouses continue to exist in the most developed societies.

---

[1] Ranging from −1 to 1, a score of −1 indicates the woman has no earnings and is completely earning-dependent on the man. A score of 1 indicates the man has no earnings and is completely earning-dependent on the woman. A score of 0 indicates perfect earnings equality between the man and the woman. The mean dependence score in Nordic countries is considerably lower than in other European countries and the United States. For example, the mean dependency measures in Finland and the Netherlands were 0.15 in 1995 and .063 in 1991, respectively. The mean dependency score in the Netherlands in 1991 was the same as the mean score in the United States in 1970. Further, the scores of African American women are considerably lower than those of other American women, reflecting the historical needs for African American women's employment alongside the lower wages of African American men (Sørenson 2004).

Much like the American women described in Hochschild's (1989) *second shift*, women from Third World societies often bear the burden of a "stalled revolution" in which gender ideology in the family has not kept pace with the realities of women's employment. These women increasingly work outside the home, yet their husbands and other family members, and society in general, retain the expectation that these women will continue to fulfill the traditional responsibilities for hearth and home.

National leaders may even issue public statements opposing migrant women's employment abroad, and the mass media may provide sensationalized accounts of the dire consequences of absent mothers who have "abandoned" their children to the increasing burden on the rest of society. Thus, women who take contract work to secure higher wages and assist in providing a better quality of life for their children are often blamed and stigmatized as selfish, neglectful mothers who have deserted their children and families. Such stigma occurs in spite of the fact that societies like the Philippines are increasingly dependent on the wages sent home by migrant workers. In 1997, migrant workers, the majority of them women, contributed nearly $7 billion to the Philippine economy, thus constituting that country's largest source of foreign currency (Parreñas 2002:41).

In conclusion, the contemporary situation of migrant workers and the implications for family continuity differ from those of previous migrant streams. Whereas in the past, migrants were unlikely to return to their home country, migrant workers today are often impeded by rigid immigration policies in their adopted county from establishing a permanent residence in their adopted country (Ehrenich and Hochschild 2002). Migrant workers today are not only less likely to establish reunited homes for their families in their adopted countries, but they may be more likely to embark upon a life of repeat passages between their adopted countries and households and those of their home societies and families. Such workers are transient, modern-day, indentured servants who can be repatriated at the economic will of the adopted country, thus remaining outsiders to the civic, economic, social, and other rights and responsibilities of their adopted country (Huang and Yeoh 1996). These burdens are borne by individual migrants, legal as well as illegal, and their families.

Care Work

One of the most pressing consequences of transnational employment is the extent to which care work comes to be bound into global capitalist systems that impact not only First and Third World economies, but also First and Third World families. Care workers are usually women who migrate to more affluent societies. These women leave behind their own families, not only to work in domestic employment, but also to extend their services to emotional, expressive care work in the households of families in other societies. In this section, I explore those patterns of care work and the resultant global care chains that can so dramatically impact the migrant women and their families.

The United Nations (1999b) identifies four sources of caring labor: women's unpaid labor, men's unpaid labor, private market labor, and public services. Providing care may be guided by economic compensation, but also by bonds of affection, a sense of altruism, or norms of obligation. Care work often involves love and emotional reciprocity, even in the case of nonfamily individuals who are compensated for their care work. For an examination of the complexities of such a relationship, Filipina women as live-in home healthcare workers, see Tung (2000). Zimmerman, Litt, and Bose (2006a:300) have articulated the value of care work for individuals and societies.

> All of us depend on the care work of others. The social value given to care work . . . has to do with societal arrangements such as how time for care work is allocated, whether care work is compensated, how care work fits with paid employment, and how care work is divided by gender. Social policy regimes govern these matters. Thus, we can say that care work is socially constructed in relation to communities, nations, and (increasingly) supranational organizations.

This care work is highly gendered. Research indicates that men's participation in housework and childcare is related to national, social contexts. The level of women's employment (as indicated by employment hours) and social policies, including parental leave (and men's eligibility for parental leave), influences men's adherence to gender ideologies and norms, the "terms of bargaining" men and women employ to arrive at gender specializations in the family, and men's actual participation in housework and childcare (Hook 2006). Chart (2000) reflects that these realignments in gender roles may even be creating a "crisis of masculinity," at least for some men. Based on interviews with 80 low-income men in a northwestern province of Costa Rica, Chart found that changes in labor markets, legislation, and social policy were undermining the traditional bases of family power and identity for men.

Ehrenreich and Hochschild's (2002) edited volume details the extent to which women's nondomestic labor is intimately bound with their domestic lives. Girls and women play dominant and critical roles in providing care for families and in communities worldwide. The most developed societies attract a bountiful supply of women who will work at low wages to perform the care work not only for children, but for elders and other dependents requiring care in the home. As in the case of domestic labor, care work is not only gendered, but manifests the complex and too often oppressive relationships among labor and the welfare state.

According to the United Nations' Human Development Report *Globalization with a Human Face* (1999b:77) in a chapter titled "The Invisible Heart," "[g]lobalization is putting a squeeze on care and caring labor" by changing patterns of time usage, challenging public spending on care, and the tendency for care labor to be low-wage labor. According to the United Nations' analysis, globalization impacts care, and consequently human development, in at least three ways. (1) Globalization encourages a shift in women's roles from domestic caregiving to labor force participation, while at the same time leading to the feminization of labor in home work, telework, and part-time work in particular. (2) The increased scope, speed, and size of markets associated with globalization tend to disconnect markets from local communities, resulting in greater reliance on families at the time families are undergoing dramatic demographic and economic changes and instabilities. (3) The same expansion of markets devalues self-sacrifice in caring for others.

By recognizing that human development involves more than considerations of income, education, health, and empowerment, and that development also involves social reproduction (i.e., care), the United Nations explicitly acknowledges the value of experiences that contribute to bonding among individuals in families. The solution to the growing dilemma of care and care labor, the United Nations posits, lies in redistributing the costs and responsibilities of care across families, nations, and the private sector.

Many contemporary societies face a care work crisis (Meyer 2000). Hancock (2002) has described the "care crunch" facing one First World society, Australia, today. In Australia, economic globalization has resulted not only in profound shifts in labor markets, but also deep individual uncertainty about employment and financial security. At the same time, an aging population and increasing divorce rate signal major demographic shifts. These forces, when coupled with adherence to traditional assumptions about the gendered nature of family roles, are compromising Australian families' ability to care for their members.

Some organizations, such as the International Labour Organization, have concluded that the way to provide for sufficient care labor in a society is to ensure that work is adequately compensated, that the work occurs within the context of regulatory guidelines to ensure competence and skill of the workforce, and that regulatory standards are enforced (Standing 2001). However, such an agenda presents a serious challenge, given contemporary capitalist agenda with regard to minimizing wages, repelling unionization, and curtailing benefits across and within categories of workers. Feminist economists, such as Barker and Feiner (2004), advocate social policies that will ensure that both familial and societal care needs are met. Ironically, doing so may well be at the expense of conventional goals of full employment, for full employment means that no one is available for unpaid care labor.

Global Care Chains

Globalization has resulted in the commoditization of care, as care work has been rationalized and bureaucratized, so as to package it better for sale in capitalist economic systems. Increasingly, affluent First World consumers can purchase for low wages the specified services which heretofore would have been provided in private venues bound by kin obligation, if not affection. Such regulated care is characterized by fragmentation and impersonality and a system of regulation that portends to deeply oppress the worker (Zimmerman, Litt, and Boss 2006b).

Global care chains are personal networks based on paid or unpaid caregiving work between people across national borders. These chains usually begin in a poor country (or in the rural area within a poor country) and terminate in a rich country (or in the urban area within a poor country). As such, care chains vary in their origination and destination (e.g., from poor country to wealthy country, from poor country to slightly less poor country). They also vary in the number and strength of links in the chain. One example is the eldest daughter in a family in the Second or Third World who looks after her younger brothers and sisters. Meanwhile, her mother, a migrant worker, works as a nanny looking after another woman's children (Beck-Gernsheim, Butler, and Puigvert 2001:68). Figure 3.2 provides another, graphic, illustration of a global care chain.

In the essay which follows this chapter, Dreby recounts the life of Paula Rodriguez, the mother of two children, who manages successive migrations between Mexico and New Jersey. Part of Paula's story includes elements of a global

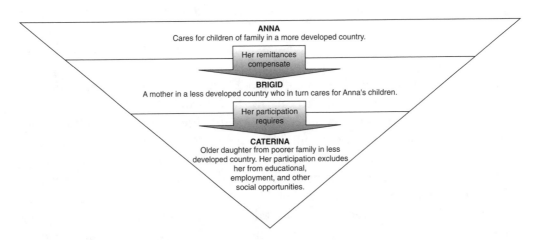

Figure 3.2 Illustration of a Global Care Chain

Source: A. R. Hochschild. 2000a. "Global Care Chains and Emotional Surplus Value." pp. 130–147 in *On the Edge: Living with Global Capitalism,* edited by W. Hutton and A. Giddens. London, UK: Jonathan Cape. Original figure designed by Martin C. Doyle based on concepts from Hochschild 2000a.

care chain, as Paula sends remittances to her brother and his wife, who must hire someone to care for Paula's children left behind.

Hochschild (2000b) has written that care work is now bought and sold to the extent that women are willing to migrate, leaving behind their families. These women do so in order to ensure higher wages than they might earn at home with, perhaps, greater security, if they can leap over currency devaluations, business failures, and other uncertainties of their home country. At the same time, however, they may be replacing anxieties surrounding economic well-being with insecurities regarding time and space away from kith and kin.

However, the exodus of women from Third World societies leaves the developing world with a global care deficit, a shortage of women to perform the very same functions for their own families in their own countries (Zimmerman, Litt, and Bose 2006b). These deficits also can arise from new care needs that grow out of childbirth, illness, or disability or out of epidemics, natural disasters, or war. Such deficits also can develop when care labor shortages develop as a result of caregiver disability, illness, or other conditions or from societal-level shifts involving female employment outside the home or caregiver emigration.

In Chapter 2, I described the growing care crisis associated with the HIV/AIDS pandemic in certain African countries. Upton (2003) found such a case in Botswana. With one of the highest rates of HIV infection in the world, deaths among working-age adults have orphaned large numbers of children, creating a serious shortage in healthy adults who can provide for their children. The morbidity and mortality wrought by HIV/AIDS also has seriously compromised the traditional fostering system in which women could rely on extended kin for support in caring for their children.

Regardless of the cause, such shifts inevitably place females as caregivers in shorter supply. However, deficits involving the movement of females from the domestic sphere are sometimes at the explicit initiative of First World and supranational interests. Zimmerman, Litt, and Bose (2006b) cite the case of the recruitment of African nurses to the United Kingdom from certain African countries, leaving the same African countries—some of which are battling the HIV/AIDS pandemic—with a critical shortage of trained healthcare workers.

These global care chains may present dilemmas for middle-class parents, as well as for the women who care for their children (Wrigley 1995). The relationships between care workers and their child, elder, or disabled charges are, under any circumstance, complicated ones. Karner's (1998) research on workers providing homecare for the elderly suggests that care laborers who care for other families' dependents can come to be seen as fictive kin, and that such relationships, when constructed as appropriate, can enable a family member (e.g., the elder) to maintain a sense of the norm of kin providing care. In a parallel fashion, such respite-care workers also derive positive feelings regarding their work. Authentic expressive bonds between employee care providers and individuals receiving such care and their families should not be dismissed. As Hochschild (2000a:140) argues, "[j]ust as global capitalism . . . creates a Third World supply of mothering, so it creates a First World demand for it."

Women's role in care work is at the very center of global dynamics that weave together gender, race, and class; migration, citizenship, and social control; the changing meaning of motherhood; and new constructions of care work and care workers' lives (Zimmerman, Litt, and Bose 2006a). In the following section, I examine the effects of global care chains on transnational parenting.

Transnational Parenting

The concept of networks, linkages, "circles of care" (Abel and Nelson 1990), or global care chains (Hochschild 2000a)—systems whereby women care for the children of others, while their own children are in turn cared for by women of even lower occupational (and wage) status—is not new. What is new is the extent to which such care chains are now global. Parents participating in transnational labor markets are often doing so in order to provide their families with economic resources that translate into a higher material standard of living and dramatically greater educational, medical, and other quality of life concerns. Does special and temporal distance from parent or parents challenge a child's physical or emotional well-being and development in ways that compromise the very advantages the transnational parent seeks to provide?

Third World children in these global care chains should not be described as abandoned or neglected by virtue of the absence of the parent. Many of these children live with either their maternal grandmothers or with other female kin. Such practical arrangements are common among Mexican (Dreby 2006) and other Central American domestic workers in California (Hondagneu-Sotelo and Avila 1997). Furthermore, migrant couples have reported satisfaction with the care their children were receiving and positive relationships with their children's caregivers at home (Dreby 2006). Single mothers who migrate and who do not have the option of maternal grandmother care may sometimes place their children with a former husband, the children's father, or with other kin. Perhaps more scholars should employ another term, such as Grochowski's (2000) concept of "strategic living communities" to refer to the complex web of family networks across borders.

Transnational contact between parents and their children can reinforce and strengthen family bonds. Parents and children write letters, telephone, and, increasingly, send e-mail messages to one another. Besides sending portions of their wages home, parents may send clothing, food, medical and school supplies, and other goods home to the family, both on a regular basis and for special holidays and events such as birthdays (Cohen 2000).

Men have historically been the one to leave families behind. *Wage fathers* are men who leave families for long periods of time to secure employment (Roopnarine and Gielen 2005). Children have experienced periodic father absences because of men's occupational demands, military service, or other situations which take them from home, as well as migrant wage labor or to forge the path for later immigration of other family members. Gielen (1993) has described such work–family patterns for Caribbean men who migrate to (and across) the United States for seasonal agricultural work, Egyptian men who pursue employment in oil industries elsewhere in the Middle East, and Indian men who leave rural for urban areas of greater employment opportunity. These situations deposit greater childcare, household, and other family burdens on women and the older generation left behind.

Dreby (2006) has examined the impact of transnational fathering on children, fathers, and families, using interviews not only with the adult parents, but also with the children, often left home in Mexico. Dreby found that Mexican transnational fathers and mothers responded to the absence from their children in similar ways, through maintaining contact through regular communication with their children and gifting or (the preferred) sending money. However, traditional Mexican gender ideologies emphasize fathers' role as financial provider and mothers' role as daily caregiver. Furthermore, these gendered ideologies are connected with honor. A man's migration to increase economic resources for his family is consistent with traditional male gender roles and brings honor. On the other hand, a woman's migration for the same reasons compromises traditional female gender roles and, therefore, a woman's honor.

Not surprisingly then, Dreby found that fathers were more likely to lose contact with their children when unable to deliver on their financial obligations. One father reported that he would only call his children when he could give them a money order number for collection. Dreby found that migrant mothers' contact with their children is not dependent on financial remittance, but rather focuses on the emotional care work they provide for their children, even at a distance. The mothers in Dreby's research expressed guilt for leaving their children; fathers almost never did.

Because of the gendered construction of mothering, concerns involving the effects of transnational parenting most often focus on the impact of the absent mother. Transnational mothering is said to "disrupt the notion of family in one place," as women improvise new parenting structures in order to provide for their children and themselves (Hondagneu-Sotelo and Avila 1997:567). These migrant mothers relinquish expectations of living with and relating to their children in a shared space, but nonetheless speak of the pain of physical separation from their children.

Such forms of mothering result from economic forces in the home country, increasingly as a result of globalization. Once again, gender shapes—and potentially destabilizes—the impact of globalization on families. Thus, parents are compromised in their abilities and satisfaction as parents by traditional gender roles. In Dreby's (2006:52) words: "If transnational fathers fail when they do not send money, transnational mothers fail when their emotional attentions are diverted elsewhere." In fact, the most common pattern for Mexican families has been and remains for the father to migrate to the United States, leaving behind his wife and children. Some transnational families begin this way, with the father later sending for the wife to join him, leaving their children behind. Dreby's research indicates that the latter is sometimes at the initiative of the wife, whose emotional distress leads her to pressure her husband for reunification, even if it means leaving their sometimes young children in the care of others in Mexico.

In spite of the risks involved in transnational employment for families and parenting, research in a wide variety of settings demonstrates that children are remarkably resilient. If shared struggle lends itself to family solidarity, children and parents in transnational families may even gain a deeper respect and appreciation for one another. For example, in research on Caribbean adults in New York whose own mothers had earlier immigrated to the United States without them, Wrigley (1995) found that, even though the mothers themselves expressed regret at having left their children behind, these adults expressed understanding that their mothers had made the sacrifice of separation in order to give the children a better life.

Parreñas (2002) interviewed 30 children of migrant mothers, 26 children of migrant fathers, and 13 children with two migrant parents. Her findings indicate that, although these children had experienced emotional hardships, they did not perceive their mothers as having abandoned them. Children's hardship was reduced when they were enmeshed in supportive extended kin and communities, had open communication with their migrant parent(s), and when they understood their parents' limited financial options which led them to work abroad.

Still, children and parents in transnational families do not have the certain satisfactions of everyday/everynight interactions with one another. Although the children in Dreby's study were by no means abandoned (most were being cared for by their maternal grandmothers), the children, especially older children, revealed emotional distress in the form of difficulty concentrating in school and preoccupation with migrating themselves to join their parents.

Parental absence, especially absence not sustained by conscientious surrogate parenting of the quality of support, communication, and understanding described above, can leave deep wounds. Long periods of physical separation due to a parent's migrant work situation, a parent's absence during war, or other situations can contribute to unfamiliarity, insecurity, and a sense on the part of the child of the parents' indifference (Parreñas 2002:42)

> There are times when I want to call her, speak to her, cry to her, and I cannot. . . . The only thing I can do is write to her. And I cannot cry through the e-mails and sometimes I just want to cry on her shoulder.

Parents also pay a price for such absences. Some mothers poignantly recount the pain of separation and the reminders that, while they are caring for other people's children, their children are far away.

> When the girl that I take care of calls her mother "Mama," my heart jumps all the time because my children also call me "Mama." I feel the gap caused by our physical separation especially in the morning, when I pack [her] lunch, because that's what I used to do for my children. . . . I begin thinking that this hour I should be taking care of my very own children and not someone else's. . . . The work that I do here is done for my family, but the problem is they are not close to me but are far away in the Philippines. . . . Some days, I just start crying when I am sweeping the floor because I am thinking about my children in the Philippines. Sometimes, when I receive a letter from my children telling me that they are sick, I look up out the window and ask the Lord to look after them and make sure they get better even without me around to care after them. [Starts crying.] If I had wings, I would fly home to my children. Just for a moment, to see my children and take care of their needs, help them, then fly back over here to continue my work (Parreñas 2002:41–42).

In speaking of her loneliness for her own children, one woman, a Filipina domestic worker living in Canada, describes herself as "bursting out of loneliness" (Cohen 2000:82).

Hochschild (2000b) believes that emotional labor is transmitted along the global care chain. This results in deficits of care when women make positive emotion investments in the children and families of their employers, to the emotional disadvantage of their own at home. Parreñas (2001) refers to this transference of motherly affection from own to employer's children as "displaced mothering" or "diverted mothering." In fact, a criticism of Hochschild's presentation of global care chains is the presumption that mothers in such chains have a finite amount of maternal care which, once expended on another's children, leaves her with little emotional labor to extend to her own children. Zimmerman, Litt, and Bose (2006b) challenge the assumption of such a fixed pool of maternal affection which invariably disadvantages a woman's own children. Instead, they cite research (e.g., Litt 2000) which supports the idea that, first, the children migrant women leave behind are often cared for in an enmeshed kinship group in which the children experience family affection from other family members. Second, Zimmerman, Litt, and Bose (pp. 19–20) argue that the affection for the children of one's employer and one's own children is qualitatively different:

> While domestic workers and nannies do form meaningful attachments to their employers' children, these feelings of "love" in most situations cannot be equated with (or exchanged for) the attachment they have for their own children.

National governments play a part in risking or assisting the quality of transnational parent–child relationships. Cohen (2000) is critical of the role of governments, through immigration and labor policies, in shaping maladjustment among families in which the mother is a migrant domestic worker. Using in-depth interviews with 21 Filipina domestic workers living and working in Canada, Cohen concluded that women's inability to immigrate with their husbands and children destroyed traditional family roles and created "serfdom-like" work environments which required the maintenance of transnational family relations over long distances for many years. In Canada, workers are allowed to sponsor spouses and children after achieving landed immigrant status, but only after three years in-country. Policies of family reunification limit such sponsorship to spouses and children and so neglect to take into account the family bonds with parents and other extended kin, a neglect that Cohen charges is Eurocentric. Further, even once unified, the families often experience tension and conflict (Cohen 2000).

In reading the accounts of children of migrant mothers, I am reminded of the literature, prevalent even in the social scientific literature through the 1960s, of "maternal deprivation." That literature was premised on beliefs that only the biological mother could provide sustaining love and affection to a child and that the outcome of maternal absence was child maladjustment. Likewise, writing on homes "broken" by divorce, the literature emphasizes that nothing can substitute for an intact, complete family composed of a mother and a father. The research on transnational parenting remains sufficiently ambiguous, so as to hasten the call for further research in this area.

Zimmerman, Litt, and Bose (2006b:19) remind us that migrant women and the families they leave behind are not merely passive victims. They argue instead for "the persistence (or transcendence) of love" between absent mothers and their children. Many migrant mothers and their children do maintain ties, and the children may well understand and appreciate the rationale behind their mother's absences.

> I realize that my mother loves us very much. . . . She would just assure us that whenever we have problems to just call her and tell her. [Pauses] . . . I know it has been more difficult for her than for other mothers. (Parreñas 2002:43)

Edgar (2004) also cautions against viewing these transnational families and individuals as expressively bankrupt. Given the dissemination of global information technologies like the World Wide Web and economies such as budget airfares, spatially disconnected families may be afforded opportunities to maintain contacts across space and time at a level greater than any other period in history. Karraker and Grochowski (2006) advocate a resiliency approach to family studies. Such an approach has potential value for the study of work–family linkages among global families in particular. For example, transition from postcommunist society has been difficult for Eastern European families. However, using a multiple case study design, Assay (2003) found former East German and Romanian families possessed qualities of strong families commonly cited in the literature:

- Commitment to the family
- Ability to grow through challenges
- Spending time together

Still, the demands of economic competition in global capitalism seriously tax the balance between work and family, even among families that are not participating in transnational employment. Giddens, Duneier, and Applebaum (2006) note the increasing time spouses and parents spend employed away from home. Average Americans spend more time at their places of employment and spend less time on vacation than in the past. Americans also spend more time commuting to and from work, school, and other activities away from home (Karraker and Grochowski 2006), all of which translates into less time with family. The most conspicuous increase in hours away from home has been among the mothers of young children. Children in those families now spend more time than at any point in history in childcare away from home.

Hochschild (1997) believes that such changes are related to global competition. She describes the strategies companies like Amerco, a profitable Fortune 500 company at the "thriving core of America's globalizing economy," must use to compete globally (p. 16). One of the key strategies involves raising productivity while lowering wages, benefits, and job security, while increasing hours on the job. Workers in some societies, including those in many Western European countries, have successfully resisted efforts to increase the paid or, in the case of salaried workers, the unpaid work week. However, such a family-friendly tide in Western Europe may be turning. For example, in 2005, the French National Assembly voted to relax the 35-hour work week rule, allowing workers to work up to 48 hours a week, the maximum work week permitted by the European Union ("France Relaxes 35-hour Week Rule" 2005). Families throughout the world face inflationary squeezes, as wages fail to keep pace with either productivity or inflation (Greenhouse and Leonhardt 2006). Global integration, represented by the increasing presence of low-cost goods from China, and a reversal in the traditional pattern of global investment (with relatively poorer nations moving into the worldwide economy as net lenders) makes national controls on inflation more difficult (Andrews 2006). Family members are faced with working more to purchase less, scaling back their material ambitions, or increasing their debt.

Yet, as Hochschild (1997) illustrates in the case of Sweden, globally competitive companies and societies can elect family-friendly or work–family balanced policies. In Sweden, parents are entitled to ten days of leave in the first two months of a child's life. Also, fathers can take leave at 80 percent pay for the first 14 days, 90 percent pay thereafter to care for a sick child. However, in response to demands from other members of the European Union, Sweden has made some reductions in family benefits for working parents, reductions which have been met with some resistance in Sweden (Hochschild 1997), where grassroots groups like The Children's Lobby, Euronet: The European Children's Network, and Support Stockings organize on behalf of family-friendly policies.

As markets and economies become increasingly placeless, globalization more profoundly affects everyday life and interaction and perceptions of community and self, including family and family relations. Changes in economic arrangements, migration patterns, living standards, and other broad societal changes related to globalization challenge and change families in such areas as the roles of women, children, and the elderly and the very foundation of marriage and childbearing and childrearing norms in the face of heretofore patriarchal societies and traditional cultures.

Summary

This chapter has explored how transnational employment and the transnational families thus created contribute to the "shuffling about, splitting, and sometimes disintegration of families" (Bryceson and Vuorela 2002:4). Heymann (2006) describes these families as "forgotten," largely overlooked while globalization progresses at a rapid pace. She seeks to reveal the fissures between families and employers and governments across borders and related issues of parental employment and effects on child health and development, family problems and crises, and other concerns at our own risk.

The situation of transnational families challenges the equation of family as synonymous with household. While transnational families live some or most of the time separated from each other, they also may strive to maintain a sense of family, even across national borders. This chapter has examined the impact of transnational employment as a way in which certain economic and family roles are transferred between less developed and more developed societies.

The increasing number of migrant domestic and other household workers participating in complex survival circuits demonstrates a way in which globalization contributes to the growing disparities between families in the Third World and those in the First World. These disparities are enmeshed not only in decisions made by families and their members to seek employment abroad, but also in national and supranational economic and political policies which severely limit migrant domestic worker's employment and family options. Furthermore, such changes are profoundly gendered, with the potential to impact both economic relations between domestic workers and their employers and between the migrant worker and her family. Women's increasing participation in the global workforce has not been accompanied by parallel improvements in the status and power of women in societies or in their families.

Care workers are usually women who migrate to more affluent societies, often leaving behind their own families not only to work in domestic employment, but also to extend their services to emotional, expressive care work in the households of families in other societies. Like migrant domestic labor, the global distribution of care work responds to economic and political dynamics between First and Third World societies. As care work has become commoditized and marketized, women leave Third World societies for employment in First World societies. Thus, global care chains ensure that families in the First World can draw on a supply of cheap, expendable workers from the developing world, while families in the developing world are left with a global care deficit, a shortage of women to perform the very same functions for their own families in their own countries.

Transnational parenting imposes particular challenges on families. A body of research is suggesting that children left behind, as well as their parents, experience emotional and other hardships. However, understanding of the impacts of transnational parenting requires cross-cultural sensitivity to kin and community ties, gender dynamics, and the potential for resiliency.

Clearly, more research is needed to ascertain how global demographics, especially migratory labor patterns, impact families in the face of tremendous economic pressures to compete and perform in an increasingly globalized economy. Further study is needed to assess how families who do not share every day/every night life in a common space struggle or thrive, shape identities and communities, relate across the family life cycle and across history, and fit into national and transnational social policy paradigms.

A Migrant Mother's Story: Paula Rodriguez
By Joanna Dreby

Paula, a heavy woman with kind eyes, grew teary when I first asked her if I could interview her about her two children in Mexico. Regardless, she agreed to the interview, which we scheduled for a Tuesday morning. Since Paula worked two full-time jobs at two different fast-food restaurants, that was her only day off from the 70-hour per week work schedule. Walking by a dark blue sheet that had converted part of the living room into an extra bedroom, we sat in the meticulously clean kitchen in the first floor two-bedroom apartment of a house by the train tracks in an upscale town in New Jersey. At the kitchen table, Paula recounted her story.

Paula had come to New Jersey about five years earlier with the help of her sister. Paula was, and is, an undocumented immigrant. She has two children, a boy aged 18 and a girl aged 15. Paula is one of six siblings, all of whom are in the United States. She and her sister live in New Jersey; she has a brother in Queens and three brothers in Texas. The family is originally from a little town outside of a small city in the state of Puebla, Mexico. Paula studied the six years of *primaria*, or grammar school, and after that she didn't work—she was an *ama de casa*, a housewife.

Suddenly, Paula started to cry, not profusely, but by closing her eyes and squinting. She said she felt ashamed about her past. After taking a moment, Paula explained that she had met the father of her children when she was about 18 years old. When her daughter was only 8 months old, he left her. She felt embarrassed because he left for no reason. One day he just went away and didn't tell her why.

After her boyfriend left, Paula moved in with her cousin Pedro and his wife Blanca in a nearby city. Because Pedro and Blanca both worked as school teachers, Paula stayed at their home in exchange for housekeeping duties. When the couple had a daughter a year later, Paula helped with childcare as well. About a year after Paula's daughter was born, she met four women who were planning to migrate to the United States. She decided to try her luck like her brothers had done before her, in *el norte*.

Paula went to the state of Washington in 1989 when her son Mateo was 4 and her daughter Cindy was just a year old. She lived with the relatives of one of her travel companions and found a job at McDonalds. Because she worked both the opening and closing shifts, Paula was home during the middle of the day and cooked for the family with whom she lived in exchange for her share of the grocery bill. By cutting daily living costs to a minimum, Paula was able to send $150–$200 a week home for the care of her kids. Paula explained that this remittance was necessary because Blanca had to hire help to care for the children in her absence.

After just 18 months in the United States, Paula went home to Mexico. "I couldn't stand it," she said. "I missed my children way too much. During the time I was away, my daughter forgot about me. But when my son would get on the phone he would ask, 'Mama, when are you coming?' and 'Mama, why did you leave me?'" The adjustment of Paula's children upon Paula's return wasn't automatic. Paula recalled that when she first came home, Cindy didn't recognize her. It took about two months of listening to older brother Mateo calling Paula mama for little Cindy to follow suit.

Back in Puebla, Paula moved into a bedroom adjoining the kitchen and, as before, took care of the cooking, cleaning, and child care while Blanca and Pedro worked. Her responsibilities expanded slowly over the next ten years. Blanca and Pedro had another daughter, whom Paula helped to raise. Blanca and Pedro also set up a store selling fruits and vegetables in the front of their house, which Paula tended to during the day.

For over two years, Paula planned her second trip north, before eventually migrating again in 1999. Paula patiently waited until her son, Mateo, graduated from the ninth grade; this time she had decided to take him with her. Paula explained that her son wasn't crazy about leaving their home in Mexico. Moreover, "My daughter often asked why [I was going to leave], but I explained to her that there was no future for me in Mexico. There I wasn't able to save any money." Paula didn't want to take her daughter with her for two reasons. First, the expense of crossing for three people, rather than two, was too much. Second, Paula worried about the danger of taking her daughter across the border. "Cindy eventually accepted that I leave, but only with the condition that I go back for her after a few months."

Paula returned to New Jersey, this time with the help of her sister. Within just a day, she started working at a local fast food restaurant. Mateo was left alone. Paula planned that he would attend high school during the day and spoke to her manager about a part-time position in the evenings. But they arrived in New Jersey in July, giving Mateo almost two months with little to do. Quickly Mateo decided he didn't like the United States or where he lived with his mother in New Jersey. That fall he never signed up for high school. Mateo turned to his uncle in Texas, who offered to take him in and cover all the costs associated with a high school education. Mateo left for Texas that January.

Within 18 months, by attending summer school, Mateo completed the two years of high school necessary for his diploma. However, he still didn't feel good living in the United States, "so much that he would call me crying," explained Paula. Mateo decided it would be best to return to Mexico to study. Paula felt badly when her son left for Texas: "Mostly because of his rejection after I brought him here. But when he left for Mexico, it hurt more because I knew the separation would be more permanent."

Meanwhile, back in Mexico, Paula said her daughter Cindy felt jealous about being left behind. "I didn't really realize this, until once when we were talking on the phone, Cindy blurted out, 'Mom, you don't love me because you took Mateo and not me.'" Paula explained to her that it is much more dangerous for a girl on the border, and that life in the United States was really no good. "Eventually, she understood that it wasn't that I don't love her, but that I had her best interests in mind."

In 2004, at the time of my initial interview with Paula, Mateo had been back in Mexico for nearly two years and almost five years had passed since Paula had seen her daughter Cindy. Mateo, now fluent in English, wanted to get a college degree in tourism. According to Paula, to achieve this end, he still needed two more years of high school in Mexico and four years of college. Paula calculated six more years of schooling for her daughter Cindy as well, who had just started studying at a private high school, financed by Paula's remittances, and who wanted to be a schoolteacher. Working two full-time jobs at the two fast food restaurants in New Jersey, Paula believed she could finance both children's educations. She expected to continue with her grueling schedule for the six years necessary to provide her children with professional degrees that could give them the independence that she never had at their age. If all went according to plan, Paula hoped she would be able to eventually return to Mexico for an early retirement.

Joanna Dreby is completing her doctorate in sociology at the City University of New York Graduate Center. This essay is based on her dissertation research on Mexican transnational families, supported by a Fulbright grant in Mexico, as well as a Carole and Morton Olshan Dissertation Fellowship. She has published her work in the *American Sociological Review, Contexts, Gender & Society*, and in *Sociological Forum*.

Critical Thinking Questions:

1. Describe the economic and social conditions that contribute to Third World women leaving their families for employment in First World households.
2. How might Giele and Holst's predictions regarding adaptation, differentiation, integration, and generalization apply to gender roles in Third World countries?
3. Using the case of Paula Rodriquez, develop a cost/benefit ratio around global care chains for:

   • the migrating woman,
   • her family, and
   • her society of origin.

   Now develop the same for:

   • the employing household,
   • the employing family, and
   • the society in which she is employed.

4. What are the quantitative and qualitative similarities and differences between the anguish expressed by transnational families (mothers and their children) and the feelings of guilt or regret expressed by some employed American women?

4

INTERNATIONAL VIOLENCE: FAMILY LEGACIES OF OPPRESSION AND WAR

⚜

Whether it is actual warfare, civil strife, the spread of AIDS, the sale of children into the sex trade, grinding poverty, or sewage flowing in front of the doorway of a shanty, violence is present whenever those with the means use their means to protect their privileges against those who want a share of them. And, to come to the unique feature of globalization, when money and time move as rapidly as they do today on the wings of a digital bird, *everyone* knows that he or she is at some risk—even those most securely ensconced in their gated villas. (Lemert and Elliott 2006:155)

THE SISTERS OF THE GOOD SHEPARD (*Buon Pastore*) provide safe houses and counsel to prostitutes in Rome who wish to leave the life. Sr. Helen Ann Sand (2004) has described the processes through which these women (some of whom are mere girls, my own teenage daughter's age) enter Italy illegally, often landing by boat along Italy's relatively uncontrolled coastline, from Africa, Asia, the Middle East, and Eastern Europe, with Albania, Romania, China, Iraq, and a growing list of African countries leading the list. Often trafficked by men who promise they will secure a position for these women caring for children or performing domestic work in an affluent Italian household, the women hope to be able to send desperately needed Euros home to their families and, eventually, achieve citizenship and reunification with their families in a less violent, more civil society than that from whence they came.

But, for anyone who enters Italy illegally, and especially for someone who is not only undocumented, but cannot verify gainful, legal employment since arriving, attaining citizenship is virtually impossible. Cut off from educational, employment, health, and other social services, the outlook for these women is dismal. Although the European Union requires member nations to control their borders effectively, and a recent four-month investigation into trafficking throughout Italy resulted in the arrest of 2,000 people, most of them foreigners, and uncovered "hundreds" of trafficking rings (Sanminiatelli 2007), efforts to stem the flow of human trafficking for sex or exploitative labor are ineffective and seem futile in light of the scale of the problem.

I have found this to be a most difficult chapter to write. Certainly, covering a range of issues related to international violence inflicted against families and their members is a daunting task, but the greater challenge was reviewing the documentation concerning how colonization and sex trafficking, rape, sexual slavery, and other violence disrupt and disturb families in the most profound and tragic ways.

I begin this chapter with a discussion of international systems of oppression, including the legacies of colonialism on families and the impact of sex trafficking. I then address the effects of war: sexual domination and exploitation, including rape in war, military sexual slavery, and other collateral violence against women and girls. I consider the marital consequences of war as well, including the marriage squeeze, heterogamous marriages, and marital instability. I also offer a discussion of military and refugee families, as well as consideration of the extent to which the greatest man-made horrors inflicted on humankind also reveal the deep promise of family resiliency. I hope this chapter captures a measure of both parts of this story.

International Systems of Oppression

Many European Americans are accustomed to conceiving of colonization from the perspective of the early history of the United States. From that point of view, colonization refers to the establishment of imperial colonies peopled by settlers from the dominant society—English from England to Australia, Dutch from the Netherlands to South Africa, and French from France to Vietnam, for example. Such is the almost romantic social legacy of people who may have shared ethnicity with the colonial power. Perhaps some of these imperial colonists were even part of the sponsored bourgeoisie. But a sizeable proportion of colonists were social castoffs and misfits—criminals, debtors, heretics, or other social nonconformists—from that dominant society.

An alternative, oppositionist perspective on colonialism began to emerge toward the end of World War II (Said 1978). Colonial administrations lasted well into the last half of the twentieth century and only within the last three decades has critical theory toward decolonization become mainstreamed (Miyoshi 1993). The concept of global Diaspora is being extended beyond reference to catastrophic dispersal of a people across wide geographic areas to include imperial, labor and trade, as well as cultural dispersion through societal domination (Cohen 1997). Sociology, psychology, history, economics, and other disciplines continue to expand the analysis of colonialism, slavery, and other oppressive legacies to include these resistance paradigms.

A review of the hardships, turmoil, and often violence faced by inhabitants of former colonies makes clear that decolonization has not resulted in economic, political, and social liberation for the formerly colonized. Former colonial societies have often faced long-standing systems of inequality across tribes, religions, races, genders, ethnicities, and other characteristics that greatly affected individuals and families. Further, former colonies were often left with abbreviated time frames in which to resolve the problems of fractured and ineffective economic, political, and social systems. Miyoshi (1993:731) notes that "peaceful progress [including to nation–statehood on the global stage] has been structurally denied" to Third World states. Former colonies, now Third World societies, simply cannot compete on a playing field dominated by the General Agreement on Tariffs and Trade, the International Monetary Fund, and the World Bank.

The legacies of colonialism die slowly, as demonstrated by the case of the Democratic Republic of the Congo. The early twentieth-century sociologist Robert Park began his career as a journalist and activist in the Congo Reform movement, seeking to address an unfolding social tragedy as that former Belgian colony sought to establish itself as a free, democratic republic (Karraker 2004; Karraker 2006). Yet, still today, the Democratic Republic of the Congo stands as an archetype of the excessive level of violence directed by military authorities against civilians. The country's natural resources continue to be plundered, while perpetrators of the genocide in Rwanda operate openly from within the Democratic Republic of the Congo's borders. Families have been particularly affected by a history of war in that nation, a history that grew out of colonialism and now stretches into a third century. The International Criminal Court, based in The Hague, is considering charges against a Congolese warlord for impressing children to serve as soldiers in that country's rebel conflict (children who are part of the estimated 300,000 child soldiers participating in armed conflicts worldwide) ("War Crimes Court" 2007). The most recent war that began in 1998 has seen Angolan, Namibian, and

Zimbabwean armed militias operating within and outside the Democratic Republic of the Congo, at a cost of almost four million lives (U.S. Holocaust Museum 2006g).

Colonialism and Families

The societal legacies of colonialism, bound as they are with violence and power, are also reflected in the social reproduction of family patterns. Colonial authorities often seek to dominate the indigenous society with critical institutions, including reinforcing family structures that will be consistent with colonial economic, political, and cultural systems. Brantley's (2003) analysis of the case of British colonial intervention in the small, colonial state of Nyasaland, Africa, is a case in point. The British colonial agents operating in this small, land-locked colonial state in the early-to-middle twentieth century enacted practices that effectively replaced family farming with low wage labor and the extended, matrilineal family with the nuclear, neolocal, highly mobile family. In another case, Pollard (2003) argued that the British successfully reshaped the family structure of Egyptian *effendiyya* (the political ruling class) to emphasize monogamy and the nuclear family, more conducive to de facto economic and political colonial rule.

Thus, the family and the gender relations within families have often been transformed by colonial powers. Brantley (2003) found that colonial agents viewed gender relations through a Western, patriarchal lens, seeing African families as patriarchal and men as the primary agents of social change. By defining the men as farmers in a culture in which women historically had far-reaching authority over feeding their families, including cultivating, harvesting, storing, and preparing all food, the British authorities undermined the existing status quo, privileging men and denigrating women by disrupting family structure and spheres of authority. The colonial agents thus ensured that men were available to perform wage labor (and to pay taxes), with the family changed to a monogamous, nuclear family consistent with British ideals of family as a husband–father with economic control over his wife and their children. These kinds of changes have disrupted and damaged women's roles and status across African families and society.

A flourishing sex trade also often has been integral to regulating the dominant colonial population in absentia from the imperial society. Briggs (2003) takes the argument even further, proposing that ideologies of family, sexuality, and reproduction direct imperialist and racial agendas. Briggs outlines how the United States operating in Puerto Rico between 1849 and 1916 engaged in colonial discourse that was both biomedical and familial, resulting in the requirement that prostitutes be registered, that they submit to medical examinations, and that they be treated if found to be infected. The historical precedence for such a model can be found in

Western programs to address matters of sexual access in military and port towns. As such, these colonial policies protected "various forms of sanctified domesticity" (i.e., white, nuclear families of the colonists), as well as armies and labor forces, while serving to "organize disorderly women, often limiting their mobility to segregated districts, enrolling them as imperial citizens through the . . . bureaucratic process of registration, sometimes restricting their clients by race" (Briggs 2003:41–42).

But not all prostitutes in colonial towns were women of the indigenous population. At the turn of the twentieth century, European prostitutes in colonial Bombay, India, occupied an intermediary status in a racially stratified sexual order. British colonial authorities managed, monitored, and segregated European prostitutes to a much greater extent than other women involved in sex work. Such a system enabled the colonial state to control the racial and sexual order more effectively through coerced medical regulation and licensing by the police and brothel mistresses. From a transnational feminist perspective, European prostitutes were an "evil" necessary to maintain access to safe sexual recreation, while maintaining acceptable racial parameters (Tambe 2005).

While "the British saw prostitution wherever they looked" (Levine 2004:159), colonial authorities also used prostitution, in all its varieties, as a means to reproduce colonial economic, family, inequality, and other social systems necessary for a successful colonial enterprise (White 2004). Prostitution disturbed the moral social order, but prostitution also helped demarcate and institutionalize social hierarchies of race, social class, and gender. On the one hand, prostitution was a "problem, but it was also both a necessity and a convenient canvas on which to illuminate the greater evils or dangers of uncivilized peoples" (Levine 2004:159). Colonial commercial interests depended on missionary Christian interests to "civilize" the colonized population, thus enabling the conforming colonized population to be subdued by Christianity and exploited for capitalist interests. Thus, agendas of social control provided opportunities to channel sexuality into rational, productive boundaries, while reinforcing the dominant and subordinate statuses of the colonial and the indigenous people, as well as the relative statuses of men and women.

On another level, contemporary scholars place prostitution in the context of rationally chosen sex work that a woman sometimes deems necessary to support herself and her dependents. In such cases, prostitution may be viewed as consistent with cultural values that permit unmarried women to control their own bodies. From this perspective, prostitution can be seen as a means to achieve or retain relative economic and social independence. Bliss (2004) arrived at such conclusions regarding the regulation of prostitution in Mexico City, from the years of the French occupation in the 1860s through the subsequent dictatorship, revolution, civil war, and reconstruction, culminating in the political and social reforms of the

1940s. Bliss found substantial contradiction between official public pronounce-
ments of prostitutes as deviant, morally depraved women who were a threat to
family and good society and the women's perceptions of themselves as acting out
of economic responsibility, supporting a network of children and others through
their earnings.

However, any prostitution exposes women to a host of short- and long-term hazards, including violence, disease, and death, as well as economic, legal, and other
vulnerabilities. In a recent study of the estimated 1,000-strong sex workforce of
young Nigerian women engaging in prostitution in Italy, Achebe (2004) documented that sex workers remain in subordinate, dependent, dangerous relationships
relative to the sex traffickers, pimps, and madams who control prostitution.

Sex Trafficking

Prostitution in colonial societies calls to mind the contemporary problem of human
trafficking and, in particular, the growing problem of sex trafficking in women and
children. Trafficking refers to the often violent transportation of men, women, or
children for exploitative, illicit purposes including slavery or undocumented work
("Trafficking in Persons Report 2006" 2006). The Palermo Protocol (UNICEF
2000:2) specifically defines trafficking as:

> the recruitment, transportation, transfer, harbouring or receipt of persons, by means
> of threat or use of force or other forms of coercion, of abduction, of fraud, of decep-
> tion, of the abuse of power or of a position of vulnerability or of the giving or
> receiving of payments or benefits to achieve the consent of a person having control
> over another person, for the purpose of exploitation. Exploitation shall include, at a
> minimum, the exploitation or the prostitution of others or other forms of sexual
> exploitation, forced labor or services, slavery or practices similar to slavery, servi-
> tude or the removal of organs.

Every year, as many as a half million women and children are believed to be
trafficked into Western Europe from poorer countries. Estimates are that in
2000–2001 women were trafficked out of Southeast Asia at the rate of a quarter
million per year and out of South Asia at a rate of 150,000 per year (Seager
2003:56). The multibillion dollar global sex trade is built on social structural
inequalities of economics, gender, and ethnicity. Such inequalities drive women and
children into global prostitution and fuel the market for sexual consumption
among men in positions of greater economic or other privilege. Sex trafficking also
draws on the economic and political disparities between regions of the globe.
Global poverty can be said to provide incentive for societies to enter the global sex

trade circuit, which is sustained by coercion, torture, rape, and other forms of violence and intimidation (Davidson 2006; UNICEF 2004).

In some countries, families sell their daughters as part of systems of oppression in which mores which view the trafficking in human beings, especially women and children, are normalized as socially acceptable. Such appears to be the case among the men involved in sex trafficking as a "family business." As Jennifer Blank describes in the essay that follows this chapter, men involved in trafficking have indifferent, dismissive, or even hostile views of their female cargo. As verified in the UNICEF (2004:6) report, patriarchal views of females as inferior contribute to the ease with which women and girls are commercially exploited. The report continues:

> Recently, the links between poverty, violence, and trafficking have been compounded by the effects of HIV/AIDS. Women and girls trafficked for prostitution are among the most vulnerable groups exposed to HIV infection. Insufficiently informed, seduced or forced to have unprotected sex, once infected with HIV/AIDS they are left without care or support. Furthermore, children orphaned by AIDS can be more vulnerable to trafficking due to the increasing poverty of their households and communities, and as a result of the stigmatization, rejection, or marginalization to which they are exposed in their communities.

UNICEF (2004) has endorsed a human rights approach to combat trafficking of women and children in Africa. The UNICEF proposal requires a national framework organized around enacting major legislation to address five areas of concern: immigration; child labor and employment; child welfare and protection; protection from abduction, torture, slavery, and unlawful detention; and prostitution and related sexual activities, including pornography, statutory sexual contact, and other sexual offenses. Clearly, effective response to the problem of trafficking will require concerted global effort on many fronts.

War and Social Disorder

Between December 1937 and March 1938, in what has come to be called the Rape of Nanking, Japanese soldiers killed an estimated 300,000 Chinese people (many of them women and children), raped 20,000 women, and proceeded to torture, bury alive, freeze to death, decapitate, mutilate, and cause to be torn apart by dogs uncounted others. The number dead exceeded those killed by bombs dropped on Hiroshima and Nagasaki (Chang 1997; "Scarred by History" 2005).

Globalization does not cause war. However, as Barkawi (2006:92) argues, "[w]ar itself is a form of interconnection." War is not only an example of globalization; war is also one of the principal mechanisms of globalization, a globalizing force. From such a perspective, war shapes cultural frameworks. War influences how people view the world, their place and the place of their nation in the world, and the experience of other places in the world. Put another way, war draws individuals from the local to an awareness of their connection to other places, including national–international identities (Barkawi 2006).

In the following section, I address issues that result from the broad category of war-related crises: international warfare, but also ethnic "cleansing" and other tribal disputes, internal insurgencies, and other armed conflicts. These conflicts impact families directly through the maiming and murder of their members, family absence during periods of service, family dislocation, and the collateral effects of economic disintegration, political upheaval, poverty, famine, and other shortages that accompany such large-scale violent crises.

The events of September 11, 2001, brought the fear of war and the deadly effects on family and personal life home for many Americans, if only for a brief time. Certainly, every reader of *Global Families* remembers where she or he was on that autumn morning. Some readers will remember frantic calls to loved ones, both those close by and those in more distant locations. Perhaps some readers experienced the loss of a brother or sister, a father or mother, a husband, wife, other life partner, kin, or friend in the events in New York, Pennsylvania, or Washington, D.C.

The continental United States has not been a battlefield location since the end of the Civil War, almost a century and a half ago. Still, as this book goes to press, over 3,000 Americans, including those serving in the armed forces and others operating as contractors, have died since March 2003 as a result of the most recent war in the Middle East, leaving reverberations of grief in every family touched by those deaths. Even families that have been spared loss of life in that conflict live with the everyday/everynight uncertainty regarding the safety and well-being of their loved one.[1] The death toll for Iraqi civilians during the same period has been highly contested, with recent estimates being around 35,000 dead ("MacAskill" 2007).

Sexual Domination and Exploitation

One of the most effective strategic weapons of war is rape. In countries as varied as Switzerland and the United Kingdom, India, and Zimbabwe, between one out of eight and one out of four women or more report being the victim of sexual assault or attempted sexual assault by an intimate partner (Seager 2003:58–59). Rape is a threat to women and girls and typically a male privilege everywhere in the world. As a tool of patriarchy, rape serves as a violent mechanism used to

---

[1]A recent book by Pauline Boss (2006), Professor Emerita of Family Social Science at the University of Minnesota, describes the particular stresses faced by families experiencing the kind of "ambiguous loss" that characterized the attacks on the United States on September 11, 2001, terrorist attacks, and the war in Kosovo.

A Nation at War by David Horsey

David Horsey, *Seattle Post-Intelligencer*. Originally published 7/12/2006.

assert male dominance. Even among intimate partners, rape is far from an uncommon experience.

Rape in War

Across the globe, rape has been used as widespread and systematic action by soldiers, paramilitary troops, or others involved in warfare. In Bosnia–Herzegovina (the former Yugoslavia), 20,000 Muslim women were raped in 1992. In Rwanda, more than 15,000 women were raped in the 1994 genocide. In Indonesia, ethnic Chinese women were targeted for rape in 1998. In the Sudan in recent years, 50,000 girls have been captured and kept as sex slaves by government forces in the northern territories (Seager 2003:99).

Brownmiller (1975), Farwell (2004), and others have conceptualized rape as both a tactical weapon of and a strategic approach to war. Rape has been used as "a weapon of terror" (p. 48), for military retaliation or reprisal (p. 52), or for "psywar" (psychological warfare [p. 87] in modern military vernacular). As such, rape in war underscores the intersections among gender and patriarchy, as well as ethnic, racial, religious, and regional political identities, and militarism. Rape in war occurs across nationalities. Hence, rape and sexual slavery in wartime can be viewed through the lenses of globalization and feminism, with long-lasting effects on family formation and quality of life. Rape, when seen as systematic, ritual pollution, such as during a pogrom of ethnic cleansing, can render substantial portions of the female population unmarriageable or can so severely depreciate her honor and status that an entire generation is impaired in its ability to form families, solidify kin networks, and ensure the care of children in conjugal pairs.

Throughout history, then, women (and children) have been viewed as regrettable, but incidental and unavoidable collateral casualties of war and conquest. (Note that virtually no attention has been given to the rape of boys and men during war.) The capture and subsequent rape and enslavement of women is a collateral acquisition, like the acquisition of territory and property (Brownmiller 1975). Brownmiller (p. 34) argues that rape provides ordinary men with a legitimate outlet in a group dynamic of conformity for exercising misogyny. Rape even can serve as an "international metaphor for [national] humiliation" and national subjugation. However, today, rape is a criminal act under international rules of war, punishable by imprisonment or death under Article 120 of the American Uniform Code of Military Justice.

Sex crimes are an integral part of war with devastating consequences for families, even beyond the physical and psychological injury to the victim. War, along with genocide and crimes against humanity, creates an atmosphere in which civilians are more vulnerable and protective institutions break down. The sexual violence that occurs at these times is even more brutal, intense, and pervasive than during more stable times. Sexualized violence, then, generates terror on not only the immediate victims, but also on their communities. The consequences of rape on societies, including rape during war, are horrific. But rape can compromise the long-term, even life-long effects on the woman or girl who survives rape, including her sense of safety and security in intimate relationships. Further, in traditional patriarchal societies, rape can create difficulties around her very ability to be accepted as an honorable women and potential marriage partner in society.

Military Sexual Slavery

Another gendered aspect of global warfare that has long-lasting effects on families is military sexual slavery. Between 1930 and 1945, especially during World War II, between 100,000 and 200,000 Asian women were forced into sexual slavery by the Japanese military. Hicks (1994) described the "comfort station" (hence, *ianfu* or "comfort workers," the name for the women who sexually serviced Japanese men serving in the military [Nozaki 2001]) in Shanghai, first of a series of officially sanctioned brothels. His research reveals the extent to which women, many in their early teen years, were coaxed or deceived, but often coerced to service the sexual desires of the Japanese armed forces. Many of these women were transported from rural villages to military bases. In the desire of nations to move forward with postwar reconstruction, these women have been all but forgotten. Even if they returned to their communities and families, these women were never repatriated in the full meaning of the word. Many carried with them extensive trauma that affected their social psychological and family adjustment throughout the rest of their lives.

Powerful testimonies compiled by the Korean Council for Women Drafted for Military Sexual Slavery by Japan have been compiled in a translated volume by Howard (1995). An article by Chung (1995) in the same volume summarizes some of the characteristics of the women thus enslaved, including the effects on their subsequent family lives. Eighty to ninety percent of the women were Korean.[2] Although, at the time of the war, the legal age for a licensed prostitute was 18 in Japan and 17 in Korea, no age restriction applied to comfort women, and girls as young as 11 were forced into sexual slavery. Most of the women had little education and came from poor farming families. Very few were married.

Not surprisingly, comfort women recall fearing for their lives (Yongnyǒ 1995; T'aesǒn 1995). The women who survived sexual slavery under the Japanese during World War II report feelings of having lost youth and opportunity (Okpun 1995; P'ilgi 1995; Yongsu 1995), being embittered (Haksun 1995) and struggling against resentment (Yǒngsuk 1995), as well as continued treatment with contempt after the war ended (Kǔmju 1995). Some grieve over continued rejection after the war by their families of origin (Sangok 1995) and their inability to bear children (Sunok 1995). The repercussions of military sexual slavery on family life were still being felt almost a half century later.

The comfort station system was part of a larger effort on the part of the Japanese government and armed forces to enforce a wartime policy exploiting Japan's long-standing colonial control over Korea (Chung 1997; Min 2003). Initially, these brothels were organized and regulated by military authorities, but, by the 1940s, civilian authorities had been placed in control (Chung 1997). However, as I discussed in Chapter 1, structural oppression theory, which examines the intersections among multiple systems of oppression, often offers a richer explanation of global contact. Even though the case of Korean comfort women reflected Japanese military and imperial policies, some authors argue that such an interpretation neglects the political and social discourse of the time. Not only military subjugation and colonization, but also reinforcement of social class and gender hierarchies, were at work (Min 2003). Nozaki (2001) and Yang (1997) argue that the case of Korean comfort women should be viewed in light of the role of Japanese masculinity, racism, and imperialism. In particular, Hicks (1995) and

---

[2]The other 10 to 20 percent of women enslaved by the Japanese were Taiwanese, Indonesian, Filipina, and Dutch. Ruff-O'Herne (1994) offers and autobiographical account of her passage from being the daughter of a wealthy Dutch colonial family to serving as a comfort woman for Japanese officers.

Mendoza (2003) emphasize that Japan's comfort system was viewed by the Japanese Imperial Army as a method of enhancing the masculine efficiency of its fighting force.

Soh's (2004) recent analysis suggests that the situation of comfort women should also be viewed in the larger context of traditional patriarchal mistreatment of daughters. Daughters fled or were driven from their homes into the public domain, where they may have had a chance to flee the domestic oppression of their father's households, but were made more vulnerable to victimization in the Japanese military brothel system. Thus, Howard (1995) emphasizes the devaluation of daughters, the prevalence of domestic violence against women and children, and the pervasive poverty in Korea at the time of the Second World War to explain why families sold their daughters into sexual servitude.

Some nations, such as the Netherlands, brought criminal charges against Japan immediately after World War II. However, Asian nations (including Korea) took much longer to take action on the issue. Eventually the Japanese established the Asian Woman's Fund (AWF) to compensate victims. Although the government of the Philippines accepted Japan's offer of redress, Indonesia, Korean, and Taiwan did not (Soh 2000b). Still, the case of sexual enslavement of women by the Japanese during World War II has received little attention in Japanese textbooks and other official war records. Until recently, testimony from the aggrieved women has been missing. However, beyond that, the Japanese response has not included authentic remorse accompanied by "apology, compensation, and historical reflection" (Field 1997:38). Perhaps this policy is consistent with Japan's postwar ideology portraying itself as a war victim (Chung 1997), but ignoring and trivializing this case has strong sexist and patriarchal overtones (Chung 1997; Nozaki 2001). Again, such reactions marginalize, and even make invisible, the lower status of women and the impact this practice had on thousands of Korean, Taiwanese, Filipina, Indonesian, Dutch, and other families.

Not until the early 1990s was debate fully engaged at the level of the United Nations to consider sexual enslavement by the Japanese as a war crime. In doing so, the debate shifted from considering these women not as prostitutes, but as sexual slaves. Thus, the debate surrounding the enslavement of *ianfu* serves to symbolically represent the view of women's rights as human rights in the arena of global politics (Soh 2000a).

Almost 50 years after the end of the War in the Pacific, in December 2000, the Women's International War Crimes Tribunal for the Trial of Japanese Military Sexual Slavery met in Tokyo. Seventy-five women from Korea, India, Japan, the Netherlands, and the Philippines testified to the long-term consequences of their experiences (Askin 2001). At least some of the initiative and effectiveness of the efforts to gain recognition and redress for these women came about through transnational feminist women's activism, with women in Korea and Japan using transnational legal means to popularize and politicize the issue at both regional and global levels (Piper 2001).

Other Collateral Violence Against Women and Girls

The poverty and lawlessness that accompanies life in a combat zone does not portend well for the quality of life of anyone, even beyond rape in war and military sexual slavery. However, a long-standing history of embattlement seems to ensure that the safety and security of girls and women will receive little or no attention. A society that exists on the brink of collapse of its civic, economic, educational, and other social systems, may have difficulty devoting economic and political resources, to say nothing of emotional resources, to concern over the well-being of a part of the population which may well be viewed as invisible and of depreciated status.

A recently released report based on research conducted in the West Bank and Gaza confirms that violence in besieged territories extends to the lives of girls and women. In a report titled "A Question of Security: Violence Against Palestinian Women and Girls" the Human Rights Watch (2006) charged that, due to the current political and economic crisis, the Palestinian authority has failed to address violence and abuse of women and girls as a priority security issue. The report documents violence ranging from wife and child abuse to rape (outside and within marriage) and incest. The report cites the practice of "honor killings" (in which men kill female family members suspected of adultery or even of having been sexually violated) and cases of rape victims being required to marry their assailants. In such cases, patriarchy, which indulges domestic and broader scale violence against women and girls, can remain uncontested, as the society struggles against external enemies.

While the Human Rights Watch study was welcomed by some Palestinian officials, perhaps a signal that some in the society are ready for a change, violence against women and girls tends to go unreported in Palestine and, when reported, unpunished or only mildly punished in a society in which a quarter of women said they have experienced domestic violence and even more (two-thirds) reported experiencing psychological abuse in their homes.

Of course, Palestine is not alone. Data collected by the World Health Organization confirms that sexual abuse continues to be a "stubborn scourge" in not only Southeast Asia and sub-Saharan Africa, but in Brazil, Japan, and Peru (LaFranier 2006). Poverty especially makes securing children's safety difficult. Legacies of violence, oppression, and cultural mores that indulge child sexual abuse create a climate of relative tolerance toward a crime with heart-wrenching consequences in a world inhabited by the HIV/AIDS pandemic and poor health and medical care.

Almost one-third of American women report being physically or sexually abused by a husband or boyfriend. In Europe, domestic violence is the leading cause of death and disability for women aged 16 to 44 years old. The World Health Organization estimates that, worldwide, 10 to 70 percent of women are physically abused by their male partners. Immigrant and refugee women are at particular risk for domestic abuse. The immigrant experience may transpose the pattern of male economic and social dominance over their wives in the host society. Further, language barriers, including inadequate interpretation services, fear of removal and legal obstacles, cultural barriers and community pressures, and reduced funding in social service areas create significant, unique risks for immigrant and refugee women (Minnesota Advocates for Human Rights 2004).

War and Marriage

Another effect of any armed conflict on families is the impact on family formation patterns. Family effects are shaped by such factors as conflict duration, mortality or injury, military and civilian population characteristics, occupation and collaboration, economic, spatial, and other hardships, and family and the societal resources for recovery. Researchers have documented several impacts of armed global conflict on patterns of marriage, including opportunity to marry, the likelihood of heterogamous unions, and the chance for marital stability.

The Marriage Squeeze

The opportunity to form a marriage is first and foremost shaped by the availability of eligible partners. Wars disproportionately remove from the pool of marriage eligibles the most suitable male partners. Men who volunteer, are drafted, or are otherwise mustered into military service during wartime tend to be among the youngest and fittest (even if sometimes the most socially disadvantaged). These are desirable characteristics not only for soldiering, but also for marrying, establishing a household, fathering children, and supporting a family.

This demographic situation has been referred to as the marriage squeeze. Studies conducted on different war experiences illustrate the impact of war on marriage rates. Goodkind (1997) has studied the deficit of male partners in Vietnam during the 1970s and 1980s, the years immediately following the withdrawal of the United States from and the ending of the war in Vietnam. As I discussed in Chapter 3, in addition to loss of male population due to war, Vietnamese men emigrated at higher rates than did women. The consequence of such a marriage squeeze was, not surprisingly, delayed and foregone marriage (Goodkind 1997; Thai 2002).

Researchers also have observed a severe marriage squeeze in Lebanon, another country beset by decades-long armed conflict. Saxena, Kulczycki, and Jurdi (2004) used the 1996 *Population and Housing Survey*, a representative sampling of 64,472 households in Lebanon (the largest demographic data set for that country since 1932). They found the proportion of single women of childbearing age doubled in proportion to men during a 25 year period ending in 1996, five years after that war ended. Saxena, Kulczycki, and Jurdi estimate the mate availability ratios (calculated as the number of single adult males available per hundred single adult females in adult age groups) declined to 75 by age 25 and to 50 by age 30.

Heterogamous Marriages

Another testimony to the impact of global forces on marriages and families can be seen in the extent of marriages between women and men from different sides of an armed conflict. While the picture of these marriages is often encumbered by stereotypes (Williams 1991), research reveals some powerful findings about the nature of marriage formation and consequent impacts on marital quality, gender roles, and other couple dynamics.

The research in this area is almost exclusively on women who marry men from the dominant—often winning—side of an armed conflict and who adopt the country of their husbands.[3] These "war brides" may well be enhancing their socioeconomic opportunity in contrast to remaining in a society which has been ravaged by war and, as discussed above, in which war has created a significant marriage squeeze resulting in a dearth of eligible men. However, research indicates that they may still face economic hardship. Further, many women struggle and grieve over the separation from their home culture and society (Footrakoon 2000).

War brides constitute a significant part of the cultural memory of some societies. For example, Esser (2003) describes the representation of marriages between Germans and Americans in German newspapers and magazines published in the American and British zones between the end of World War II (1945) and 1949. Esser argues that these marriages were used to demonstrate and enhance positive relations between former combatants. He also argued that portrayals of these marriages in flattering light contributed to popularization and dissemination of the American dream. Part of this portrayal included the representation of the modern German woman as stylish and devoted to her husband. These same portrayals usually ignored such issues as marital instability, violence, or other problems.

Some research suggests that the intersection of marriage and national conflict has the potential to affect previous levels of tolerance among ethically diverse groups. Kandido-Jaksic (1999) studied attitudes toward ethnically-mixed marriages and

[3]Some research has examined the extent to which racist ideology is sometimes relaxed when the dominant regime finds itself in need of workers or future population growth. See Kallis' (2005) research on the simultaneous ban on marriage and sexual relations between Jews and people designated Aryan in Nazi Germany.

mixed ethnicity offspring among people of former Yugoslavia. The war in the Balkans and the subsequent separation of that region into more nationalistically seg-regated countries may have resulted in a decrease in social tolerance toward different ethnic groups and nationalities. However, using Bogardus' Social Distance Scale, Kandido-Jaksic found that the offspring of ethnically-mixed marriages appear to be uniquely unwilling to adopt negative attitudes toward other ethnic groups.

Other research by Kunovich and Deitelbaum (2004), using 1996 data from Croatia's Center for the Investigation of Transition and Civil Society, suggests that ethnic conflict promotes both in-group polarization (attachment to Croatian nation-alism) and out-group polarization (distrust of "others"). Kunovich and Deitelbaum suggest that out-group polarization, in particular, is associated with a return to con-servative values, including attitudes toward gender roles and family policy on issues such as abortion and divorce. These findings suggest that heterogamy may, through the next generation that is produced by such unions, decrease the level of prejudice and increase the level of tolerance for diversity in a society.

Marital Instability

Although the literature is both scant and sometimes contradictory, American mili-tary service, in general, and the lived experience of war, in particular, affects not only opportunity to marry, but also probability of subsequent divorce. Pavalko and Elder's (1990) classic research on the effects of military service during World War II drew on longitudinal studies for men representing 624 marriages, concentrating on men who grew up in California. Pavalko and Elder found higher divorce rates among men who served in the military during World War II and among those who experienced combat than among men who did not serve or experience combat. Pavalko and Elder also found that prewar marriages were more likely to dissolve than were those formed during the war. Finally, they found that men who entered the service later had higher rates of divorce.

Pavalko and Elder explain the greater risk of divorce among servicemen in terms of psychological factors, such as posttraumatic stress syndrome; social psychological factors, such as combat bonding; life course factors, such as age-differentiated marital obligations and the presence or absence of children; and soci-etal factors, such as home-front mobilization. Research on more recent military cohorts sometimes confirms a negative association between military service on marital stability, especially during wartime. Using data on 3,800 men from the National Survey of Families and Households for 1987–1994, Ruger, Wilson, and Waddoups (2002) found that participation in combat increased by over 60 percent the risk of marital dissolution for American men serving in the military. However, for that cohort, the time of marriage (before, during, or after the war) did not affect dissolution.

In contrast, using the 1992 *Survey of Officers and Enlisted Personnel* during the period of the Gulf War, Angrist and Johnson (2000) found no effect of deployment of American male soldiers on divorce rates. However, the same study found a marked increase in divorce rates for female soldiers who were deployed. This finding suggests that women's deployment and subsequent family absence places a greater strain on marriage than does husband's deployment and absence. Given the greater responsibility women have for the expressive aspects of marriage and family life, the greater negative impact of their absence is not surprising.

In sum, the effect of military service on subsequent divorce in American marriages during wartime has been found to be strong for those marriages formed during World War II and especially during those formed during the Korean War (Ruger, Wilson, and Waddoups 2002). However, the effects on dissolution for subsequent cohorts, the impact of time of marriage (before, during, or after they war), and gender effects are more variable.

Although the research is limited, challenges to marital stability also have been observed among other populations who were either internally displaced or sought refuge in exile during civil and regional wars. Drawing on a 1987 survey of 254 divorced and 799 currently married women, Aghajanian and Moghadas (1998) attribute at least part of the increase in divorce rates in Iran since the 1960s to eight years of war, as well as to social and legal changes in that country. In another study, Laliberte, Laplante, and Piche (2003) analyzed data collected in N'Djamena, Chad, in 1993–1994. Their findings confirm the higher risk of divorce (and even transition from monogamy to bigamy) among internally displaced individuals, compared to refugees. Perhaps, in comparison to refugees, those who remain behind have fewer resources available for survival strategies, whereas those who seek to leave must marshal a more creative range of options, including family solidarity, or, in the most extreme cases, death. In contrast, however, Granot (1995) did not find higher rates of divorce among couples living in the zones in Israel (e.g., Tel Aviv) that experienced the greatest war-related anxiety surrounding Scud missile attacks when compared to couples living in areas less affected by the attacks. Further research is needed to examine the effects of war on marriage, including the place of unique national histories and cultures and contemporary factors, such as pervasive media coverage.

The impact of war on marital stability may not transmit to any great extent across generations. In a study applying multivariate, event-history techniques to the 1988 German Youth Instit interview data, Diekmann and Engelhardt (1999) found only slightly higher risks of divorce among individuals who grew up in a family dissolved by war, when compared with individuals who grew up in two-parent families. (As to be expected, Diekmann and Engelhardt did find significantly higher rates of divorce among individuals who had grown up in families dissolved by divorce.) Diekmann and Engelhardt speculate that it is not the absence of a parent per se that contributes to the higher rate of divorce, but that differences in personal investments in marriage for those who lost a spouse to death, versus those who lost a spouse through divorce, contribute to the intergenerational transmission of divorce.

In conclusion, the lived experience of war and the potential ensuing confusion and breakdown in social institutions has great potential to compromise marital and family stability. Even in a society with strong economic, legal, political, and religious institutional support for marriage and family, as was the United States in the nineteenth century, the beginnings and endings of marriages were sometimes fluid and occasionally contested. For example, Schwartzberg (2004) analyzed the records of widows who filed for the same soldier's Civil War pension. Schwartzberg found separations (both short- and long-term), as well as abandonment and desertion among working-class couples sometimes served as informal divorces, setting the stage for subsequent bigamous marriages (and hence, contested pensions).

Family Resiliency in the Face of International Violence

The book will probably never be written that can fully capture the devastating effects of war on families. The memory of the horrors of World War II is still alive for some readers of *Global Families*. Nazi Germany and its collaborators murdered approximately six million of the nine million Jews living in Europe. In addition, Nazi policies systematically killed Poles, Russians, and Slavic peoples; Roma ("gypsies"); people with mental and physical disabilities; homosexuals; and political, religious, intellectual, and other groups, including Communists and Socialists, Soviet prisoners of war, Jehovah's Witnesses, and dissident Christians (U.S. Holocaust Museum 2006h).

The U.S. Holocaust Memorial Museum estimates that more than a million Jewish children were murdered by Nazis and their collaborators. Babies and children were particularly vulnerable to morbidity and mortality due to malnutrition and starvation, insufficient clothing and shelter, and exposure to crowded, unsanitary living conditions which provided opportunities for the spread of infectious diseases. Also, as the youngest members of society were the least usable commodities for forced labor, babies and children were quickly separated from more productive members of society and swiftly murdered (U.S. Holocaust Memorial Museum 2006f).

The term *genocide*, literally created in 1944, refers to "massive crimes committed against groups" which through "a coordinated plan of different actions [aim] at the destruction of essential foundations of the life of national groups, with the aim of annihilating the groups themselves" (U.S. Holocaust Memorial Museum 2006k). Today, the U.S. Holocaust Memorial Museum continues to track contemporary genocides throughout the world, including:

- Burundi, where a civil war in 1993 resulted in the deaths of 200,000 and the displacement of over 500,000 (U.S. Holocaust Memorial Museum 2006d).
- Chechnya, where massive military action from Russia has devastated the country, through indiscriminate bombing of populated areas and massacres of civilians (U.S. Holocaust Memorial Museum 2006e).
- Darfur, where tens of thousands of civilians have been murdered, thousands of women have been raped, and two million people have been driven from their homes. Thousands of these die each month from living outside the areas of conflict in harsh desert environments with inadequate food, water, shelter, and health care (U.S. Holocaust Memorial Museum 2006j).
- Rwanda, where extremist members of the Hutu majority have managed a campaign to exterminate the Tutsi resulting in the murder of 800,000 people in 100 days and the rape of thousands of women (U.S. Holocaust Memorial Museum 2006i).

Families Surviving War

War and genocide displace individuals and fracture families in the most awful ways. After all, what better way to destroy a people and a society than to separate individuals from families and loved ones or to rape, torture, or murder parents and children, siblings and elders. Such extreme violence denies families safety and security, nurturance and socialization, as well as intimate care and continuity. However, under such circumstances, some families exhibit remarkable levels of resiliency.

For instance, Cohen's (2006) work documents how, during the Holocaust, the ghetto was the final location where a reasonable semblance of the traditional family structure was maintained by European Jews. Ghetto families' abilities to maintain emotional bonds and construct new family structures were not only keys to survival under the most austere circumstances, but also served to reverse Nazi policies intended to degrade and dehumanize Jews.

Even though literature often describes the inadequacies of Holocaust survivors as parents (especially around issues of attachment and detachment), research findings are contradictory, at best. Using self-reports, Kellerman (2001) found few differences between the quality of parenting by Holocaust survivors and a control group. In fact, the most recent, large-scale studies of survivors of wars and of their children have repeatedly found both the survivors and their children within the normal range of family relationships. The best research in this field compares survivor and nonsurvivor families (see Krell, Sueffeld, and Soriano 2004) and employs a life history approach (see Stanger 2005). Much of this research draws on family narratives (see Rosenthal 2000; 2002a; 2002b).

Yet, the stories of family resilience in the face of diaspora conditions are often lost or hard to retrieve. Even though the accounts of slave and former slave families are particularly difficult to find, in part due to the prohibitions against literacy for slaves, some accounts of the survival of such families remain. See Genovese (1974), Stevenson (1991), and West (2004) on families enslaved in the United States. Sadly, however, just as the toll on personal life is so high in such families, the loss of family stories is likewise high.

Modern technology, including the Internet and other computer-assisted technologies, may provide a means for processing and disseminating such accounts. The U.S. Holocaust Memorial Museum established a Web project which records survivors' experiences during the Holocaust. Among the stories included in the "Behind Every Name a Story" project is the account of Miriam [Rot] Eshel. Miriam was born in 1930, the second child and oldest daughter of a Jewish family living in Irshava in the Carpathian mountains in what was then Czechoslovakia. In 1944, Miriam's family was forced to move to the Jewish ghetto in Munkacs, 30 kilometers away, before being deported to Auschwitz, where Miriam was separated from the rest of her family. Miriam was later transported to a labor camp near Stuffhof and from there forced with 1,000 other women on a death march, from which only 100 survived, to be liberated by the Russian army. Of 11 family members, only Miriam and a younger brother survived (U.S. Holocaust Memorial Museum 2006a). After the Holocaust, Miriam made her way to Israel (then Palestine), where, in 1953, she married Jacob, another Holocaust survivor (U.S. Holocaust Memorial Museum 2006b). A moving poem, written in honor of Miriam's strength, by her husband Jacob, appears on the U.S. Holocaust Memorial Museum Web site (http://ushmm.org/wlc/en/).

Without a doubt, ghettos, resettlement camps, forced labor, and extermination camps can fracture families. However, powerful stories have emerged, providing testimony to the resiliency of families and their ability to retain intimate bonds against all odds. Krohn (1998) has recounted such a story, of her father's family, which had not been together since the 1930s. Sixty-three members of this extended family, including all ten first cousins, gathered for a reunion in Chicago, Illinois, arriving from across the United States, England, and South America. The story that emerged was one of family continuity, as, over the years and three continents, members of the family remained connected through regular correspondence and occasional "too short and always emotional" (Krohn 1998:2–3) meetings. Krohn recorded impressions of that reunion:

> When we finally met this summer, there were many powerful moments: We noted similar family features. . . . We observed the expressions of awakening on the faces of the younger generation as they listed to elders speak about their wartime experiences. . . .
>
> Other highlights included seeing my ten-year-old niece find her niche in the group; hearing English, the common language, spoken with German, Spanish, and British accents; seeing . . . the fantastic family trees a cousin brought for each reunion attendee.
>
> After the reunion . . . family members returned to their respective homes [and] resumed their daily lives with greater awareness of how one cruel dictator had affected the lives of so many. They also returned home with a stronger, more caring sense of family.
>
> It made me realize that I will never be alone in the world with all of that family.

Such accounts speak to the resiliency of extended family bonds across space and time. In 1981, the annual International Conference on Children of Holocaust Survivors began meeting. The first large-scale congregation of children whose parents had survived the Holocaust offers the second generation the opportunity to engage in intergenerational exchange, as well as contact, with researchers and mental health practitioners working in the field of survivorship (Peskin 1981). By the last decades of the twentieth century, psychologists, social workers, and other professionals affiliated with organizations like the Institute on Working with Holocaust Survivors and the Second Generation had begun to examine the impact of the Holocaust on not only first generation survivors, including their needs as they age, but also the impact of the Holocaust on the next generation. Bergmann and Jucovy's (1982/1990) work and Lemberger's (1995) volume *A Global Perspective on Working with Holocaust Survivors and the Second Generation* brought together research and resources for a population that spans the globe and every continent.

Much research on the impact of war tends to focus on psychological impacts on and the resiliency of individuals. For example, Brajsa-Zganec (2005) has investigated the prevalence of depressive symptoms among children displaced by the war in the Republic of Croatia. She found that the debilitating effects of long-term exposure to the war were lessened by social support (instrumental support, support to self-esteem, and belonging and acceptance) and tended to be greater for boys than for girls.

In another study using in-depth interviews with a sample of 55 volunteers from the 1934–1939 German birth cohort, Larney (1994) found a considerable variety of experiences and responses to growing up in Germany during World War II:

> [E]ngulfed in war, the individuals within those societies had to adjust to the events they experienced. They had to adopt coping strategies that allowed them to psychologically as well as behaviorally manage the events of war. (p. 206)

The participants in Larney's study had direct, personal experiences with bombings, death of parents and other loved ones, and loss of homes, possessions, and safety associated with the destruction of and changes in family and other social institutions. The participants in Larney's study also reported that their roles as children changed as they were required to adopt productive roles in the family. That, in turn, affected their education and ambitions, as well as family life itself. As a result of growing up during World War II, the men and women in Larney's study exhibited lifelong frugality, attitudinal conservatism and traditionalism, and risk-avoidant frames of reference.

While Elder's (1974) research had suggested that hardship of an economic nature leads to an increased focus on family, Larney's research indicates that individuals who experience the most severe effects of war may shift from values emphasizing family and altruism toward values emphasizing purely personal self-interest. Larney suggests that the family focus Elder observed among individuals during wartime may be temporary. Such a conclusion would be consistent with other research on the importance of the family during hard times such as the Great Depression in the United States (Farber 1971; Elder 1974), the psychological effects of war (Quester 1990), the effects of war on life course (Mayer 1988), and the place of strategies for coping with war (Elder and Clipp 1988), including situations in which a family member is a prisoner of war or missing in action (McCubbin, et al. 1974).

Military Families

In addition to families experiencing war and others intimately familiar with genocide, military families represent global families in a very clear sense. Since World War II, the concept of American foreign service has expanded to include increasing numbers of families with members involved in military service, the diplomatic corps, international and multinational business enterprises, and a wide range of governmental, nongovernmental, and not-for-profit organizations. Likewise, the information, socialization, and advice offered to those families have shifted to reflect the changing demographic composition of these types of transnational employment.

For example, 50 years ago, the wives of men serving in the United States Army could read in *The Army Wife* (a book dedicated "To Army Brides of Today and

Tomorrow" [p. iv]): "Never in the history of the United States Army have American troops been allocated on such a global basis" (Shea 1954:268). Yet, the chapter dealing with assignment of the family beyond the continental United States dealt with topics such as "How to Keep Cool Despite the Thermometer" when living in 'the tropics', "Clothing for the Artic" when living in Alaska, Newfoundland, Labrador, and Greenland, "Servants in Japan" when living in that country, and shopping in postwar Europe, as well as "Schools, Medical and Recreational Facilities" in [then French] Morocco, Turkey, and Saudi Arabia. American military families facing the death of a service member were counseled to avoid:

> outward display of mourning except in the observance of the military customs of the Service. There are no drawn shades, crepe-hung doors, muffled bells, or hushed voices, despite the deep sorrow of the family of the deceased. . . . Death is accepted as an inevitable happening, and while everything possible is done to show consideration to the bereaved family, post life goes on in an uninterrupted manner except during the actual funeral services (Shea 1954:319).

In contrast to admonitions to traditional conjugal couples, today's military families are far more likely to be headed by single parents, often women, and to receive advice that better reflects the complexity of their lives. The advice offered in current guides, such as the pink-camouflage-covered *Married to the Military* (Hosek 2002) and *Help! I'm a Military Spouse—I Want a Life Too!: How to Craft a Life for YOU as You Move with the Military* (Hightower and Scherer 2007) offer advice on such contemporary matters as pursuing a career (even starting a business) and marriage enrichment seminars. Spouses are directed to such Web sites as *CinCHouse.com* (standing for Commander in Chief of the House) and spouses, husbands as well as wives, are encouraged to "find a niche" involving "purposeful activities outside the home" (Sick 2007).

In cases in which both parents are serving, parents are required to maintain a Family Care Plan, specifying custody and financial arrangements in the event both parents are deployed ("How to Survive Double Deployment" 2003). As demonstrated in the days following September 11, 2001, those deployments can be announced suddenly and, as recent events attest, can be extended for unpredictable lengths of time.

A small but growing body of literature examines the impacts and adjustments of "military brats and other global nomads" (Ender 2002). For example, Morten Ender (2000; 2006), Chair of the Sociology Department at the U.S. Military Academy (West Point) has amassed a body of original qualitative and quantitative research on growing up as a dependent child in a military family. Ender's (2002) chapter titled "Voices from the Backseat" is a reference to the nomadic life experienced by American army families as they move from base to base every three years.

Such a global, nomadic life affects families in a number of ways. In the summer of 2004, the Military Family Research Institute and the U.S. Department of Defense Quality of Life Office commissioned a study on the adaptation of adolescents when a family member is deployed into combat. This qualitative study yielded findings consistent with other studies demonstrating the potential for resilience among families and members under stress. Particularly with support from the parent at home, the adolescents in this study adapted to the absence of the deployed parent with maturity and by assuming additional family responsibilities. At the same time, the adolescents in this study were well aware of the dangers associated with combat. Some adolescents experienced disruption in their lives due to interruptions in financial, transportation, or other everyday circumstances. Others exhibited certain behavioral changes, including changes in school performance and traits associated with depression (Huebner and Mancini 2005).

Refugee Families

Although families in the U.S. military face such hardships as frequent moves from place to place, separations that sometimes last for years, and the uncertainty of knowing if the service member spouse or parent will return home from a combat assignment, military families often have in place a certain set of institutionalized supports. Refugees and their families often have few such supports, although, today, the support for refugees (e.g., in places like Minnesota) are certainly greater and more systematically delivered than such services in previous eras.

Including those internally displaced, between 35 and 45 million people throughout the world are living as refugees. Men (and often boys) disproportionately bear the costs of direct engagement in armed conflict.[4] However, the burden of providing for families during war or other times of severely diminished resources disproportionately falls to wives (and widows) and mothers. Further, while women constitute at least half of the world's refugees, men have greater opportunities for seeking asylum (presumably because women have more limited involvement in direct action). The largest number of refugees originates from and are hosted by countries in the Middle East. Four and a half million people have fled the conflicts in Afghanistan and another 4.1 million have fled the conflicts in Palestine. Iran hosts 2.5 million refugees, while Pakistan hosts two million, and

---

[4]Seager (2003) explains that constructions of femininity and masculinity are challenged by the inclusion of women in military positions. Still, women began to be trained and serve in combat positions throughout the world, including in Argentina, Austria, Brazil, Israel, Italy, Taiwan, the United Kingdom, and the United States in positions ranging from flying combat missions and, in Norway, serving as a submarine commander. The highest proportions (14–15 percent) of women in the active armed forces are found in Australia, New Zealand, South Africa, and the United States. Gender-typing persists, however, in United Nations peace-keeping operations, where women constitute over half of the general service staff, but only a quarter of local and professional staff, and less than five percent of civilian police and military personnel.

Street Family, Potosi, Bolivia by David Parker
David Parker/Minneapolis Institute of Art

Jordan hosts 1.6 million. The largest number of internally displaced people is found in the Sudan (4 million), with over 2 million each in Colombia, Angola, and the Democratic Republic of the Congo (Seager 2003:98).

The lives faced by the children of refugee families are particularly troubled. For example, as a result of the Vietnam War, more than two million people fled Indochina after 1975. While at least ten percent died in the process, more than 1.6 million refugees survived to seek asylum in the surrounding countries. Nearly 60,000 of these were unaccompanied minors (Freeman and Hũu 2003:3). Children seeking refuge may do so while accompanying a parent, older sibling, or other adult, but may also be alone. Freeman, an anthropologist, and Hũu, a U.S.-educated social worker with a specialization in child welfare and protection, and himself a refugee from Vietnam, have chronicled in their own words the life experience of children living in refugee camps. Their research focused on unaccompanied minors who had either been orphaned by the death of one or both parents or who had become separated from their parents. Some of these children fled on their own, while others had been sent on these high-risk escapes by parents. Between 1987 and 1995, Freeman and Hũu visited 18 camps that housed Vietnamese people.

There they found extreme neglect and abuse, with adult detainees and camp guards alike abusing the children physically and sexually. Camp officials would remove children from their families and place them in foster care and would move certain family members to other camps or across camp areas, thus disrupting further children's daily routines. In these circumstances, Freeman and Hũu (p. xiii) found children who were "traumatized, frightened, and depressed . . . who did not know what was going to happen to them next." The children's narratives reflected "both uncertainty and the disarray in their lives." At the very least, these children reported missing their parents and wishing to return home. Some clearly came away from the experience with deep psychological damage typical of children with long exposure to traumatic events: numbness, sadness, fear, and rage.

The quality of adjustment to even the most devastating of refugee experiences seems, like other family stressors, to be mediated by the quality and experience of previous family relationships, as well as external role models and threats. An original study of the "dreams, drawings, and behavior" of Palestinian children living in refugee camps in the West Bank revealed that children were expressing less fear, confusion, depression, victimization, and alienation, while developing more internalized loci of control in the years since the Intifada. Further, they were articulating values of bravery and solidarity in the face of hatred and revolt against the authority represented by Israeli soldiers (Nashef 1992). Thus, the refugee experience shapes families across generations, in quite direct ways, through children.

Summary

This chapter has examined a range of issues related to international violence and families, including family legacies of oppression and war. Colonial authorities often seek to dominate the indigenous society with institutions, including monogamous, nuclear family structures and gender relations that will be consistent with colonial systems and which are to the advantage of the colonial system. Some writers argue that a flourishing sex trade likewise serves a broader social agenda and regulates ideologies of family, sexuality, and reproduction, as well as imperialism and racism. The multibillion dollar global sex trade is built on gender, national, and other inequalities that drive women and children into prostitution and fuel a world market for sexual consumption.

While globalization does not cause war, war represents a particular manifestation of global political, economic, cultural, and other forces. Rape in war demonstrates the convergence of patriarchy with militarism and yields the potential for the rape of women and children to be used as a strategy of terror and subordination during periods of armed conflict. Likewise, military sexual slavery, as exemplified by the "comfort women" enslaved by the Japanese during World War II, reveals the interconnections between gender and militarism, with tragic consequences for the quality of life for the women involved. Perhaps, not surprisingly, in societies which have a long history of living with international violence, the physical and sexual well-being of women and children has low priority.

War changes the marriage experience, first by "squeezing" the ratio of men to women available for marriage and, second, by increasing a society's probability of heterogamous mate selection. Many of the latter face hardships, in light of the status differences between husbands and wives. Although the literature is both scant and sometimes contradictory, American military service in general and the lived experience of war not only affects opportunity to marry, but also probability of subsequent divorce.

Also, war displaces individuals and fractures families. However, even under such circumstances, some families exhibit resiliency, as illustrated by documents from Holocaust survivors and their families. Military families and their adjustment are a special case of work–family linkages in a highly mobile world. Including those internally displaced, between 35 and 45 million people throughout the world are living as refugees. These families, especially the children, face unusually severe social psychological hardships.

Sex Trafficking: A "Family Business"
By Jennifer Blank, M.A.

Trafficking in persons has distorted women and children as commodities in the global market to be bought, sold, and consumed by tourists, the military, organized crime, law enforcement agencies, traffickers, recruiters, and pimps (Hughes 2001b). Between 700,000 and 4 million women and children are trafficked internationally each year, at an annual shadow profit of seven billion dollars specifically from sex trafficking (Hughes 2001a:9). Such a lucrative business has attracted the attention of many governmental and nongovernmental agencies (NGOs), but sex trafficking continues to grow and flourish.

Globalization, poverty, and violence against women are just a few of the macrosocietal issues associated with human trafficking. This essay briefly addresses why trafficking is such a growing, profitable business and why people, particularly men, become involved in what is often a "family business."

Globalization Fosters Sex Trafficking

The majority of women and girls trafficked into the sex industry are minority women from Third World countries. Many of these women and girls suffer from the feminization of poverty, gendered violence, and oppression of migrant populations in the host countries.

Global corporations provide the lowest common denominator of wages and social services in order to best compete in the global economy (Mies 1994). Such a "race to the bottom" allows the service sector, particularly the sex tourist industry, to prosper and enables trafficking and prostitution to grow in southeastern Asian countries, Central and Eastern Europe, the independent states of the former Soviet Union, and Africa. In addition, as populations are relocated because of war, political repression, and economic displacement, women fall victim to trafficking in concert with poverty and lack of access to education and training, political power, and legal and other protection (McMahon and Stanger 2002).

The propensity to commodify sexual/erotic relations with women and children has intensified in Third World countries. Itzin (1992:65) believes that this industry "especially exploits Black and Third World women and children, trading on race discrimination and perpetuating racist as well as sexist stereotypes." For the same reasons, Southeast Asia, Latin America, and Africa have become favored destinations for sex tourists. Foreign sex workers are subject to much more harassment and abuse than local sex workers because of their vulnerability from being socialized into an ethos of female self-servitude and self-sacrifice. In addition, women who are trafficked are often located in environments in which people of their racial or ethnic background are considered inferior and are thus subjected to additional discrimination and abuse.

Abusive, violent treatment in the sex trade is overlooked because trafficked women are seen as merchandise; they can be used repeatedly as a source of ongoing profit for years while also being expendable. Once they fall ill, are too old, or contract HIV, trafficking women can be disposed of and replaced at low cost for high profit (Bales 1999; McMahon and Stanger 2002). However, people in the business will invest significant effort to retrieve their women who run away, thus conserving their capital investment. Furthermore, if women are able to escape and return to their home country, which is almost impossible, the women risk being shunned by their families. Found by traffickers, the women are thrown back into the prostitution/sex trafficking ring, or they are murdered.

Dehumanization and Commodification in a "Family Business"

Women become involved in the business because they follow recruiters/traffickers who promise lucrative jobs in factories, as employees in restaurants (often fronts for prostitution), or as "entertainers" in the sex and tourist industries (McMahon and Stanger 2002). Women may be coerced, deceived, or kidnapped and sold into the sex industry, but young women also are openly recruited for work in prostitution (Global Alliance Against Traffic in Women 2001, Anderson and O'Connell Davidson 2002, McMahon and Stanger 2002). A small minority of young girls also are sold into the sex industry by their parents or other relatives and recruiters in order to pay off family debts (McMahon and Stanger 2002).

The demand for young women for commercialized sex work is very high. Some customers, especially Chinese and Sino-Thais, are willing to pay large amounts of money to have sex with virgins (Bales 1999). These men prefer to have sex with virgins, first, because a girl's virginity is thought to be a strong source of *yang* (coolness), which quenches and slows the *yin* (heat) of the aging process. Second, virgins are assumed to be free of the HIV virus (Bales 1999). Of course, the number of times "virgins" are repeatedly sold makes the latter problematic. My research, summarized in this essay, indicates that commodification and dehumanization of women and girls are inextricably linked in what has often become a lucrative "family business" (Blank 2003).

In 2003, I conducted research in London, England, and specifically focused on traffickers involved in the sex industry. This research involved open-ended interviews in a qualitative study that focused on men who traffick. I addressed general questions on prostitution, attitudes about women who were trafficked for sex, and the men's experiences in the business. This essay focuses on Ahmet, a trafficker with a high level of involvement in the business (and considerable candor during the interviews), but also draws on the experiences of Demitri, a pimp, and Cyril, a bouncer in a club frequented by operators in the sex trafficking trade in London.*

My research revealed that the reality, opinions, and justifications of men involved in sex trafficking are created and maintained by personal experiences of the business within *their* world. Before they became involved in the business, these men saw themselves as an "excluded" population. They believe that they were never given legitimate opportunities to obtain material success. These men viewed greed, money, and power as motivations for maintaining a financially and personally successful life.

Trafficking is a low-risk, high-profit, sometimes "family business." Ahmet said he first became involved when he was 13 years old. He "apprenticed" under his father, first by trafficking drugs, guns, and refugees from Albania. When I asked him why he became involved in the first place, he said, "My dad owns the boats. He wanted [us; Ahmet and his brother] to [become involved]." Ahmet did not become involved in trafficking women until his family was not earning enough money to pay off the debt from their boats. He told me:

> It was my idea. My mates told me about it, and it was just a way to make extra money. So I rented a boat from my dad and did it myself. I was about 14 and making 250,000 [American] dollars a month. When my dad saw me making the money, he wanted to do it too.

His family's involvement in trafficking women was motivated by money and power. He told me, "I had to do it. I had to help out my dad for a better life for myself." He also claimed:

> If I had the opportunities and all the doors open, I would have done that, but we didn't have it, and we aren't accepted in this society. I'm just a dirty Albanian who rapes and kills, and we have to fight back to make a decent living. I would have no other choice. I'm not gonna scrape toilets for 5 pounds [British sterling] an hour.

Ahmet wanted a better life. The same was true for Demitri and Cyril. When asked why they got involved in the business, Demitri said, "For me, it has always been about the money—do you know what I mean? It's about making money." Cyril's reasons were very

---

*The names of the men have been changed to protect their identities.

similar. He got involved because of "the excitement, the money, [and] the fun. It was the money." He was 15 when he entered the business, because he was "seeing an older woman and she asked [him] to look over her and the money came in and it was easy." Each man, regardless of his current position in the business, joined for the money and the power they gained from trafficked women. The women were mere commodities, the means to an end of financial prosperity.

Of course, the tragedy of trafficking humans intersects not only with gender and economics, but also with race and ethnicity. The intersecting systems of domination and oppression do not have equal effects on women in Third World contexts. Mohanty, Russo, and Torres (1991) argue for the need to recognize and explore Third World women's experiences, including their place in colonial, imperialist, and minority capital systems. Additional research and legislation must address the broader scope of the trafficking business beyond prostitution, including forced labor, debt bondage, domestic servitude, forced marriage, and child labor.

Effective social action to combat trafficking requires international cooperation on a global scale, as well as understanding the economic incentives and value systems of sex traffickers engaged in this "family business." For example, the United States has implemented a strategy to combat trafficking through the "Three P's": Prevention of Trafficking, Protection and Assistance for Victims, and Prosecution and Enforcement against Traffickers (Hughes 2001a). First, trafficking must be prevented through culturally sensitive and nationally targeted educational campaigns to promote awareness. Trafficked persons must be guaranteed protection from their traffickers and provided with legal, social, educational, and other assistance from government and social service agencies, while being assured that prosecution of the traffickers can be accomplished without placing the women at risk for deportation or other public sanctions.

Jennifer Blank earned the Master of Arts degree in Criminology at Middlesex University in London. This essay is based on original research conducted in London clubs with men involved in the sex trafficking business. Since returning to the United States, Blank has presented her work on human trafficking and slavery at meetings of the American Society of Criminology and to educational groups. With Emily Troshynski, Blank is the co-author of "Interviews with Sex Traffickers" (*Trends in Organized Crime: Interviewing "Organized Criminals,"* edited by van Lampe, forthcoming 2007, *Transaction*) and "Trafficking Women for Prostitution: Attitudes and Perceptions of Sex and Violence" (*Feminist Criminology*, forthcoming 2007).

Critical Thinking Questions:

1. Referencing Blank's essay on sex trafficking as a "family business," what are the macrosocial contexts of sex trafficking? Speculate on the impacts of a woman's life as a trafficking person on her broader life chances, including opportunity for family life.

2. Some scholars (e.g., Lorentzen and Turpin 1998) have written of war as a gendered experience. How does the gendered nature of war impact family life?

3. Account for the differences and similarities in marital quality for those who experience military service during wartime and those who do not.

4. Identify three variables that could account for family resilience in the face of international violence. You may reference a summary of the literature on family resilience (e.g., Chapter 3 in Karraker and Grochowski 2006) or a brief discussion of the term (e.g., pages 137–40 in Seccombe 2006).

5

FAMILIES AND WORLDWIDE CULTURE SYSTEMS: EFFECTS OF MEDIA AND CONSUMPTION ON NORMS AND VALUES

DEMOGRAPHIC TRANSITIONS ARE CHANGING the death, birth, and migration patterns of families worldwide. The transnationalization of employment alters family structures in profound ways, including the migration of some family members for labor and the consequent changes in marriage and care work systems. Likewise, as I have discussed in earlier chapters, some families are challenged by international violence, including the legacies of colonialism, the damage inflicted by warfare, the trafficking in human beings, and the distinct risks faced by refugees and their families. Even nonviolent expressions of globalization can shred cultural customs and family values. Such challenges not only tear at livelihoods and family relationships, but also influence family attitudes and values.

I was prompted to write this chapter by concerns that many in the media, politics, and the pulpit, and even my students, have expressed regarding the threat of globalization to family norms and values. Do global forces compete for family loy-alty? Does globalization corrupt traditional family values and norms through some sort of transcendent global culture?

Hyperglobalists and global transformationists have argued that one powerful fea-ture of globalization has been the permeation of Western individualism, materialism, and secularism into non-Western cultures. Some believe the current violence directed at the West is an effort on the part of more tradition-bound societies to reject spiri-tual decadence and to lay claim to culture and values that emphasize religious funda-mentalism, patriarchy, and other traditional values. But such competition between the sacred and the secular is not limited to the East. Marty and Appleby (1991) have asserted that both the Christian right and Islamic fundamentalism have much in common. In *Jihad vs. McWorld*, Barber (1995:205) draws parallels between certain tenets of Islamic fundamentalism and other forms of "fundamentalist opposition to modernity," including fundamentalist Protestant movements in contemporary American society. Barber (1995:211) asserts that certain Islamic fundamentalist clerics "are not so far from . . . the Christian Right's campaign for a return to nineteenth-century family values—family values understood as direct emanations of church going, school prayer, and a Protestant Christian America."

In the West, cultural leaders, including the two most recent popes of the Roman Catholic Church, have expressed grave concern regarding the impact of globalization on family values. In affirming "the marriage covenant, whereby man and woman establish a permanent bond," Pope Benedict XVI extols not only traditional norms regarding family structure, but also a conviction that such a structure "is a great good for all humanity" ("Pope Extols Virtues of Traditional Families in a Changing Spain" 2006:A9). On the one hand, contemporary families, faced with demographic transi-tions, transnational employment, and international violence need all the help they can get. However, although such statements may comfort those who hold certain tradi-tional beliefs about families, genders, and sexualities, these statements leave little room for the rich diversity of intimate bonds that serve families confronting postmod-ern global realities. In the extreme, such statements may even provide support for those who seek religious endorsement for discriminatory behaviors against lesbigay, single parent, and other families that do not conform to such a marriage covenant.

Globalization impacts families in sometimes subtle, but always critical, ways by changing the cultural context in which families operate. I begin this chapter with an analysis of the impact of global media, then consumption, on families. As a result of revolutions in information technologies and multinational economics, "mass" media and consumption are increasingly becoming "global" media and consumption. Technological advances are expanding the potential for communica-tion and transportation, reducing time and space barriers between people with access to cell phones, the Internet, and inexpensive travel across national borders.

Cultural images and products distributed throughout the world have the potential to educate, entertain, and almost instantaneously inform a much larger and more geographically dispersed audience than at any other time in human history. Some of the developments in communications and computer technology have lowered economic and other obstacles to communication and interactions across societies. Thus, these more globalized exchanges have the potential to provide new pathways to knowledge about world events and even to foster understanding and sympathy across national and other borders.[1]

Agents of globalized media and consumption also have the power to exploit, while persuading and seducing huge numbers of families and their members into new material and nonmaterial culture systems, compromising the indigenous customs and mores, and increasing the gap between families who have access to novel cultural resources and those who do not. Global pessimists (e.g., Albrow 1997) argue that the erosion of barriers between cultures is propelling the world toward a massification of culture on a global scale and an erosion of the sense in which culture represents the unique historic experience of a people who share a common national, regional, or other territory. In doing so, changing media and consumption systems can be a source of conflict and change across genders, generations, and other family divisions, especially when those images offer a previously disenfranchised group, such as women or youth, a different vision of society. Some of these changes may oppress. Some may liberate. And they may do so in an uneven pattern across a society's members, as witnessed by the unequal access to computer technologies in the United States today.

Such a massification of global culture is aggravated by a tendency toward monopolistic control over media, consumption, and other cultural systems. What some critics have called cultural imperialism sets the stage for the introduction of Western images and products to the recipient nations to the advantage of the United States and Western nations. The United Nations Educational, Scientific, and Cultural Organization (UNESCO) has acknowledged the inequity in the export of cultural goods between the northern and southern hemispheres and the threat such inequity poses to vulnerable cultures. In the *Proceedings of the International Symposium on Culture Statistics* in 2002, Mounir Bouchenaki, Assistant Director-General of the Culture Sector for UNESCO (2003:19), opined:

> Globalization in trade has undeniable consequences for cultural diversity, pluralism, and intercultural dialogue. Cultural diversity also heightens the sense of identity as the source of creativity and living culture. Globalization can contribute powerfully

---

[1]Ronald Bosrock, founder and director of the Global Institute, and author of a weekly column on globalization in the business section of the *Star Tribune*, holds such an optimistic view of globalization. His work is described in Chapter 6.

to bringing people closer together. But in doing so it must not lead to worldwide cultural uniformity or the hegemony of one or a few cultures over all the others.

Scholars continue to document escalation in the flow of cultural content across national borders. Culture, in particular mass culture, has been conceptualized as a commodity, in much the same way that the products of factory labor are commodities (Adorno 1991). Lash and Lury (2006) describe a "global culture industry" in which material objects (e.g., designer labels, sportswear) vested with globally recognized brands mass marketed through global capitalism have become powerful transnational cultural symbols. Scholars are only beginning to explore how these transnational cultural symbols are affecting gender and family norms and values.

UNESCO collects data on a wide variety of selected cultural goods and services, including heritage goods, books, newspapers and periodicals, other printed matter, recorded media, visual arts, and audiovisual media. UNESCO defines core cultural goods and services as:

> Consumer goods which convey ideas, symbols, and ways of life. They inform or entertain, contribute to build collective identity and influence cultural practices and . . . the overall set of measures and supporting facilities for cultural practices that government, private and semipublic institutions or companies make available to the community. Examples of such services include the promotion of performances and cultural events as well as cultural information and preservation (libraries, documentation centres and museums). (UNESCO 2005:84)

UNESCO (2005) estimates that between 1994 and 2002 the value of cultural goods and services exchanged across national borders increased from 38 billion to 60 billion United States dollars (USD).[2] By 2005, UNESCO estimated the global market value of cultural and creative goods at 1.3 trillion USD and growing. The magnitude of these cultural exchanges only continues to increase, and dramatically so, with the growth and dispersion of the World Wide Web and other computer mediated communication technologies and multinational and even transnational economic institutions.

Over a half century ago Park (1950; 1952) delineated five processes of what he called "sociation" at work when cultural groups encounter one another: contact, competition, conflict, accommodation, and assimilation. These concepts have been successfully applied to cultural contact between the immigrant and host societies, including policies to control guest workers, legislation to counter trafficking, and tension in religious tolerance (Karraker 2004; Karraker 2006). The extent to which

---

[2]These estimates are based primarily on official customs declarations and may not reflect all foreign sales of cultural goods and services (UNESCO 2005).

globalization has resulted in the Westernization of world cultures—and consequently in cultural contact, competition, conflict, and assimilation, as well as clash, displacement, or even annihilation—remains somewhat contested. Skeptics on globalization contend that transnational movements of populations and individuals and the flow of cultural features across the global landscape have always impacted cultural identity. They argue that commercial and public service broadcasting, the press, and even the news, often has a local or national quality (MacKay 2000).

Hyperglobalists argue that worldwide cultural diversity is losing ground to more homogeneous Americanized or Western culture. Clearly, the international flow of cultural goods and services is dominated by a very few countries. The largest single exporter of cultural goods in 2002 was the United Kingdom at 8.5 billion USD, followed by the United States at 7.5 billion USD (see Table 5.1). Together, the United Kingdom and the United States account for almost 30 percent of the world's core cultural exports. Likewise, the largest single importer of cultural goods in that year was the United States at 15.3 billion USD, followed by the United Kingdom at 7.8 billion USD (UNESCO 2005).

While Featherstone (1990:2) acknowledges the tendency to see American mass consumer culture as the prototype of homogenized, cultural imperialism "riding on the back of Western economic and political domination," he does not see single,

Table 5.1 Top Five Exporters and Importers of Core Cultural
Goods, 2002 (in U.S. dollars)

Top 5 Exporters	USD
United Kingdom	8,548,772,100
United States	7,648,414,300
Germany	5,788,930,800
China	5,274,900,700
France	2,521,273,300
Top 5 Importers	**USD**
United States	15,338,583,000
United Kingdom	7,871,901,800
Germany	4,162,119,700
Canada	3,829,892,500
France	3,406,846,100

Source: UNESCO 2005: Tables I-1 and I-2.

unified global culture. Rather, he emphasizes that third cultures can exist beyond the usual bilateral exchanges between nation–states. Featherstone (p. 6) writes rather of the "extension of global interrelatedness" advanced by continual cultural interaction and exchange.

Smith (1990) traces the rise of such transnational cultures from the aftermath of a divided Europe following World War II through the formation of a transnational European Union with economic, political, and even cultural traits that transcend any single nation–state. Smith (p. 176) speaks rather of a "post-industrial global culture" as:

> a pastiche of cultural motifs and styles, . . . operating on several levels simultaneously: as a cornucopia of standardized commodities, as a patchwork of denationalized ethnic or folk motifs, as a serious of generalized "human values and interests," as a uniform "scientific" discourse of meaning, and finally as the interdependent system of communications.

The globalization of culture is often viewed as an issue of Americanization, or the transmission of material and even nonmaterial aspects of American culture and society worldwide. In MacKay's words (2000:48), "cultural goods flow to the rest of the world, inculcating United States or Western values in those in recipient nations." But Featherstone (1990) cautions that a view of culture as global does not necessarily presume a society that transcends a weakened system of nation–state societies. Rather, Featherstone conceptualizes global cultures (in the plural) as "transsocietal cultural processes which take a variety of forms . . . and . . . which sustain the exchange and flow of goods, people, information, knowledge, and images which give rise to communication processes which gain some autonomy on the global level" (1990:1).

Of course, the concept of global culture, even a unified global culture, is not new. Media theorist Marshall McLuhan (1964) coined the term "global village" a half century ago. What is being transmitted through globalized media and consumption goes beyond marketing products and services, to transmitting and potentially socializing powerful messages about what is beautiful and desirable, what is good and valuable. Spybey (1996) argued that the resulting world culture socializes individuals into different patterns of knowledge and awareness which may displace traditional, local institutions in favor of novel, transnational ones.

These cultural transmissions influence age and gender roles, childhood and sexual socialization, and youth and other family cultures. For example, Izuhara and Shibata (2002) found that Japanese women who had immigrated to Great Britain tended to relinquish values of family reciprocity in favor of individualist values. Contrary to traditional Japanese cultural expectations, these women do not expect their children to support them in old age. In the words of one such woman, 60 years old, living in Britain since 1958:

> When I need old-age care, I'll sell this house if financially necessary, and move to a nursing home. Although I want to leave the house to my children, they may also suggest that I sell it. My son's partner said, "Don't worry about your sons. They both have a job. Just look after yourself." Even between parents and children, we need to respect each other. Old-age care is hard work even for professional nurses, not to mention ordinary individuals . . . Even if I have to sell this house, I would hire a professional helper. (p. 164)

Thus, elements of a worldwide culture force families to confront the reproduction of Western social institutions through patterns of values and norms shifting across global boundaries. In this chapter, I consider the implications of global culture on family life, including the significance of the media, especially television and digitized technology, and patterns of mass consumption. I conclude with a discussion of the impact of global forces on family norms and values.

Global Media in an Era of Information Revolution

Appadurai (1996) has examined the creation of various landscapes on the global scene. In Chapter 2, I addressed the first of his landscapes, *ethnoscapes*, or flows of people. In Chapter 3, I considered the indirect impacts of *finanscapes*, or flows of money in currency markets and stock exchanges, and *technoscapes*, flows of industry, machinery, and production facilities, both of which have implications for transnational employment. The present chapter examines *mediascapes*, flows of images and information produced by newspapers and magazines, television and film, and the potential of those cultures to reveal *ideoscapes*, flows of images associated with political ideologies.

Beck-Gernsheim (2001:62) describes the mass media as a "driving force behind transnational life plans." She also states:

> More persons throughout the world see their lives through the prisms of the possible lives offered by the mass media in all their forms. . . . [P]eople are beginning to imagine other worlds and to compare them with their own. So life for the ordinary person is no longer determined just by the immediate situation, but increasingly by the possibilities that the media (either directly or indirectly) suggest.

As stated earlier, media broaden access to experiences in which individuals cannot actually participate. Globalization changes the human impact of media by increasing the scope and scale of media reach and influence, enabling the viewer to witness events in virtually any part of the world.

Cultural imperialism, the increasing domination of indigenous ways of life by American, European, or Western ways of life, extends to the worldwide media. Cosmopolitan or Western images presented in the media may prompt consideration of new visions of culture and society, including social and family structure, gender and intergenerational relations. Worldwide, over 40 percent of television programming hours originate in the United States and the language of this programming is English (MacKay 2000:63). Allen and Massey (1995) contend that the globalization of the mass media, prompted by new communication technologies, has resulted in the standardization of culture on a worldwide scale. Hence, media can play a powerful role in compromising the integrity of local culture.

The massification of media may be a consequence of an oligopolistic worldwide media. Five firms—Bertelsmann, Disney, News Corporation, Time Warner, and Viacom—are not only the largest in the world in terms of sales, but also are the most fully integrated across news and entertainment production and hardware and software businesses (MacKay 2000). For example, Australian Rupert Murdoch's News Corporation owns 132 newspapers and is one of the three largest newspaper groups in the world. News Corporation also holds major film, television, and video production and broadcasting divisions, including 22 television stations (covering 40 percent of households in the United States), Fox News Channel, 25 magazines, and several major book publishers (pp. 58–59). Significant from a global perspective, News Corporation owns major stakes in several American, Asian, Australian, German, Indian, Japanese, Latin American, Spanish, United Kingdom, and other global television, cable, satellite, radio, and music video networks (Herman and McChesney 1997).

The rise of a sizeable middle-class consumer base in developing countries in central Asia and even in the least developed countries in sub-Saharan Africa has generated tremendous expansion of the mass media in societies in those regions. A globalized mass media sells consumer and cultural goods while transcending the ability to entertain and educate. Globalized mass media can symbolize and promote a sense of community identity and engage emotions regarding national character across local, national, and regional borders. Globalized mass media can mobilize societal support for social movements (e.g., the student protests in Tiananmen Square in 1989) and extend cultural identity to a broader, even transnational, public through television, films, magazines, and other widely distributed venues (Ong 1999). Such appears to be the case as mass marketed popular films distributed worldwide are shaping race and sexual orientation identification beyond local communities (Gabilondo 2002).

Thus global media have the capability to construct what Morley and Robins (1995:64) call "electronic communities" beyond local, regional, and national borders. Modern global media can be said to be "constructing new geographies [while] bringing together otherwise disparate groups around the common experience of television . . . [and] bringing about a cultural mixing" (pp. 128, 132). Unfortunately, however, the impressive potential of global mass media to transform societies and families in less advantaged parts of the world in terms of education and literacy, health and wellness, and other quality-of-life issues is yet to be fully realized.

Television as Global Media

Broadcasting technologies, in particular, have played a pivotal role in connecting audiences, often composed of relatively isolated individuals and families, at a mass societal level, thus "promoting national unity at a symbolic level" (Morley and Robins 1995:66).

Not only are broadcasting and other media pivotal in shaping national culture and civic engagement in national life, they also link individuals and their families to broader constituencies. These macrolevel linkages occur, at the very least, on a symbolic level. Morley and Robins (1995:64) argue that the new globalized media and electronic technologies play a substantial role in the "transnationalization of culture" by "disrupting established boundaries . . . and . . . rearticulating the private and public spheres in new ways." In doing so, global media can play a profound role in viewers' images of the stranger or the "other." At the same time, Morley and Robins caution, such viewing experience ensures neither identification nor sympathy with the viewed, given that the viewer is separated and insulated by the very technology that permits viewing.

Perhaps nowhere is the explosive potential of global media imagery—and the potential impact on families—more evident than in the increasing availability of television, with its unique characteristics of accessibility, immediacy, and privacy. Worldwide, the number of television sets per thousand individuals tripled in the last three decades of the twentieth century, from 81 television receivers per 1,000 inhabitants in 1970 to 240 television receivers per 1,000 inhabitants in 1997. As shown in Table 5.2, significant differences persist among continents (at 446, Europe has the highest and, at 60, Africa has the lowest number of receivers per 1,000 inhabitants), and among developed, developing, and least developed countries (at 548, 157, and 23 receivers per 1,000 inhabitants, respectively) (UNESCO 1999).

In some markets, the host society has acted to regulate the representation of television programming produced in or originating from another society. For

Table 5.2 Television Receivers per 1,000 Inhabitants, 1997

World Total	240
Continents	
Africa	60
America	429
Asia	190
Europe	446
Oceania	427
Groups of Countries	
Developed	548
Developing	157
Sub-Saharan Africa	48
Arab states	119
Latin American and the Caribean	205
East Asia and Oceania	253
Southern Asia	54
Least developed	23

Source: UNESCO 1999: Table IV.S.3.

example, in response to criticisms that children in places like Canada know more about New York City than they do about Toronto, the Canadian Parliament adopted broadcasting legislation in 1968 and again in 1991 which has as a primary objective "the maintenance and enhancement of national identity and cultural sovereignty," with the result that the amount of foreign broadcasting in Canada is higher than in the United States, but less than that in other industrialized societies (Tremblay 1992:1).

In cases of other widely distributed cultural icons, distributors have responded by recasting and re-visioning the original television program concept. For example, by 2002, the award-winning children's educational television show *Sesame Street* was distributed in 20 markets, including China, Egypt, and Russia. In some markets, characters derived from the local society are drawn to reflect those populations and customs. For example, the South African version of *Sesame Street* has a character named Kami. Kami is five years old and HIV-positive. Kami's mother had died of AIDS, and Kami is depicted as living with a foster mother (Orecklin 2002).

As a primarily domestic medium, readily turned on and tuned in, television is often a critical part of family leisure activity. As such, the social functions (and dysfunctions) of television include structuring the day and punctuating family time and family activity (Morley 1986). As the presence of television is extended and expanded to families worldwide, these globalized images of mealtime, homework, leisure, and bedtime may reshape the rhythms of daily family life in peculiarly Western, capitalist ways. Established family rituals, such as attentive deference to elders as they communicate knowledge and skills or conversations around meals about the days' events, may be reorganized around normative authority reflected in televised situations or conversations regarding demand for marketed products.

To the extent that televised images disproportionately represent Western culture, television brings a hegemonic image of values and norms into families' homes (or, in less developed societies, community gathering places). In the words of David Walsh (2006), psychologist and founding president of the MediaWise Movement, a program of the National Institute on Media and Family, "Who tells the stories defines the culture." Families are thus faced with cultural images that may enrich, but also compete with or even challenge local, traditional values and norms.

Wired and Wireless Families on a Global Scale

As I discussed earlier, global cultural flows of the type generated by television can produce both cultural homogeneity and cultural complexity (and even social disorder), as well as transnational cultures that can transcend the interests of nation-state societies. After all, information flow can be among the most difficult aspects of a society to control. As any parent who has attempted to control her child's Internet use can testify, information has a way of oozing around any efforts to contain it.

Castells (2000), author of *The Rise of the Network Society*, studies the history, politics, and technology surrounding the emergence of new social structures associated with what he calls *informationalism*. Led by television broadcasting, the new information technologies of informationalism have resulted in a "communication explosion throughout the world" (p. 361), including microelectronics, computing machines and software, and telecommunications. Like the media sources described above, computer mediated communication technologies challenge conventional boundaries of space and time. In particular, the Internet and the World Wide Web have the capacity to revolutionize every aspect of social life, including community and family, socialization and work, self and identity.

As with other forms of technology, access to the Internet is very unevenly distributed worldwide and even within societies. The junior senator from Illinois, Barack Obama (2006:140–141), in observing a live-action map at the headquarters of Internet search company Google, which depicted all the Internet activity across the world, wrote:

> [T]he physicist in Cambridge, the bond trader in Tokyo, the student in a remote Indian village, and the manager of a Mexico City department store were drawn into a single, constant, thrumming conversation, time and space giving way to a world spun entirely of light. Then I noticed the broad swaths of darkness as the globe spun on its axis—most of Africa, chunks of South Asia, even some portions of the United States, where the thick cords of light dissolved into a few discrete strands.

What has been termed the digital divide exists not only locally and globally, but also along age, social class, gender, and race lines. Worldwide, the typical Internet user is urban, higher-income, and male. Eighty-eight percent of Internet users are in industrialized countries, whereas industrialized countries compose only 15 percent of the world's population. Africa has the fewest Internet users. Not surprisingly, Internet costs are highest in the least developed parts of the world (Seager 2003:82–83).

A digital divide exists within certain populations even in more developed countries. A recent study of the digital disparity for immigrant youth in California (Fairlie, et al. 2006:14–15) revealed that the technology gap is significant and widening. In 1997, 43 percent of native-born individuals had home access to a computer, but only 33 percent of immigrant individuals had such access. By 2006, the respective percentages were 70 and 56 percent. In 2006, even though 70 percent of native-born individuals have access to a computer at home, only 56 percent of individuals living in immigrant households have access to a computer at home. Gaps exist within immigrant groups as well, with the highest percentage of home computers found among youth in immigrant Asian households and the lowest (36 percent) found among youth in immigrant Latino households.

Education and income are the two largest variables associated with differences in computer ownership. However, desire to own a computer, associated with employment in technology-related occupations, is also an important factor in home computer ownership. In order to reduce the growing digital divide, Fairlie, London, Rosner, and Pastor (2006) advocate not only programs to make computer ownership more affordable and school-centered programs to make computers more home accessible, but also community education programs to socialize the entire family—parents as well as children—on the value of digital technology.

Castells (2000) cautions that the social meaning of Internet-mediated communication is complex. On the one hand, Rheingold (1993), author of *The Virtual Community*, sees the new Internet-mediated communication technologies as having the potential to draw people into on-line interaction around shared values and concerns, with new virtual communities providing face-to-face meetings, friendly exchanges, and even aid and assistance in the form of material and other support for their members. As I described in Chapter 3, migrant and other transnational families in which one or more members are employed away from the family can use not only telephones and innovations in lower-cost long-distance calling, but also the Internet to enhance communication across time and space.

Some research indicates that the Internet seems to encourage the maintenance of social networks. Hampton and Wellman (2004) found that access to computer-mediated communication tends to increase contacts among individuals who were just beyond the reach of usual, everyday contact. Further, the Internet and other computer-based technologies extend communication across wider expanses of time and space than otherwise possible, but also provide access to transferable skills for education, employment, and the formation of other social capital.

However, if any member along the family chain does not have access, cannot afford, or cannot use the technology, the potential of transnational families to network in an increasingly globally wired world is diminished. Also, in contrast to the perspective that a wired family is a closer family, some critics (e.g., Slouka 1995; Wolton 1998) express concern regarding the potential of such communications to dehumanize relationships, at least in everyday life. Psychologists have found greater Internet use to be associated with a decline in size of social circle and a decline in communication with family members in the household, thus generating a possible increase in depression and loneliness for some family members (Kraut, et al. 1998).

Although the role of information and communication technologies in global development has been the subject of analysis at the international level (see UNESCO 2005; United Nations 2005b), the transnational impact of those technologies on families has not been deeply assessed. The importance of global mass media for families lies, broadly, in (1) the ability of the media to structure time and space and (2) the role of the media in socialization. Any definitive conclusions regarding the impact of the Internet would require far more controlled, systematic study on more populations than seen to date. However, Castells (2000) may be correct in concluding that the Internet is best suited to developing and maintaining many weak ties (as opposed to fewer strong ties) at relatively low material cost. New communication technologies have the potential to dramatically transform time and space and, accordingly, human life and relationships by enabling families whose members are miles or even continents away to remain virtually connected.

Global transformationists contend that cultural transmission is complex, nuanced, and sometimes contradictory. Marling (2006) argues that local cultures—in everything from language and eating habits to education systems and land use—are remarkably resilient and even resistant to the importation and wholesale adaptation of American or any other predetermined cultural direction.[3] Castells agrees, and cites the example of the adaptation of the telephone to social relationships: "The telephone was adapted, not just adopted. People shape technology to fit their own needs" (2000:293).

Cellular and mobile phone technology has had particularly significant and rapid impact on families. For those with access, this technology enhances children's, parents', and other family members' abilities to remain in contact, securing lower long-distance rates for families living apart, and even permitting family members to locate one another in crowded spaces. Not insignificantly, phone technology still serves as a primary means to call for help. Families' access to communication and other technology is linked to other patterns of global consumption.

Global Consumption and Families

Lawson (2001a:306) and others make the point that "[t]he majority of [the world's] consumers live in the global north." That fact means that individuals and families in the developed, northern hemisphere are the focus of enormous, global marketing organizations. However, once again, advertising and other marketing efforts across national borders make mass consumer systems global consumer systems (Mattelart 1994).

Such global marketing seems to rely on and generate a system of increasingly universal values in which consumers are socialized into the hegemonic consumption of products. Globalization promotes a particularly universal, insatiable consumerism because, in a world in which capitalism serves as the globally dominant economic system, consumers' desires are never satisfied. Globally derived, mass consumption thereby becomes a primary part of the construction of identity and lifestyle (Miles 2000).

Several studies reveal the extent to which global patterns of consumption have in fact been co-opted by the local culture via face-to-face relationships. For example, Billington, Hockey, and Strawbridge (1998) have examined the preference of young men in the Congo who are members of a low-status group (the *sape*) to consume global goods. These men wear clothing with ostentatious designer symbols and display in their cars global products, such as internationally marketed soft

---

[3]For an interesting discussion of the preservation of *local* culture in land use even in the face of Western tourism in Venice, Italy, see McGregor (2006:319):

> . . . tiny streets that led everywhere within an islanded neighborhood and nowhere beyond it . . . posed no problem. Obviously, Street of the Priests meant street of *our* priests, Boatyard Street referred to *our* boatyard; there is only one neighborhood warehouse, one parish church. . . . [Today t]hough the street names are carefully painted on uniform white blocks at nearly every corner, Venetian postal addresses make no mention of them.

drink cans. Billington, Hockey, and Strawbridge argue that these young men are not merely imitating Western culture. They are using these cultural artifacts as a means of establishing a high-status identity and, thereby, enhanced social power.

Lest cultural diffusion appears to be an exclusively North to South phenomenon, consider that Americans may also seek to purchase the latest fashions and technology in order to appear to be innovators or early adaptors of cultural trends. For example, in recent years, Australian wines have begun to replace French wines as among the most desirable on American and even some European tables.

While some societies and cultures may push back against the forces of global capitalism and even develop functional alternatives, the pervasiveness and invasiveness of mass marketed, iconic goods make this a Herculean undertaking. For example, "Barbie," that most successfully marketed idol of hypersexualized, hyperconsuming American femininity, was banned from sale in Iran in 1996. In doing so, Iranian political authorities were indicating their perception of the power of American consumer goods to cultivate, compromise, or corrupt traditional culture in that Middle Eastern society. A "counter-Barbie" named Sara was introduced in Iran in 2002. However, even at a cheaper cost, sales of the chastely-dressed Sara are poor, and consumers seem still willing to pay $40 for a Barbie doll on the black market ("Dolls No More American Whore" 2002). A new doll developed by a toy company based in the United Arab Emirates was introduced in 2003. About the same size as Barbie, "Fulla" comes dressed in a long, black *abaya*, but no bikini. The storyline that accompanies the doll portrays her as a doctor and teacher who likes sports and respects her parents. The "real test [of the doll's success in the Middle East] will be . . . whether this is something that only adults will collect or whether [it's something] kids will want" (Shah 2007:E3).

Baudrillard (1988), Ritzer (2005a), and others have argued that American means of consumption, which include not only dolls and others specific projects, but also superstores, megashopping malls, cybermalls, as well as television shopping networks and family-oriented theme parks, are imposing themselves in ways that compromise family intimacy. George Ritzer, taking a postmodern view of society, sees a relentless, globally ubiquitous propulsion toward an extreme version of Weber's formal rationality in mass consumption patterns. In a series of works beginning with *The McDonaldization of Society* first published in 1993, to *Expressing America* published in 1995, and continuing through *Enchantment in a Disenchanted World* (2005a), Ritzer sees what he has termed "McDonaldization" in the exceedingly bureaucratized, highly efficient, predictable-if-mundane, technology-driven, and above all rational, escalation of fast-food eating places (Ritzer 1996) and credit card retail purchasing (Ritzer 1995; 2005b). In this way, the massification of not only consumer goods, but also consumer leisure experiences, moves the family further from cherished, spontaneous, intimate connection and closer to anonymous, standardized, rationalized interface.

In this context, the family should not be viewed as a purely private domestic institution. Rather, the family sits at the apex of every other public institution, including religion, government, education, and most certainly economics. For example, globalization changes dietary cultures. Men living to greatly advanced ages in Crete have a lifelong pattern of nutrition following the traditional Mediterranean diet, rich in home-grown, unprocessed natural fruits, vegetables and grains, with liberal doses of healthy fats from olive oil and fish, but sparse on foods heavy in saturated fats from meat and dairy products. In contrast, the "new generation," represented by teenagers in the same culture, demonstrates a decided preference for an American-style diet, heavy in processed foods, sugar, and saturated fats resulting in a diet typical of what some have called a "worldwide epidemic of heart disease" (Schmickle 2006:A7).

Like Baudrillard (1988), as well as Bauman (1992) and Featherstone (1991), Ritzer views postmodern society as a consumer society. These theorists argue that the focus of capitalist society has shifted from concern for the means of production to the means of consumption. In Ritzer's words (2005b:282): "Although producing more and cheaper goods remains important, attention is increasingly being devoted to getting people to consume more and a greater variety of things."

This shift requires an increasing emphasis on marketing and advertising, including infomercials, telemarketing, and even product placement in television shows and movies. Baudrillard (1988) even describes the new means of consumption as a new kind of labor. In Ritzer's (2005a) analysis of the McDonaldization of society, the consumer engages in labor to arrive (and wait in line) at fast-food destinations. Once there, the consumer performs tasks related to serving of and cleaning up food choices, which were previously performed by paid employees. All the while, the hapless consumer is increasingly besieged by objects of consumption.

An American family traveling anywhere in the most developed (and many parts of the developing world) is rarely far from McDonald's golden arches. Others are not persuaded of the global extent of consumer McDonalization, or at least the validity of that most American metaphor, McDonald's restaurants. Although effective as a rhetorical device, McDonald's is not the ultimate, ubiquitous global symbol that Ritzer (1993) and others have made it out to be. In *Globaloney*, Veseth (2005) charges that McDonald's, although highly visible to Americans abroad searching for recognizable branded symbols (another such symbol is Coca-Cola) in the global landscape, is ultimately bound by ethnocentrism. Veseth (p. 125) supports his claim with evidence that the number of reasonably authentic Italian restaurants outside of Italy is more than double the number of McDonald's in all the world, that the signature fast food in Great Britain is Indian curry, and that

McDonald's is no more and perhaps less globally ubiquitous than Chinese cuisine. In other words, observers:

> constantly encounter images of home as they travel the world, and they associate them with their particular visions of globalization. Their reactions to what they find are likely to differ, however, because, although they see the same world, they process the images through different cultural filters, which yield predictably different conclusions. [The observer] assumes that the fast food he finds abroad is the same as at home and takes comfort from that. But he's wrong. In fact, McDonald's menus are not all the same . . . what made the original McDonald's distinctive was price and efficiency. (pp. 126–127)

Veseth argues that cultures today remain diverse and complex. If so, then families may be faced with less pressure from global mass culture than the McDonalization thesis would suggest. Further, the local construction of meaning for community, household, and family life attached to such cultural icons as McDonald's should not be overlooked. Reflecting a family development theme:

> Some women in East Asia . . . seem to use McDonald's stores as a "sanctuary" from male domination. . . . McDonald's has become a gathering place where children and grandchildren are specially celebrated. . . . McDonald's is the home of "conspicuous consumption" . . . but it is also the great leveler. . . . [In Taiwan] the choice of McDonald's (versus a restaurant owned by a mainland Chinese family) makes a [political] statement about independence from mainland influence. (p. 134)

To the extent that the interaction behind the fast food, the credit card payment counter, or the theme park concession is carefully scripted, patterns of interaction surrounding the new means of consumption can best be described as "simulated," resulting in a loss of authentic interaction (Ritzer 2005b:284).

Some of these new means of consumption have further, specific, identifiable effects on individual consumers. Parents, in particular, face social dilemmas: short-term advantage in responding to mass marketing appeals or long-term costs associated with sometimes deleterious effects. As in the case of the shift from the traditional Mediterranean diet in Crete, fast-food establishments encourage people to eat unhealthy foods. Credit cards encourage people to spend beyond their means. Shopping malls stimulate people to buy things they do not need. Television, cybermalls, and mass distributed catalogs enable people to shop without space and time constraints. (Ritzer 2005a, 2005b) and Baudrillard (1989) both describe American society as emotionally hollow, in which every place seems like every other: meaningless, monotonous, superficial, a reminder of Gertrude Stein's (1937/1973:289) pithy description of Oakland, California: "There is no there there."

Lipovetsky and Charles (2005) frame the problem of hyperconsumption as patterns of consumption that absorb and integrate ever increasing aspects of social life. In hyperconsumption, individuals consume less to enrich their social status and more for the individual gratification, hedonism, and pleasure. Such a condition, Lipovsetsky and Charles argue, generates anxiety, tension, and anguish, as the individual fails to find comfort in increasingly uncertain times void of traditional systems which, previously, had restrained individualistic impulses. Baudrillard (1990) and Ritzer (2005b) depict these hyperconsumptive experiences as occurring in the context of enchantment, magic, and spectacle. Ritzer (p. 285) writes of these new means of consumption as "fragmented" and "discontinuous." He writes, "We find ourselves adrift in an ecstatic system in which fast food restaurants . . . and their endlessly different, but surprisingly similar, products whirl about us. We are lost in a world of relentless, but meaningless, expansion."

What is the impact of this enchantment on parenting and families? Is a good parent the parent who succumbs to the seduction and provides his child with the fullest measure of enchantment? What is the impact of parental competition to mount the most extravagant birthday party at a themed restaurant, complete with a fantasy-character host. Is a family failing or ensuring a special form of relative deprivation if the parents do not provide the children with a Disney or other theme park holiday?

Some social critics argue that these new means of consumption can be injurious to family cooperation, connectedness, and intimacy, even beyond the social class implications for parents who are unable to conform to the pressures of this mass consumerism (or who financially "express," thereby overextending themselves in an effort to do so). Lemert and Elliott (2006) argue that both this mass consumer capitalism and globalization (and, I would argue, the emphasis on enchantment) have had dramatic impacts on eroticism, sex, and intimacy. Global capital, ideas, and ideologies, coupled with increasing geographic mobility, form increasingly global views of sexuality through worldwide advertising, mass media, and information culture and technologies. In particular, Lemert and Elliott cite the increasing consumer emphasis on youth, sensuality, playfulness, and physical attractiveness. They fear that some of these increasingly global exchanges may be replacing family norms and values favoring family cooperation and durability with wide-ranging views of enchanted consumer culture.

In contrast, global patterns of distribution also offer the potential to provide, on a large scale, a wide variety of goods, but also information, that can significantly enhance the material quality of life and well-being for families worldwide. Mass distribution of materials for health, literacy, and other areas of life may be more effectively and efficiently distributed, perhaps even with increased economies of scale, if markets are defined in global terms. The successful global marketing of products like Coca-Cola soft drinks, but also world health efforts to eradicate scourges, like polio and small pox, as well as female genital mutilation (FGM), gives but a hint of the potential for the worldwide distribution of goods and services.

In 1998, the United Nations (1998/1999:4) convened a *Workshop on Technology and Families* in Dublin, Ireland, to provide an opportunity to examine the impact of technology on families. The development and diffusion of technology has "contributed immensely to the improvement of living standards of millions of people in many parts of the world," resulting in reduced poverty, improved health, greater opportunities and choices, and access to products that have enhanced the quality of life. The report continues to say that technology also has the potential to strengthen the family unit. As stated in the introduction to the United Nations report:

> The effect [of technology] is to alter, often dramatically, how people live, how they earn their living, what their prospects are—for better or for worse—and how they relate to each other in and through their social institutions. Technology impacts the institution of the family through various channels, among them the education system, the mass media, the world of work and social services, in particular those relating to health and social well-being. (p. 2)

The report concluded that technology, including computer and other digital technology, changes the ways families nurture and socialize children and alters the quality of relationships among spouses, parents, children, and siblings, as well as near and extended kin. In the next section, I explicate the effects of global media and consumption on family norms and values.

Cultural Globalization and Families

Globalization and the third culture referenced earlier argue questions of connectivity, modernity, imperialism, deterritorialization, moral distance, and cosmopolitanism (Tomlinson 1999), as well as questions of family connection, autonomy, and authority in such arenas as gender, mate selection, and intergenerational systems.

Every family in every society—to a greater or lesser degree—is confronted with the problems that globalization portend for culture (Nederveen Pieterse 2004). Lemert and Elliott (2006:154) remind us that "the changing world all about is filled with risks—risks that prevent any life, even among the well-heeled, from reclining into self-satisfaction." If nothing else, the increasingly frequent "bumping up against" diverse folkways and mores, languages and traditions presents families with challenges and opportunities on an escalating scale. Moreno argues:

> The changing demographic characteristics of our society, as well as the increasingly global nature of all enterprises, are rapidly propelling us into ever more frequent

close encounters of the cultural kind with persons quite dissimilar from ourselves. We are largely unprepared to adequately cope with this quiet but significant revolution taking place in our society and our world. (2002:1)

Families are the primary agents through which their members can acquire the skills to contend with globalization. In fact, Bourdieu (1998) fixes the family as central in the acquisition of various forms of capital, including cultural capital. Cultural capital is articulated through the family in the form of socialization of values and norms, habits and customs which then, in turn, enhance or inhibit the accumulation of educational, economic, and other forms of capital. The family that can provide access to many diverse cultures can enable its members to accumulate symbolic capital in the form of language, education, and other traits that increase cultural adaptability.

In Wallerstein's (1990:54) world-system analysis, culture is an "ideological battleground," but one in which might arise "a new rendezvous of world civilizations." The globalization of culture compromises local cultural integrity and challenges traditional family patterns in favor of global cultural homogeneity—or even just pervasive change along nontraditional lines—in families. Perhaps in no area is this more obvious than in the effects of cultural globalization on gender in families.

Globalization and Gender

Beyond influences on socialization and double standards concerning gendered norms, the patterns of family life associated with globalization challenge adult gender roles. Abdi (2006; forthcoming 2007) uses a feminist perspective and a multimethod approach, including interviews, participant observation, focus groups, and literary analysis, to reveal how the Somali civil war in the late 1980s and the subsequent migration, resettlement, and transnational experiences of Somali men and women underscore changing gender dynamics on ideological, economic, and social levels.

[T]he absence of formal institutions in the aftermath of the conflict rendered women's economic pursuits in the informal sector salient for family survival. In the American setting, refugee women's access to public assistance, and/or jobs in the lowest tier of the economy, where most refugee men are also clustered, has led to a male perception of women's "empowerment" in America. . . . new discourses supported and driven by mostly male community leaders demonizing women's "transgressions" of cultural and religious boundaries, which are seen as "emasculating" Somali men. (Abdi 2006:iv)

Abdi's findings on the shifts and conflicts surrounding gender norms and values, as experienced by Somalis living in the United States, are presented in an original essay, "Contested Norms and Values in Transnational Families," at the end of this chapter.

Still, research indicates that traditional standards and even double standards regarding gender roles can be remarkably resilient, even in the face of globalization (perhaps because sexism is so globally pervasive). For example, Timera (2002) found that Sahelian girls are required to conform to parental and community expectations that they remain in the parental home until marriage and that they perform well in school in order to prepare to be a good wife and mother. Likewise, in her essay, Abdi posits that boys and young men, rather than girls, are more likely to have the opportunity to adopt the cultural practices of inner city youth, therefore bringing young males into more direct confrontation with the older generation.

However, girls may come to conflict with family and community, as seen by the cases brought by some of these girls against their communities and their parents over issues of female circumcision or forced, arranged marriage to a member of the local immigrant community. On the other hand, Timera found, boys are unlikely to be sanctioned for marriage to a white French girl, and they leave school and enter the labor force at an early age. In contrast with girls, boys are less likely to come into conflict with family and the local community. Boys, who seem to be in harmony with their parents and local communities, are more likely to come into conflict with French public law. Thus, apparently, identity formation in the adopted society is differently gendered in the negotiations between immigrant parents and their children. In the next section, I address some of the challenges—and promises—of cultural globalization for parent/child relationships in the family.

Globalization and Parenting

In no area is the contention between cultures more evident than in the case of parents attempting to navigate between two (or more) cultures in rearing their children. While some parents manage to ensure the retention of the home culture, others struggle mightily with the attractions and distractions of the new culture for the younger generation.

Al-Ali's (2002) research on Bosnian refugees relocating to the United Kingdom and the Netherlands after the wars in the former Yugoslavia in the 1990s reveals the lengths to which families will go to maintain native culture, even in the face of displacement and resettlement in a safer, and perhaps more attractive (at least to the younger generation) Western culture. The parents in Al-Ali's study, while taking pride in their children's developing skills in the English language, express concern about their children's losing touch with their Bosnian culture and language. One woman, Amra, reported, regarding her daughter Selma's enculturation:

> Selma speaks perfect English. She sometimes corrects me. Her teachers all say that she is doing really well. But her Bosnian was getting worse with time. So now I am spending a few hours almost every day reading Bosnian stories to her, practicing writing and talking. (pp. 91–92)

Some of the parents in Al-Ali's study were even taking advantage of an official curriculum on Bosnia language, history, geography, music, and art provided by the Bosnian consulate in London. Perhaps not surprisingly, some of the parents in Al-Ali's study report significant resistance from their children, who may refuse to attend the Bosnian educational programs on weekends. Some of the parents relented, no longer requiring their children to participate in the Bosnian programs.

Similarly, Timera (2002) writes of the dilemma of second generation Sahelian youth, children of African parents born and raised in France. She describes poignantly the situation of the relatively recently migrated parents, who remain deeply committed to their home villages in Senegal, Mali, Mauritania, and other regions through associational, religious, and national identities. While a significant part of the reality for parents is their ghettoization as an ethnic and religious community of migrants, Timera's research reveals that the assimilation and integration of this group is contested on intergenerational and gender stages. For example, Timera describes, on the one hand, how parents have a well-constructed identity socialized in their native country. The parents' task for themselves upon reaching France is the transformation of identity through adaptation and acculturation. On the other hand, the children of migrants face a contradictory socialization process, beginning in the family with values and norms (e.g., names and prayers, language and body language, dietary habits and table manners, religious practices and celebrations, dressing customs and hygiene standards) that form the social structure of the parents' community.

At school, children of migrant parents may be devalued. In the case of Sahelian youth, these children certainly experience being "the other" and realize their foreignness in the dominant French society. The school promotes French values and norms, pointedly marking the difference between the parental culture and the culture of the next generation. Schools' objective to foster assimilation into the majority culture of French society may not be readily apparent to the immigrant parents. Timera refers to an identity crisis, as these immigrant children traverse between home and school. In the next section, I place the effects of globalization in the larger frame of family values.

Globalization and Family Values

Conversations with parents around the world suggest that American goods, from blue jeans to Coca-Cola through rap music, are an essential part of those parents' negotiations with their children. American women traveling abroad are often surprised at the extent to which men in other countries assume all American women are sexually adventurous. After all, those same men see such a titillating image thus represented on reruns of television shows like *Baywatch* (a television show which, in reruns, along with its star, David Hasselhoff, is evidently wildly popular in Germany) and a constantly shifting parade of scantily-clad music celebrities. Western, and more particularly American, culture seems omnipresent in global society.

As I discussed earlier in this chapter, new communication technologies have expanded the potential for families to extend their world in terms of not only education, entertainment, and information, but also communication and even interaction. A father can track his son's travels through Greece via his online credit card charges. In case of an emergency, a daughter can reach her mother from a cellular phone across the globe. Worldwide spheres of consumption play increasingly powerful roles in the formation of identity and lifestyle, including family values and norms, as illustrated by Ritzer's (2004b) concept of McDonaldization.

However, in a book titled *How "American" Is Globalization?*, Marling (2006) responds "less than you think," but "more than you know." Marling deconstructs the assumption of cultural Americanization in the global context. He finds that the diffusion of technology (e.g., automatic teller machines [ATMs], franchising, and innovations, such as bar codes and computers) not only changes the means of production and consumption, but also expresses American norms in areas such as work and leisure, convenience and credit, family and community. However, the uncertain success of such quintessential American icons as Euro-Disney, suggests that some culture traits do not translate well, even to other Western cultures. Further, although Americans often assume that culture traits diffuse more rapidly from the United States to other countries, one trip outside the United States challenges that assumption. For example, as ubiquitous as cell phone technology appears in the United States, that technology has been adapted faster and more extensively in Europe and other locations, initially at least because land-line phone costs were so much higher in Europe.

Similarly, Miller (1997) argues that, through indigenization, local cultures are continuously changing—digesting, incorporating, and assimilating—as they encounter cultural elements from other societies. For example, in an engrossing ethnography of the construction and deconstruction of white masculine identities among youth in northeast England, Nayak (2003) recounts the ability of young

men and women to splice Englishness with whiteness and various ethnicities ranging from Anglo-Irish and Scotch-Irish to Anglo-Italian and various distinctions of
color. Significant to these identities are global systems of music, fashion, and sports.
However, for these youth, contact with the global is complicated and often played
out in local spaces, including local music clubs, playgrounds, and basketball courts.
Nayak concludes:

> [W]hilst youth cultures draw inspiration from the global marketplace when it comes
> to dress, music, hairstyles and fashion, these values are invariably approached at the
> prosaic level of the "local," where the inflections of race, class, gender, and so forth,
> remain evident. . . . There remains compelling evidence that youth cultures continue
> to be complex, place-related phenomena. (2003:176).

In sum, Nayak finds compelling evidence that youth cultures are local place-
related, while at the same time complex, porous, open-ended meeting places. In
these cases, family culture clashes may be seen as a product of intergenerational
conflict, but one which is exacerbated by the exposure of youth to a dizzying array
of global images.

Such may have been the case for the parents of the alleged bombers in London
in July 2005. According to news accounts, the parents were shocked at their sons'
possible involvement in a global terrorist movement. The family of one of the
alleged bombers said it was "devastated" by the attacks and baffled by their 18-
year-old son's involvement in terrorist activities (Frankel and Whitlock 2005).

Still, generalizations about differences in receptivity to cultural adaptation
across generations are risky. Even though the desire to fit into the new culture in a
host society may be strong among both old and young, children almost always find
adaptation to a new culture easier than do older generations—whether Sahelians in
France, Bosnians in the United Kingdom, or Hmong in Minnesota—and may
adapt more easily than do their parents to the new society. The young also may
make active attempts to distance themselves from being different, as well as from
their parents' strong ties to the native society and repeated desires to return.

Acculturation appears to increase the risks involved in parenting across two cultures (Martinez 2006). For example, some research suggests, albeit inconclusively,
that acculturation is linked to psychological problems, including depressive symptoms
(e.g., Katragadda and Tidwell 1998) and suicidal thoughts (e.g., Hovey and King
1996). Some more powerful research offers more compelling evidence that acculturation, as indicated by English-language adaptation and participation in other aspects of
the dominant culture, places first- and second-generation youth of Mexican origin at
increased risk for alcohol and substance use, conduct problems, early sexual activity,
juvenile arrests, and other problem behaviors (Gonzales, et al. 2002).

Hmong Familes, Frogtown by Wing Young Huie
Wing Young Huie/Minnesota Institute of Art

Some research reveals the lengths to which some groups will go to manage and retain their native values. For example, in research on British Asians in the Swaminarayan Movement,[4] Barot (2002) found transnational families whose adherence to shared beliefs about religion, business, and welfare (including values and norms emphasizing contributing to the common good of movement members and endogamous marriage) have resulted in an effective business network and a high level of family welfare that has extended over a century and across four continents.

The explanations for negative associations with acculturation include decreased family cohesion and parental authority and increased conflict between youth and their parents (Gonzales, et al. 2006), as well as greater exposure to negative stereotypes and discrimination and increased susceptibility to deviant peer role models (Gil, Vega, and Dimas 1994; Rotheram-Borus 1989). Further, according to Baca (2006:1E), "[t]he most recent waves of immigration have brought new Americans

---

[4]The Swaminarayan Movement takes its name from Sahajananda Swami, a Brahmin from Utter Pradesh, India. The movement originated in the nineteenth century as India was transitioning from Mogul to British colonial rule and developed in response to perceived moral decline. Followers from a range of castes aspired to salvation through adherence to the teachings of the charismatic Swami and supported social changes that would result in improvements in the ritual and social status of lower- and middle-rank caste members (Barot 2002).

into a culture that is more complex, more technology- and bureaucracy-driven than it ever has been. And when immigrants' command of English is lacking, sometimes they turn to the closest available interpreters, their children." Bicultural families, especially in cases where the children are becoming acculturated at a much faster rate than the parents, may find themselves in situations in which the roles of parents and children are reversed or compromised. For example, in Minneapolis, Minnesota, during the 2005–2006 school year, students spoke 94 different languages. Given the diversity in languages spoken in family homes, some immigrant children are placed in the position of serving as interpreters for their parents in the marketplace, but also in the child's own teacher conferences and personal counseling sessions, and even in the doctor's office as interpreters for parents seeking medical care.

Although children can derive a sense of responsibility and maturity from these roles, they also may become overburdened, and parental authority may be compromised (Baca 2006). However, youth also may share their parents' regret at absence from the home country. Anisa, a 15-year-old living in the Netherlands, still grieves over the culture she left behind in Bosnia. Anisa states:

> Bosnia is so different from the Netherlands. I am looking forward to the summer when we will go back to Sarajevo. It is so much more fun there. I go out with my friends and cousin all the time. People are so much nicer and warmer there. Most of my best friends here are from former Yugoslavia, not just Bosnians. We try to have fun here as well. But here everything is so expensive and my parents won't let me stay out as late as in Sarajevo. And the food . . . I hate Dutch food! Have you tried our pies? (Al-Ali 2002:92–93)

This contrast in rates and levels of adaptation can result in parental disappointment and even intergenerational conflict, as demonstrated in Al-Ali's research. Such differential rates of adaptation to the new society—and estrangement from the native culture—may even set the stage for alienation between children and their parents, as the former adapt more readily and more comfortably to the values and norms of the adopted society.

Far beyond the usual meaning of assimilation, some families and their members engage in what Al-Ali (2002:21–22) calls reverse cultural alienation, that is, "the tendency to alienate oneself from one's original cultural background as opposed to the more common form of cultural alienation in which newcomers feel estranged and out of harmony with their new adopted surroundings." Al-Ali posits that this reverse cultural alienation may be most common among elites who more closely identify with elites in the host society and who may feel comfortable speaking other languages. They welcome living in the host country and may avoid others from the native country out of concern for becoming ghettoized expatriates.

Izuhara and Shibata (2002) have observed this phenomenon among Japanese migrant women living in the United Kingdom with their English husbands.

Globalization shapes "the fluidity of intra- and interfamily relations in the face of far more fixed cultural norms" (Bryceson and Vuorela 2002:24). Therefore, appreciating the effects of globalization on real families requires understanding how families live out cultural values and norms in everyday life. Unfortunately, globalization tends to take a top-down approach (Flusty 2004), emphasizing the sublimation of the local, regional, or national to transnational economic or political processes and revealing the global context of immigration, colonization, and other social processes. However, such a hyperglobalist or world systems approach overstates the significance of economic and political systems and understates the importance of cultural systems in everyday/everynight life. In other words, the smaller scale contexts and practical consequences of global forces on families are overlooked. The permutations of globalization on real families require examination of everyday practices and of members with multiple identities in diverse localities. Theoretical and methodological creativity, including more research of an ethnographic or other observational nature, are needed to reveal what Flusty calls the inside out or from below implications of globalization on families.

Bauman (1992, 2001, 2004, 2007) and Lemert and Elliott (2006) are among the social scientists who have tried to unravel the impact of globalization and postmodernity on individuals, their identities, and their relationships. Those authors charge that globalization does have "deadly" consequences in terms of emotional costs and culture. They see a world increasingly characterized by individualism, which is a:

> current preoccupation with the self in terms of narcissism, emotionalism, the manipulation of individual needs or desires, and a quest for self-realization and self-fulfillment . . . with traumatic consequences for people's emotional lives and relationships. (Lemert and Elliott 2006:10–11)

Lemert and Elliott see heightened individualism in the shift from custom and tradition to what they call the "internal world of the individual" and the production of competing polarities of freedom and alienation. For Lemert and Elliott, the consequences of globalization can be seen not only in accelerating patterns of international contact and worldwide social problems and in rapidly expanding communication technologies and more rational consumption patterns, but also in more diverse cultural cosmopolitanism life worlds and relationships that are more experimental, open, and privatized than in the past.

The "new individualism"—Self with a capital "S" (Lemert and Elliott 2006:18)—has personal and cultural implications, more felt in the developed world, but of increasingly universal reach due to globalization and revolutions in communication technologies. This new cultural identity is highly "privatized," meaning that the individual is required to be independent and autonomous.

Bauman (2003) terms these "liquid" relationships, associations that are temporary and frail and destined to produce a sense of anxious impermanence in the actors as they seek secure bonds which they are unable to establish and maintain in an uncertain world. In *Wasted Lives*, Bauman (2004) describes as an inevitable consequence of globalization a greater emphasis on rapid response to changing cultural, economic, political, and other forces. Ultimately, such rationally-grounded relationships, organizations, and networks trend toward expendability.

Perhaps with an overlay romantic view of family and intimacy, Lemert and Elliott (2006) grieve the loss of secure, reliable intimacy and bemoan the arrival of fleeting, casual, impersonal, clandestine sexual encounters as a symptom of the narcissism and psychic withdrawal, all enabled by the new technology, which allows one to establish sexual contacts and engage in experimental encounters in a whole new way. But, is this not just new technology laid over old patterns? How different is this, really, from anonymous sexual encounters experienced by men as they traveled away from wives and families and landed in different ports, countries, and communities, as part of their mobile work lives? One major difference is the extent to which these options are increasingly available to women, as well as men. As seen in the dramatic increases in American women's participation in the labor force during World War II, nothing shifts gender roles as quickly and as radically as an urgent macrosocial situation. However, although globalization has clearly generated significant shifts in gender roles, greater egalitarianism is a long-term trend in gender roles across societies.

Any discussion of the impact of globalization on family culture should be framed around the reality that geographical place has never been perfectly correlated with community and identity.

> [C]ommunities can exist without being in the same place—from networks of friends with like interests, to major religious, ethnic or political communities. . . . the instances of places housing single "communities" in the sense of coherent social groups are probably—and . . . have for long been—quite rare. Moreover, even where they do exist, this in no way implies a single sense of place. (Massey 1994:153)

Globalization challenges scholars and citizens to re-vision space and place, community and identity which does not necessarily deny the uniqueness of local space, but which sees culture and space as:

- Dynamic, rather than static, processes
- Associated with boundaries, as well as linkages to the outside
- Characterized by internal conflicts

Still, in many ways, postmodern families are increasingly on the frontier of a globalized world, at an "interface between two (or more) contrasting ways of life" (Bryceson and Vuorela 2002:12). These transnational families are "frontiering" in the sense that they are breaking new cultural ground. Families must be able to hold values and priorities, norms and strategies in ways that take into account changing demographies, employment, and other realities in a global world. Thus, global families are challenged to use creative approaches to structuring family life, including gendered ways of organizing care work and responding to violence and other threats. In doing so, families face new stressors and possible conflicts in the face of oft-reduced intimate connections in which associations and identities are more open to negotiation in postmodern, globalized cultures.

Summary

Globalization impinges on the reproduction of social institutions, values, and norms and the conduct of everyday life among families whether or not they are experiencing transnational population shifts. Families increasingly experience flows of cultural goods and services across national borders, with a clear tendency for Western (particularly English-speaking) nations to dominate as both cultural exporters and importers.

The mass media not only inform, entertain, and educate; they also virtually extend reference points beyond that which the individual and family actually experience. In doing so, mass media (especially television) can create "electronic communities," essentially transnational mass culture, considering the oligopoly of mass media production. Transmitting cultural messages to families beyond the local, regional, and national through international levels thus situates families in global context.

The globalization of culture also involves ever broadening and deepening patterns of mass consumption, which impact family values and norms. Therefore, globalization affects families not only in terms of the goods and services available for consumption and the information disseminated concerning economics and politics, but it also affects the environment, health, medical, and other critical issues of family life. Globalized culture is a powerful force in shaping attitudes and behaviors; systems of stereotyping, prejudice, and discrimination; likes and dislikes; and values and norms. Globalized culture offers an enormous, some say homogenized, range of entertainment and information options, but also influences our deepest belief systems in terms of gender and age roles, parenting and other family relationships, and youth and other civil rights and social movements.

Contested Norms and Values in Transnational Families
By Cawo M. Abdi, Ph.D.

Following a civil war brewing since the late 1980s that reached its climax in 1990, Somali women, men, and children fled from their war-torn country to seek asylum in countries in the Horn of Africa. Some eventually found their way to other places, including the Americas, Europe, and Australia. Dispersal of families became the norm, rather than the exception. Somali refugees went not necessarily where they would like to go (e.g., Canada), but rather where they could go (e.g., Scandinavia). To escape the war and precarious life in remote refugee camps in Kenya, Ethiopia, or Djibouti, Somali people used legal routes, such as family reunification and government settlement programs, as well as illegal routes, paying traffickers, traveling with false documents, and/or taking dangerous boats to cross the Mediterranean. This dispersal has resulted in family networks that often span more than two countries, and has also led to myriad challenges for the Somali family.

Drawing from research in Canada, the United States, and Kenyan refugee camps, this essay examines some of these challenges faced by Somali families. I collected original data in Minnesota from 2001 to 2005 and conducted in-depth interviews, participant observation, and focus groups with over 300 Somalis of both genders and different ages. My research illustrates how the dispersal of Somalis around the globe, in regions where the language, religion, and ethnicity of the majority differs from that of this group, is affecting their identity by challenging some of their norms and values. Refugees' accommodation and resistance to these new practices result in a complex web of gender and generational power contestations and discourses within the community.

From the onset of displacement, refugees face problems requiring rapid and innovative adjustments to new realities. To provide an example, the role of men as providers is greatly undermined in the context of civil war, when these men are either absent, partaking in the war, or are the first to leave the country. The latter is due to the nature of civil war, when men are the first ones targeted for killing.[1] Thus, migration challenges gender norms dictating the roles of men and women in the household, which, in turn, inform the gender power relations within the household and society.

My research revealed that these new challenges, though real, did not really shift Somali gender power relations. In the period of transitions, when refugees were still settled in temporary areas within and immediately outside of Somalia, the wider context of refugee life did not change. That is to say, refugees were still within or very near the country of origin, where strong cultural and religious edicts dictated the subordinate position of women. Even though the Somali civil war undermined the gender order, the war did not translate to overt gender power contestation between the sexes, at least in the early stages of the conflict.

Conditions undermining gender power relations become more drastic when the settlement area is not only distant from the country of origin, but also when the gender practices

---

[1] Women also are killed in war. In addition, as discussed in the previous chapter, they are also subjected to gender violence, including rape and torture.

prevailing in the place of settlement greatly differ from the practices in the country of origin. My interviewees report that the main factors destabilizing traditional Somali gender order are the institutions catering to newcomers and the socioeconomic opportunities and challenges refugees experience in their new place of residence. For instance, similar to the previously mentioned challenge to the male "breadwinner" role in transit settlements, the new context in developed countries, such as the United States, offers new opportunities in the form of public assistance for refugee women and their children. Most of these women arrive with low human capital in terms of education and other transferable skills, making initial integration into the American workforce difficult. I found that these new sources of income for women with children become arenas of dispute and conflict within families, with claims that women's access to these opportunities are destabilizing the Somali family, and that these opportunities are allegedly leading to conflict and higher divorce rates within the community.

Interestingly, rhetoric on the disruption of Somali traditional gender practices brought about by settlement in a Western country is not limited to those dependent on social assistance for their livelihoods, but rather is a widespread belief among Somalis, including women. When the economic opportunities refugee women access in the Diaspora, in the forms of welfare and/or employment, are not deemed the culprit in gender disruption, Somali men fear that the institutions and values of the mainstream community may be triggering a revolt among women in contesting Somali gender relations. Some men argue that, in addition to economic opportunities, the legal system in place in the West encourages women to break up their families whenever they feel they are being denied anything. These claims, in fact, border on paranoia, with some refugees going as far as asserting that the Western system wants the breakdown of the Muslim family. While it is more the men who resent and dwell on the dangers confronting the Somali family in the West, many women also support these claims. Most of these men and women place the responsibility for the danger the Somali family faces in the Diaspora on women's shoulders, saying women are abandoning their cultural and religious practices under the influence of Western values made by and for a different type of society.

A contradiction between what was regarded as sacred in the Somali context, that is, women's culturally and religiously sanctioned subordination to men, and the new institutions and gendered practices in the countries of settlement (especially in the West), has led to a vigorous debate about the future of the Somali family in the Diaspora. A proverb often cited by my interviewees states: "*Naagi waa saar, saarna kaligii geed kama boxo*" (women are vine, and vine does not grown on its own),[2] and is currently challenged by Somali women's prominence in the economic and emotional sustenance of their families since the collapse of the Somali state. From my research, I conclude that the Somali civil war exposed the contradictions between gender rhetoric and practice and the prominent role women played and still play in society, roles unacknowledged and thus invisible in a patriarchal society.

---

[2]This proverb is often stated to support women's dependence on her father, husband, or brother during the life course, thus justifying the necessity for women to remain dependent, and therefore subordinate to men at all times.

In addition to gender, a topic considered most pertinent for the Somalis in the Diaspora related to the wedge emerging between young people and their parents. Many parents expressed the danger of losing their children to the mainstream culture, perceived as greatly different from that of Somali culture. Intergenerational conflict is nothing new in society, including migrant and refugee communities. However, this conflict is exacerbated by the often myriad other settlement issues refugee communities confront in their new homes. For example, consistent with their low socioeconomic status as recent refugees with low human capital, the residential areas available to most Somalis in the West are in urban inner city areas. Concentration in these areas means that young Somalis, especially boys and young men, adapt some of the cultural practices of inner city youth in terms of dress and behavior. Because these poorer areas are subject to more police scrutiny, and because the opportunities for extracurricular activities that their parents can afford or that are available in such neighborhoods are limited, refugee/immigrant youth perceive their new country as one that excludes them. They often identify with those most marginalized in these societies. For example, in the American context, many Somali youth identify with African American youth, who, like them, are often concentrated in poorer neighborhoods and who feel excluded from the "American dream."[3]

Unlike the youth, Somali parents, whose upbringing was in a completely different society, panic at the future prospects of their children in their country of settlement. Most parents I interviewed asserted that they escaped their war torn country to provide better opportunities for their children. They detail the sacrifices they made to come to the West, in the hope that their children's futures would be brighter than their own. Again, parents fear that the new institutions in the West are disrupting cultural childrearing practices. The parents fear power reversal between parents and children. Illustrating this dilemma for parents, a male community worker in his late 30s stated:

> Here the child is raised by the state . . . The state is the authority. In Somalia, it was different. When you are a child, the highest authority is your parents. Other higher authorities were the teachers, the koranic one, and the school one. You could not smoke cigarettes in front of them; you could not misbehave in front of your teacher, just like your parents. Here the teacher is nothing. He is just a service provider; he is selling something to you. The parents are just here to provide you services, food, shelter; and, if you don't like them, you can even complain to the school, or you can call 911. What exacerbates this is the existence of cultural barriers, language barriers with the parents. Here the kid has become the authority; so when there is a meeting with the teacher or they go to the hospital or to a governmental agency or to an office, it is the child who is interpreting. The parent does not know anything.

This excerpt highlights refugees' interpretation of the intergenerational conflict existing between parents and children. The speaker was, in fact, an educated man, and most parents expressed this conflict in more daunting language, with some expressing regrets of bringing

---

[3]It is also true that male Somali youth in many urban areas (Toronto, London, and Minneapolis-St. Paul) are in conflict with African American youth. Many incidents of violence and confrontations in schools and outside have been reported.

their children to this new land, while others detail plans to return with these children before they lose them to the "system."[4]

The gender and generation conflicts within the Somali family as a result of forced displacement and settlement in the West are currently salient in the debates on the family as highlighted in Chapter 5. This debate is occurring in a transnational context, with emerging developments often circulating between Somalia and the countries of settlement in the West. The debate is even discussed on Somali Web sites. There, diverse viewpoints are presented, though opinions often dramatize changes deemed inherently to be undermining Islam and Somali cultural practices. Inevitably, these conflicts will continue as the second generation of Somalis in the West come of age in the next decade.

Cawo M. Abdi, Ph.D., is a Somali–Canadian scholar who completed her doctorate in sociology at the University of Sussex in the United Kingdom as a Commonwealth Fellow. She is currently a visiting lecturer in the Department of Sociology and the Institute of Global Studies at the University of Minnesota, Minneapolis. Her next work, "Convergence of Civil War and the Religious Right: Re-Imagining Somali Women," was recently published in summer 2007 in *Signs: Journal of Women in Culture and Society.*

Critical Thinking Questions:

1. What are the potential benefits of a globalized media and consumption to families of the northern hemisphere? To families of the southern hemisphere?

2. Valid, reliable empirical evidence concerning the impact of global mass media, including computer mediated communication such as the Internet, on global families is sparse. Outline the research design for a study that would deepen our understanding of the impact of global mass media and consumption on socialization in the family.

3. Are you a skeptic, a hyperglobalist, or a transformationalist regarding the impact of cultural globalization and families? Do you agree or disagree with the contention that *McDonaldization* increasingly threatens global families' abilities to forge an authentic culture for their members? As some cases offered in this chapter suggest, societies are remarkably able to construct local meaning from even the most American of cultural icons. How might a globally-presented aspect of Western culture (e.g., McDonalds restaurants) be adapted by families to improve the quality of family life?

4. Frontiering refers to "interfacing between two (or more) contrasting ways of life." To what extent do the gender roles described in Abdi's research demonstrate that globalization fosters frontiering in family values and norms around gender roles?

---

[4]Intergeneration a conflict is gendered, with most problems identified with boys. Girls often experience intense scrutiny compared to boys. Girls are thus closer to their families and remain more connected to Somali tradition, even if this is one adapted to the new country. Boys, on the other hand, enjoy great freedom, coming and going as they see fit, something that was okay in Somalia, but is now said to be leading to the deviant behavior of some youth.

6

Positioning Families in Global Landscapes: Families, Policies, and Futures

Ronald Bosrock, John H. Myers Chair of Management and founder and director of the Global Institute at Saint John's University in Collegeville, Minnesota (College of Saint Benedict/Saint John's University Faculty and Staff Profiles 2006) believes that "globalization can change [the] world for [the] better" (2006:D8). While acknowledging how far globalization must reach to reveal true improvements in the quality of family life across the globe, Bosrock writes that globalization holds:

> out hope that an expanding worldwide economy would go a long way toward closing the gap between poor and rich nations. . . . Opening world markets to free trade and the free flow of capital and labor has contributed much toward the weaker countries of the world in the world economy. Globalization has highlighted issues such as the poverty among women, child labor, and the scandalous lack of basic medical care throughout much of the underdeveloped world. (D8)

Bosrock argues that global equity and stability are prerequisites to the enjoyment of economic benefits in developed societies. Hence, the developed North and West have a vested interest in improving economic opportunity in places like Mexico and other Central American nations, as well as in reducing the threat of violence in significant parts of Africa and the Middle East.

Although, in each chapter in *Global Families*, I have attempted to alert the reader to the potential benefits of globalization for families, a dominant message of the previous chapters has been the extent to which globalization challenges, compromises, and places at risk families and their members. In terms of the family consequences of globalization, I have discussed how global changes in death, fertility, and migration are shaping family structures in ways that impact family dynamics, including patterns of dependency. I have demonstrated how employment transcends traditional definitions of national borders, serving workers' desires to improve their families' economic opportunities, yet often at the expense of the quality of family life in marital, parenting, and other family relationships. I have considered some of the international sources of the greatest family hazards caused by war, human trafficking, and family dislocation. Finally, I have sought to reveal the extent to which mass communication and marketing increasingly means global communication and consumption, with significant consequences for family norms and values, especially around parenting.

In this, the final chapter of *Global Families*, I examine international efforts to improve the quality of life for families across the globe in the second decade of the United Nations Year of the Family. I describe the work of selected organizations—supranational, but also regional and national organizations—in order to reveal the critical position of a gender-sensitive lens on social policy, including development programs that seek to affect family well-being. I place family rights in the broader context of human rights and ask: What is the prognosis for the institution and relationships of family in a global society? Where national borders are increasingly contested on political, economic, cultural, and other grounds, is the world moving toward a postfamily global society, or does family remain a cornerstone for societies, regardless of the global milieu?

Beyond the Second Decade of the Year of the Family

My stand in *Global Families* is consistent with that of the United Nations. In 1998, the United Nations reiterated the need for a continued emphasis on the needs of families in an era of rapid change, including globalization.

> Rapid changes are underway in the forms and styles of family life. The major changes in societies, such as industrialization, urbanization, secularization, commercialization

and *globalization* [italics added], are powerful forces influencing family life. In many parts of the world, children are denied their right to be loved and cared for as well as their right to food, health care, and education. Many face domestic violence within their families, the most common form being the gender-based violence. The number of women working outside the home is increasing. The population is aging. The position of the extended family is declining so that the demands on the nuclear family are growing. Unemployment is high and widespread, with catastrophic consequences for the dignity and self-esteem of both men and women and for family solidarity. (United Nations 1998)

In speaking to the follow-up to the International Year of the Family, the United Nations General Assembly (United Nations Programme on the Family 2003b) affirmed six objectives:

1. Increase awareness of family issues among governments and in the private sector.
2. Strengthen abilities of national institutions to formulate, implement, and monitor family policies.
3. Stimulate efforts to response to problems both affecting and affected by families.
4. Undertake reviews and assessments of the conditions and needs of families.
5. Enhance effectiveness and generate new family programs at local, national, and regional levels.
6. Improve collaboration among national and international organizations that support families.

Furthermore, the United Nations Programme on the Family (2003a) urges that every social policy on the family should take into account changes facing families in the areas of family structure, aging, migration, and the HIV/AIDS pandemic. Achieving such lofty objectives will require an investment in and by social science that goes beyond culture-specific or comparative research to include study of international, transnational, and global family concerns.

Idealistic declarations and position statements of the United Nations and other supranational organizations are a crucial starting point for achieving international consensus regarding human rights and other important social values. These organizations and their actions have the potential to impact the quality of life for families. But, in an essay titled "The Global Human Rights of Families" which follows this chapter, Marsha Freeman, Director of the International Women's Rights Action Watch at the University of Minnesota Human Rights Center, argues that such public statements still fall short of resulting in meaningful, assessable social change. Freeman states: "In short, while everyone celebrates the family, few take care of it."[1] Social policies mean little without enforcement or structural change.

Again, Gendered Family Realities

In 2006, in her Presidential Address before the American Sociological Association, titled "Great Divides: The Cultural, Cognitive, and Social Bases of the Global Subordination of Women," Cynthia Fuchs Epstein (2007:1) stated: "Categorization based on sex is the most basic social divide." Each chapter in *Global Families* has confirmed that the consequences of globalization, and hence, effective social change to improve the quality of life for families in today's global society, are inextricably bound to issues of gender.

An organization like the Center for Women Policy Studies in Washington, D.C., which recognizes the need to build support for U.S. foreign policy that ensures women's human rights and works, concerns itself with such family-friendly issues as immigration and poverty, HIV/AIDS, reproductive rights and justice, and trafficking (Center for Women Policy Studies 2006). Bodies like the United Nations Commission on the Status of Women have moved beyond their original mandate to examine and monitor the status of women worldwide. The Commission also has attempted to serve the common good of women and their families in several areas addressed in *Global Families*. For example, the Commission has worked with organizations, such as the International Labor Organization (ILO) and the World Health Organization (WHO), and through international treaties, such as the Convention for the Suppression of Traffic in Persons, and to press for improvements in the quality of life for women, girls, and their families (Hawkesworth 2006).

In doing so, Hawkesworth (p. 112) argues, the United Nations has provided a "free space of feminist activism," with global implications. Indeed, Seager's (2003) atlas of feminist organizing in the world confirms that, in the last decade, nations throughout the world—from Afghanistan, Botswana, and Chad through Europe and North America—have enacted legislation to guarantee equal rights to men and women and, in the case of countries like the Netherlands and South Africa, to gays and lesbians as well. In a book in a larger series on globalization, Hawkesworth (2006:1) quotes a statement from Women in Development Europe (WIDE): "Feminism in one country is not sustainable—we need feminism on a global scale."

---

[1]For an elaboration on family social policy from a domestic, American perspective, see the final chapter, "From 'Family Values' to 'Valuing Families'" in Karraker and Grochowski's *Families with Futures: A Survey of Family Studies for the Twenty-first Century* (2006). That chapter includes a "Principles and Checklist for Assessing the Impact of Policies and Programs on Families," originally adapted by Karen Bogenscheider from a version originally published by Theodora Ooms and Stephen Preister and presented at the Family Impact Seminar in Washington, D.C., in 1988.

Thus, any response to globalization must involve globally-based social movements. Global movements can support and advance transnational initiatives involving agents of developed nations concerning population, family labor, and other issues. The case of recent Korean–Japanese coalitions to provide recognition and restitution to comfort women, discussed in Chapter 4, testifies to the power of feminist movements that cross national boundaries to effect powerful social change. At the same time, any effort at global action must recognize the significant divides in global movements that can be seen between North and South, capitalist and socialist, across regions more or less developed, and among countries constituting diverse cultural, ethnic, racial, religious, and other identities. Snyder's (2006) qualitative study of women's peace organizations meeting at the 1995 Fourth United Nations World Conference on Women reveals that transnational activism among groups representing diverse circumstances is best advanced when the very process of intergroup conflict is used constructively to build coalitions leading toward effective, and equitable, cooperation. Snyder argues that a commitment to such transnational, global movements requires, first, examination of inequalities in decision-making (such as those that may exist between participants from Northern and Southern countries), which in turn can provide opportunities to test commitments to coalitions. Second, escalation in long-standing areas of conflict (e.g., around racism) indicates a need to address issues of dominance, which in turn can provide an opportunity for meaningful dialogue. Third, negotiation of priorities, some of which originate in different cultural and ethnic contexts, can increase understanding of differences within coalitions, thereby increasing opportunities for collaboration. Fourth, conflict resolution strategies, such as those required to bring indigenous and refugee groups together, in and of themselves can aid in the formation of collective identities and relationships for further collaborative efforts.

Global social movements face diverse traditions and agendas, as well as significant inequalities in experience, power, and resources (such as those seen between North and South), but can use inclusive and participatory processes to constructively engage conflict. In doing so, globally-oriented social movements have the potential to increase not only the depth and complexity of their knowledge surrounding women's and family issues, but also their strategic authority. At the same time, Liu's (2007:921) research, in which she compares Chinese and Indian women's movements in the wake of the agenda adopted by the United Nations Fourth World Conference, "challenges the dominant assumption that global thinking can substitute for local thinking." Liu's research indicates that, although national women's movements may build from international agenda, the direction and efficacy of national social movements depend on political contexts (e.g., democratic versus authoritarianism) unique to each society.

A similar caution applies to movements to advance the quality of family life worldwide: When it comes to social action, one size cannot fit all. For example, many on the political right would not agree that feminist or gender-based movements will advance profamily agenda. Likewise, translating concern regarding human rights into effective international law and policy and meaningful social justice around issues addressed by the United Nations Commission on the Elimination of All Forms of Discrimination Against Women (United Nations 1999a) requires knowledge of a society's culture, as well as the voices that are speaking—and silenced—for that culture (Merry 2005). For example, the success of efforts to require companies to support men's participation in childcare in Sweden rests in a broader sociopolitical context that promotes gender equality. Haas and Hwang (2007) found that father-friendly companies in Sweden had adopted corporate values consistent with the domestic sphere, while affirming a high value on the entree of women into the public sphere. These findings do not bode well for societies, such as the United States, in which the values of corporate cultures often compromise family interests, and public opinion often seems ambivalent regarding women's participation in the labor force.

Women continue to earn only one-tenth of the world's income while working two-thirds of the world's working hours and continue to constitute the majority (70 percent) of the world's poor (Heyzer, as quoted in Seager 2003:102). However, I hope readers of *Global Families* share a measure of my optimistism for constructive social change. Women are slowly gaining entitlement to fuller participation in economic, educational, political (including military), religious, and other institutions and to self-determination in terms of marriage (including divorce) and reproductive health rights while obtaining freedom, at least in law, from licensed domestic and sexual violence (Seager 2003). For example, in 1996, the International War Crimes Court, The Hague indicted eight Bosnian Serb military and police officers in the rape of Muslim women, the first time sexual assault has been addressed separately as a war crime. In 2000, the United Nations Security Council passed a resolution which mandated the equal participation of women in peacekeeping. Other landmarks in the early twenty-first century include:

- Vietnam banned polygamy and dowry.
- Chad made sexual violence, including genital cutting, a criminal offense.
- In Jordan, a new law allowed women to initiate divorce.
- The Scottish Episcopal church voted to allow women to become bishops.
- Bahrain permitted women to vote and run for all elected offices.
- About 20,000 Columbian women participated in a peace march, demanding an end to the civil war in that country.
- The Norwegian government enacted legislation requiring that companies ensure at least 40 percent of their board members are women. (Seager 2003:102–103)

Rae Lesser Blumberg (1988:115), a sociologist who has studied and worked with Third World economic development programs, has found that the intersection of gender and development provides insights into the interfaces "between macro and micro, between social structures and human lives." Blumberg charges that gender insensitivity characterized the viewpoint among those in positions of authority who were, in Blumberg's words, "oblivious to the gender division of labor and rewards within the household." For example, her analysis indicates that macrolevel development policies to address the African food crisis failed to take into account women's economic place and power at the microlevel. These policies set in motion a "chain of consequences" (p. 116) in which women were economically undercut, beginning with diminished abilities and disincentives for women to engage in food cultivation and production.

Epstein (2007:17) concluded her Presidential address (cited at the beginning of this section) with a powerful statement regarding the relationship between gender and society:

> The most productive societies are those with porous boundaries between categories of people. . . . Small groups of men may prosper by stifling women's potential, but prosperous nations benefit from women's full participation and productivity in societies.

Not only women and societies, but also their families benefit from women's liberation. Further, globalization—with the greater movement of families within and across national borders, the increase in transnational employment, the fluidity of social arrangements necessitated by war and other social upheavals, and the dramatic culture shifts occurring in the early twentieth century—may well be just the social process to stimulate the kind of "porous" boundaries of which Epstein speaks.

Social Policy, Development, and Family Well-Being

In each of the preceding four chapters, I have offered a compendium of research on the many ways families are affected by globalization. In turn, these chapters reveal a pressing need for consideration of family impact when formulating social policies at national, international, and, especially, transnational levels. Based on the research I offer in *Global Families*, a family-sensitive global policy agenda must include five urgent policy priorities, each premised in family impact on a global scale.

1. Accelerate the urgency of global responses to the HIV/AIDS pandemic, while generating an understanding of the escalating deficits acquired by global societies, from Australia to Zimbabwe, when generations are left without care.

2. Revise immigration, refugee, and asylum policies, to reduce the uncertainty of family reunification, while making visible the assets that women like those at Sarah's and their families can contribute to an adopted country.

3. Scrutinize migrant employment practices to reveal the underlying macrosocial order underlying migration for work, as well as the manifest and latent consequences for families, like that of Paula Rodriguez, the home, and host societies.

4. Immediately end violence against women and children, including violence as a collateral effect of war and during periods of civic unrest, using research that will unmask the social foundations of rape, trafficking, and other forms of violence in norms and values, including patriarchy.

5. Charge supranational bodies with analyzing the negative effects and promoting the positive effects of global media and consumption and seek ways to develop sensitivity around the challenges families face as they encounter global culture, especially through mass media and consumption.

In each area, I advocate development of family impact statements, along the lines of environmental impact statements, consistent with a family ecology approach, which sees families as embedded in interlocking global systems composed of economic, political, cultural, and other social systems. At a basic level, however, policies and practices will need to be premised in a more inclusive definition of family, one that transcends the definition of family as a unit formed around a man and a woman and their relations by blood, marriage, or adoption. A global concept of family must be inclusive, making room for the rich array of relationships among children, adults, and elders who are bound together by rights and obligations, even across space and time.

Even though I see these initiatives as embedded in social justice, the means to achieving meaningful change at a global level is difficult and complicated. Certainly, social policy, development, and family well-being are fundamentally bound together. And policies that support social development are often linked to improvements in the quality of life for families. However, such is not always the case. For example, Haney's (2003) analysis of state, market, and domestic relationships in Eastern Europe documents the link between retrenchment in welfare entitlements and benefits and economic marketization and privatization in a global context. By the early 1980s, nations such as Hungary were moving away from large, comprehensive welfare systems which included such programs as universal family allowances, a three-year paid maternity leave grant, and local childrearing assistance grants. Not coincidentally, Hungary joined the International Monetary Fund. The International Monetary Fund, along with the World Bank, urged nations like Hungary to adopt policies that would restrict eligibility through the application of means and income tests. Haney (2003:163) concluded: "[T]he international agencies' reform model targeted national-level social entitlements in an attempt to dismantle the universal tier of the welfare state." The consequence of such vigorously pursued supranational agenda is greater family risk.

Some critics see governments as largely incapable of or unwilling to engage issues such as transnational migration from the perspectives of those most affected. These critics (e.g., Piper 2003) see nonstate actors, including nongovernmental organizations (NGOs) as playing pivotal roles in advocating from the bottom up to exert pressure on governments and policymakers to take into account the well-being of transnational families. While doing so, NGOs and other organizations attempting change in the quality of family life on a global scale must first frame societal problems such as poverty and hunger in meaningful ways. As Terezinha da Silva, president of the *Forum Mulher* (Women's Forum) in Mozambique, offers: "I don't like the phrase 'fighting poverty.' Poverty is too wide a topic, and it can mean different things to different people." (Moya 2006:22) Poverty and other problems facing global families are complex, embedded in often disparate economic, as well as political, cultural, and other social factors.

These organizations frequently confront additional challenges, including the gendered effects of social problems like civil wars. Again, da Silva offers that women are most often the collateral victims of war. However, more national and even local organizations like *Forum Mulher* are increasing their effectiveness by cooperating and sharing experiences and resources with other organizations that focus on women's issues, as well as networking with other NGOs, political groups, government representatives, and trade unions and with academic and donor organizations.[2] The Global Women's Action Network for Children, launched in 2006, is another such organization, bringing together "thoughtful, committed, powerful women from around the world" (Edelman 2006:1) who represent governments and the United Nations, business and nonprofit organizations, cultural and educational groups, and many faith, national, and racial assemblies to work on behalf of the world's children.

Tension between family rights and responsibilities and the national and international bodies that might seek to regulate them may well be fundamental. Sigle-Rushton and Kenney (2004) describe one such area—public policy—regarding the often conflicting parental responsibilities for work and care. Sigle-Rushton and Kenney differentiate among 15 members of the European Union on the basis of state provision of publicly-funded early childhood education and care. In five countries (Sweden, Finland, Denmark, Belgium, and France), childcare is not a private, family responsibility, but a collective, societal responsibility. These five countries

---

[2]For example, a thematic session at the annual meetings of the American Sociological Association in Montreal in August 2006 explored the potential impact of the declaration on women's rights, including gender-based and sexual violence, HIV/AIDS prevention, childbearing risk reduction, and sexual health and reproduction (Simonen 2006).

have extensive early childhood education and full daycare for a large proportion of children. The childcare programs in these countries are integrated through educational and social-welfare systems and access is almost universal.

Following Hochschild's (1989) argument that little meaningful change has occurred in the ratio of men's breadwinner/caregiver responsibilities, Sigle-Rushton and Kenney (2004) foresee an increase in what they call dual earner/dual career families. They already see signs, at least in the European Union, that social policies are moving in that direction. In support, they cite the 1997 Treaty of Amsterdam, which seeks to make equal opportunities for men and women a basic aim of all policymaking. Although the research is incomplete, such "gender mainstreaming" appears to have support, as witnessed by increasing numbers of nations enacting policies that would encourage fathers and mothers to participate more equitably in parental leave and by surveys (e.g., the *Employment Options for the Future* study) which demonstrate that, even with the lost earnings, men would prefer to reduce their hours worked. Such is the case in countries like Sweden with long-standing support for gender equity in domestic and labor spheres.

Bodies like the Organisation for Economic Co-operation and Development (OECD) share a broad commitment to democratic government and the market economy and work toward dissemination of research on a range of economic and social issues (OECD 2006). The OECD publication, *Babies and Bosses* (2002), targets the challenge of balancing work and family life as a global issue and explores how policies in this area contribute to the structure of labor markets and other social outcomes. The OECD's findings indicate that family-friendly policies including childcare, child-related leave, and tax benefit policies can benefit societies in a variety of ways, including not only improved child development and greater gender equity, but also more secure family economics. Other supranational government bodies like the European Union (EU) have adopted policies of gender mainstreaming. Through the European Commission, the EU will address gender inequality in 21 specific areas, including migration, employment, education, trafficking, and development (European Commission 2006).

How then do individual societies around the world measure up in terms of some of the indicators of family well-being? On one important indicator, the provision of parental leave connected with childbearing or adoption, the Project on Global Working Families (2002) at Harvard University (described in some detail in Seccombe's [2006] earlier volume in this series) found that, of 168 countries whose policies on this matter were surveyed, 163 guaranteed some form of paid leave to women connected with childbearing (and, in some cases, adoption). The Project found no national policy granting paid leave to new mothers in three of the least developed countries: Lesotho, Papau New Guinea, and Swaziland. Shamefully, the

United States also has no national policy regarding maternity leave, and women in Australia only recently became entitled to one year unpaid leave.

A national paid child-related leave is among 20 policies that the Project has identified as among those that countries can index to promote societal equity regarding working families. In addition to paid leave for childbearing and child-rearing, the full list addresses issues of access and support for children, adults, and older adults, including those with special needs and disabilities, to educational, health, community resources and, in the case of older adults able to work, employment opportunities, as well as availability of caregivers for health and other care of children, other dependents, and self. For example, Lawson (2001a: 374) has stated: "Clearly, the global human condition, and especially the well-being of the world's families, is . . . the key problematic for the helping professions of the twenty-first century."

Lawson (2001b) offers a framework for family-centered policies and practices applicable to a global world. His framework engages governmental bodies at the local, state, national, and international levels and considers the importance of local mobilization for collective action, matters of place in need and opportunity, global issues of space–time compression, and intercultural contact zones. Lawson's futuristic model of social welfare emphasizes the importance of "coordination, synchronization, and alignment" (p. 365).

Many economists and social policy experts contend that, even in the face of criticism, the World Bank and certain other supranational organizations continue to have an almost monopolistic control over strategic policies of international development. Goldman (2005) argues that this is the case because organizations like the World Bank have transformed themselves into powerful forces with the intent of advancing neoliberal global social policy. Critics of the World Bank fault, among other things, the failure of the Bank to distribute resources equitably so that women and others previously underrepresented on the global development stage have access to the Bank's resources. Gender-based and feminist critiques of economic development policy emanate from feminist economic theories which critique free markets (Strassman 1993), socialism (Folbre 1993), and public/private connections (Jennings 1993). By deconstructing economics (Ferber and Nelson 1993a, 1993b; Williams 1993), questioning classical economic assumptions (England 1993), taking into account women's experience (Solow 1993), and asking "economics for whom?" (Longino 1993), mainstream economics is potentially being reshaped by feminist theories (Blank 1993).

The period ushered in by the United Nations Women's Decade in 1976 saw greater appreciation of the connections between women's subordination in the domestic sphere, including women's childbearing, caring, and other domestic roles, and women's inequality in the broader society. While the United Nations

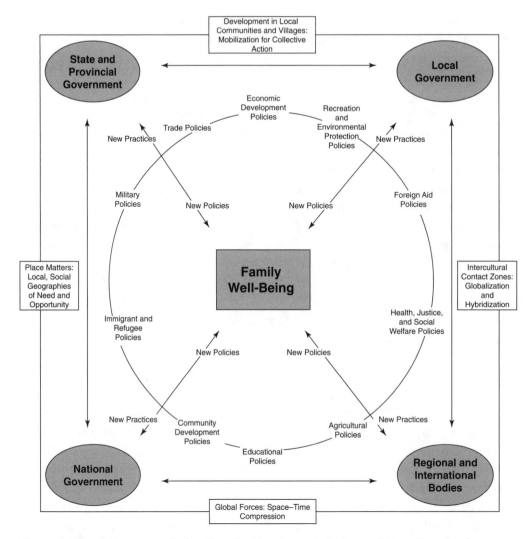

Figure 6.1 A Framework for Family-Centered Policies and Practices in the Global Age.

Source: Lawson 2001a. Adapted with permission from K. Briar-Lawson, H. A. Lawson, and C. B. Hennon, *Family-Centered Policies and Practices: International Implications* (New York: Columbia University Press, 2001). Figure 6.1 processed by Martin C. Doyle.

(1997) Research Institute for Social Development has called for a "more gender equitable macroeconomic agenda," as suggested in Chapter 2, development theory views Third World women as reproducers of human capital. From this perspective, population control is critical not only to modernization through demographic transition, but also to subsequent economic development and the eventual reduction of poverty.

In fact, conformity with World Bank strictures on population control has often been a condition for a country receiving loans from the International Monetary Fund. By the 1980s, structural adjustment policies (SAPs) directed by the World Bank (working closely with the United Nations) had as their goal prescriptive population control as a key element in broader development. At the same time, SAPs became associated with cuts in countries' spending on social services and subsidies, to the effect that women are forced to bear increasing responsibilities for health-care of their family members. Meanwhile, families are being required to assume more of the direct health costs for immunizations and preventive care, as well as prenatal care and education (Purewal 2001).

Some of the latent dysfunctions wrought by such SAPs have been found to include reduced time in lactation and, consequently, shorter intervals between births. Other consequences relevant to the family include increased morbidity and greater transmission of infectious diseases, and increased infant and child mortality. These changes result in greater strain on the household productive capacities of women, who bear disproportionate responsibility of care of family members (Afshar and Dennis 1992; Purewal 2001; Sparr 1994; Stewart 1991).

Some organizations have mounted efforts to draw attention to the deleterious effects of such policy strategies as shifts away from food subsidies and basic preventative and curative healthcare and toward the privatization of healthcare and the influence of transnational corporations in health-related issues. In other words, women too often serve as the "safety net" for decline in development policy support for social welfare programs (Purewal 2001:105), thereby limiting women's ability to care for their families, as well as to achieve literacy and higher education and to derive income from outside the family.

Purewal (2001) is critical of the emphasis on fertility "disincentives" (e.g., mass sterilization programs, denying food ration cards) in places such as India. She argues that these tactics misrepresent the sources of population growth (in-migration) and permit the exploitation of Third World markets by transnational corporations. She concludes her critique of World Bank and other international initiatives aimed at population control by noting the official World Bank position:

> Fertility decline requires that issues of gender equity, poverty, and wealth distribution be seriously addressed. . . . the World Bank has taken the position that "it is possible for fertility to decline . . . without much change in those social, economic, and health variables generally believed to be crucial preconditions for demographic change" (World Bank 1992, as quoted in Purewal 2001:111).

Purewal, Rowbotham (1992), and others charge that SAPs too often represent both a misconceived notion of women's place in development and, in terms of human rights, "the denial of reproductive rights by development and population policies" (Purewal 2001:97). These critics often favor a gender and development approach, which emphasizes women's roles in economic production (and income generation) originating not only from their part in the labor force, but also in productive activities that maintain the domestic front (Purewal 2001). Such an approach may be more consistent with an acknowledgement of the intersections between family rights and human rights.

Family Rights as Human Rights

The United Nations (2005b) *Millennium Declaration*, adopted in 2000, entrusts member nations to engage in global partnership to address these basic human rights:

- Eradicate extreme poverty and hunger.
- Achieve universal primary education.
- Promote gender equality and empower women.
- Reduce child mortality.
- Improve maternal health.
- Combat HIV/AIDS, malaria, and other diseases.
- Ensure environmental sustainability.
- Develop a global partnership for development.

But globalization makes citizenship and civic entitlements contested terrain. Land (2004) offers a cogent analysis of the changing definitions of citizenship in law and practice, particularly as they apply to women and children, which, by extension, apply to families as well. For example, beginning in 1993, the Women's Human Rights Program of Minnesota Advocates for Human Rights (2006) has joined with organizations in the Commonwealth of Independent States, Central and Eastern Europe, Haiti, Mexico, and Nepal to document violations of women's rights in areas including workplace discrimination and sexual harassment, domestic violence and rape, and sex trafficking. The Women's Program has a particular interest in education and rights and abuses of immigrant and refugee women. Each of these areas impacts not only women and girls, but their families as well.

Closely related, the *United Nations Bill of Rights for Children* embodies ideals that affirm:

- order and regulation in family life,
- protection of basic human rights, and
- human dignity in the lives of families [and their members] so they can grow and live productive and rewarding lives. (Roopnarine and Gielen 2005:11).

But children's rights have usually been placed in the context of social beliefs about children's capacities and their place in the family and society. By the end of the nineteenth century, patriarchal authority over children was giving way to legislation to protect children, even to the point that in England, by 1889, cruelty and neglect of a child had become a criminal offense. Likewise, by the middle of the nineteenth century, legislative bodies had begun to establish minimal age for employment laws, as well as laws regarding ages for compulsory education. By the early twentieth century, children in France, Germany, and Great Britain gained legal entitlement to school meals and medical inspections. The first attempt to codify these and other rights for children occurred in 1924 when the League of Nations endorsed *Codifying Children's Rights*, although Land makes clear that this document specified what nations *should* do for children, not any rights to which children could lay claim.

By 1959, the United Nations adopted the *Declaration on the Rights of the Child*, which included statements concerning children's civil and political rights, but only with regard to the right to a home and a nationality at birth. The United Nations *Convention on the Rights of the Child*, adopted in 1989 and binding on those ratifying nations, spoke not only to children's need for "care, protection, and adequate provision" (Land 2004:60), but also for participation. Today, the United Nations Committee on the Rights of the Child reviews each member nation's progress on children's rights each five years. By the year 2000, all member nations had ratified the *Convention*, except two: Somalia and the United States. The unwillingness of American politicians to join the rest of the civilized world in affirming basic human rights of all children is reprehensible, all the more so because of the "profamily" stance so many American public officials adopt.

The standards embodied in the *Convention*, which apply to all persons under 18 years of age, are guided by general principles of nondiscrimination, best interests of the child, right to life, survival, and development, and respect for the views of the child. Articles establish specific civil rights and freedoms, including the right to name and nationality at birth, preservation of identity, access to information, freedom of thought, conscience, and religion; freedom of expression, association, and peaceful assembly; and freedom from violence, abuse, neglect, torture, or cruel and inhuman treatment. Other articles specify children's rights to basic health and welfare; education, play, leisure, and cultural activities, with special consideration for children with special needs and those in emergency situations such as refugee or war conditions. The *Convention* also specifically denotes children's rights regarding family, including parental responsibilities, rights of children separated from their parents and deprived of family, and adoption procedures, including rights to contact and reunification. Regarding children's right to be free from physical punishment, parental rights to use corporal punishment with their children vary across nations. However, physical punishment of children is now illegal in at least nine European countries (Land 2004).

From 1951, the *European Convention on Human Rights*, through Articles 8 and 12, grants every European the right to privacy in family life and home and the right to marry (Land 2004). Clearly, international and transnational precedent—or at least inclination—exists to establish globally applicable policies regarding families and their members. In 1995, Euronet: The European Children's Network, a coalition of networks and organizations, formed to campaign for the interests of children and aiming toward "building a Europe with and for children" (Euronet 1997:1). Euronet's organizers were specifically concerned that issues such as free movement of children through the new European Union and the information revolution—both global concerns as I have shown—were being inadequately addressed during European Union policy discussions. A small body of research is growing on the global plight of children's education and labor needs, their disadvantaged status as street children and child soldiers, and the particular problems as refugees and child slaves. (See Ansell 2005.)

Thus, the rights of children, families, and humanity are inextricably bound. And, given the rate at which GLBT families are being formed, made visible, and becoming politically active on national and transnational stages, the rights of those families and their members must be next on not only national, but also global political agendas. In a treatise on global justice, Mandle (2006) defines global justice in terms of respect for basic human rights which should guide policy concerning a wide range of issues domestically, as well as globally. As Berger and Berger (1983) argue, globalization changes the role of the family with respect to the state. With globalization, the prevalence of transnational economic, political, and other social forces increases, often at the expense of national autonomy. With the rise of global interests, the family no longer serves as the primary agent mediating between private and public life. At the same time, families and their members are forced to become more self-reliant (Beck and Beck-Gernsheim 2002).

State resistance of globalization can have exacting effects impinging on family dynamics. For example, before the fall of the Soviet Union, with its state-controlled economy, a state decision was made not to import expensive foreign contraceptives or to develop facilities to manufacture modern contraceptives. According to a Soviet state demographer, in 1988 the number of abortions (6,500,000) exceeded the number of live births (Segal 2003).

The national politics of abortion is another such case. Beginning in the late 1960s in Britain and with the U.S. Supreme Court decision in Roe v. Wade in 1973, laws guiding access to abortion trended toward liberalization (Francome 2004). However, Smyth's (2005) analysis of Ireland reveals the extent to which globalization serves as a prism through which to view antiabortion legislation. Smyth presents antiabortion legislation as affirmation of Irish ideals of the centrality of family for women, but also as resistance to laws that would move Irish practice closer to that of England, and rejection of liberal (American) discourse on individual privacy. Using qualitative analysis of newspaper accounts and parliamentary proceedings, Smyth reveals abortion law as a meaningful symbol of Irish Catholic national—even glocal—culture and identity.

Thus, the futures of families in global societies are affected by other transnational movements and, in particular, by movements to advance the cause of women's rights throughout the world. For example, at the 9th Interdisciplinary Congress on Women, held in Seoul, South Korea, June 19–24, 2005, Esther Nganling Chow and others brought together feminist scholarship that Chow (as cited in Lorber 2005:5) described as "a prism through which we envision a transnational, transethnic, translingual, and cross-cultural kind of feminism in both thinking and doing, in both scholarship and practices that go beyond the limitation of one country." While English and Western references still predominate, such conferences can stimulate informed agenda for social policies and social action around family issues as well. Such convergence can reveal the extent to which issues previously seen as national or regional become global (Lorber 2005).

Organizations like the International Women's Rights Action Watch (IWRAW 2004:1) and affiliated bodies of the United Nations have an ongoing charge to monitor and report "implementation of women's human rights under the International Covenant on Economic, Social, and Cultural Rights" (a Committee of the United Nations). The IWRAW operates in accordance with six other international rights treaties articulated in the United Nations' Universal Declaration of Human Rights, including treaties dealing with the rights of children and with racial discrimination. The Commission on the Elimination of Discrimination Against Women (CEDAW) (United Nations 1999a), adopted in 1979, deals with many of the issues addressed in *Global Families*, including equality in marriage and family law (Article 16), employment (Article 11), exploitation (Article 5), and development (Article 3).

Across the globe, politicians of every persuasion complete for claim to be best representing the interests of families. *Familialism* refers to the promotion of pro-family ideas and political initiatives ostensibly intended to strengthen families. (Offering couples who complete a course in premarriage counseling a discount on their marriage license is an example of familistic legislation.) Too often familialism is used to provoke opposition to human rights in areas such as access to contraception, abortion, and other health concerns, as well as civil rights for gay, lesbian, and transgender folk and their families, and still, across the world, the rights of girls and women. Further, policies cited in defense of the family are not always only or even primarily about family issues. Instead, family "reforms" can serve to advance any number of other agenda, including colonial rule (Haney and Pollard 2004).

Such familialism is, in part at least, ideological metaphor. After all, if the reality of "family" is so contested, what does it mean to be "profamily?" Karraker and Grochowski (2006:405) favor shifting the conversation from a rhetoric of "family values" to one of "valuing families."

> Families do not merely survive but thrive when they have adequate economic resources, nutrient dense nutrition, access to regular physical activity, healthful environments, good health (including mental health) care, decent housing, freedom from violence of all kinds, and family-friendly workplaces. Furthermore, every family needs a network of family, kin, and friends, along with neighborhoods, community, and schools, to foster a sense of respect and a connection among families and their members. In short, families thrive when the whole society has viable investments in every family.

The Universal Declaration of Human Rights, adopted by the General Assembly of the United Nations in 1948 proclaims in Article 16:

1. Men and women of full age, without any limitation due to race, nationality or religion, have the right to marry and to found a family. They are entitled to equal rights as to marriage, during marriage and at its dissolution.
2. Marriage shall be entered into only with the free and full consent of the intending spouses.
3. The family is the natural and fundamental group unit of society and is entitled to protection by society and the State. (United Nations 1948)

Further, in Article 25, the Declaration provides:

1. Everyone has the right to a standard of living adequate for the health and well-being of himself and of his family, including food, clothing, housing, and medical care and necessary social services, and the right to security in the event of unemployment, sickness, disability, widowhood, and old age or other lack of livelihood in circumstances beyond his control.
2. Motherhood and childhood are entitled to special care and assistance. All children, whether born in or out of wedlock, shall enjoy the same social protection. (United Nations 1948)

In light of such lofty visions, what then, is the prognosis for family in a global society? In a world in which national borders are increasingly contested on political, economic, cultural, and other stages, are we moving toward a postfamily global society or does family remain a cornerstone for societies, regardless of their position in the global milieu?

Conclusions: A Postfamily Global Society?

In *Global Families*, I have demonstrated how globalization places families at substantial risk. At the same time, the social processes of globalization—demographic transitions, transnational employment, worldwide culture shifts, as well as international violence—ensure that family structures will be more diverse and family relationships will be more flexible, even as they become less localized. Clans and other kin groups will continue to have declining influence, as seen in fewer kin marriages and freer mate selection, greater sexual freedom, wider recognition of women's rights in marriage initiation and family decision-making, and the extension of children's rights. This leads some to question: What, if anything, will bind people together into intimate, caring bonds in such postmodern, global societies?

Even though globalization in this new world order may bring benefits to families, globalization also places families, their members, and consequently the greater society at significant risk. People can no longer depend on sets of assumptions, beliefs, and values that traditionally gave certainty and predictability to life and solidarity to social relationships. Meanwhile, the individual is faced with a complicated set of societal controls and constraints in the form of the educational system, the labor market, and other institutional forces. In essence, personal lives are constructed in a risky, unpredictable social environment void of past supports such as kin networks, yet constrained by powerful social forces (Beck and Beck-Gernsheim 2002). Beck and Beck-Gernsheim argue that the same trend toward individualization that characterizes societies also characterizes family relationships. In other words, they see the family shifting from what they call "a community of need" to an elective association, that is, a "postfamilial family."

Beck and Beck-Gernsheim cite the situation of women as it has been evolving from the end of the nineteenth century and accelerating beginning in the last half of the twentieth century with changes in women's education, occupation, legal, and life cycle situations. As women can no longer depend on a husband (or children) to support them later in life, they must make individual choices and plans for their security and lives separate from the family. They say that the interests represented in the family can no longer be viewed as homogeneous and, although individual men and women are still linked to the family, the gendered nature of expectations and interests, burdens and opportunities means that individual women (and men) must create lives of their own. In such postfamilial families, the adults and the children spend increasing amounts of time outside the home abode, in employment, education, leisure, and entertainment.

As I have documented in previous chapters, such social trends are exacerbated by globalization. Edgar (2004:7) agrees that the individualization occurring worldwide has resulted in situations in which "traditional forms of authority have doubtless weakened, and individuals increasingly have to negotiate their own moral stance, plus their relationships and their personal work and family biographies." Edgar affirms that individuals and families are differentially capable of managing the risks associated with global restructuring. Family empowerment is, he argues, limited by such factors as poverty, religion, and persecution.

But Edgar (2004) is among those who reject such extreme postmodernist positions on the family in a global world. In an article aptly titled "Families as the Crucible of Competence in a Changing Social Ecology," Edgar (1999) described in apt terms the family's continued centrality as the social location through which both human capital and social capital are acquired. The family remains the pivotal location for acquisition of personal development as the social network in which the child (and other family members) is embedded, learns skills, and has access to economic and other social resources within the community and beyond, in the national social context. Further, Edgar argues, decisions regarding such family processes as mate selection (including the decision to remain single), parenting, residence, and employment are embedded in systems of resources and negotiations in which the family is a key mediator.

In contrast to this rhetoric, and to the debate on what they call the "antisocial family," Barrett and McIntosh (1991) remind us that *family*, wherever and however it is constructed, has important appeal on several levels involving emotional security for its members. Barrett and McIntosh see the family as, first "offering a range of emotional and experiential satisfactions not available elsewhere" (p. 21). While kin by ascription lacks choice and implies constraint, such relations provide an opportunity for a level of psychic support unavailable elsewhere in society. Besides, they contend, there can be pleasure in that which is simply familiar. The appeal of the family also resides in its location as the optimal and rewarding place for bearing and rearing children. Barrett and McIntosh argue that a married couple or (I add) a constellation of two or more committed adults, whether married or not, can most reliably provide material and social psychological support for the youngest members of society. That some families may fail to do so is that much greater the tragedy of postmodern life.

While explicating the crisis facing the comfortable family form of romantic myth, Barrett and McIntosh remind us that any currently dominant model of family is time- and culture-bound. That very romantic myth, they argue, is in fact a family form articulated among late nineteenth-century bourgeoisie in Western Europe. To the extent that we hold such an image of the family as the salvation for our social and personal problems, the family as an institution is doomed.

Can the family not be seen as the "maker of the future," as Boulding (1983) contended? In an article of that title, Boulding wrote of the agency of families who

Hall Family at Farmer's Market by Mark E. Jensen
Mark E. Jensen/Minnesota Historical Society

seek to maximize the resources available to their children and other family members in any community. As Robert Putnam argued in *Bowling Alone* (2001), the better a family's connections in the community, the better a family's life chances. In a civil society, parents, grandparents, and other family members build social assets through such actions as volunteering and political activity. Such civic engagement builds family assets, but also benefits the common good in a civil society. And Edgar (2004:14) reminds us:

The family is the filter through which issues such as border protection, terrorism, public transport, and education are interpreted. Moreover public interest in issues changes as cohorts change. . . . [But] [k]inship is still more important than citizenship, and for most people citizenship has practical meaning [only] through kinship.

In *Familiaris Consortio*, a statement on the role of the Christian family in today's world, the late Pope John Paul II (1981:74) said:

[The family now finds its role] extended in a completely new way: It now also involves cooperating for a new international order, since it is only in worldwide solidarity that the enormous and dramatic issues of world justice, the freedom of peoples, and the peace of humanity can be dealt with and solved.

Hutton and Giddens (2001) see globalization as testing and complicating families in ways much like the Industrial Revolution and urbanization eroded extended family ties. However, in similar ways, globalization also stretches and tests patriarchal control of family members. Globalization's new culture systems, such as the Internet and inexpensive travel back and forth across great distances, likewise will tax family intimacy and authority.

In May 2000, I was introduced to a young man, about age 14, waiting on the steps of the main reception building at Città dei Ragazzi. Founded in 1944 by the late Monsignor John Patrick Caroll-Abbing, Città dei Ragazzi (Boys', and later Girls', Towns) remains a refuge and a home for children and youth who find themselves alone on the streets of Rome, Italy. Those who find their way to one of the pastoral communities on the outskirts of Rome have always been "unaccompanied minors"—orphaned, homeless, or displaced. However, rather than being separated from their families as armies swept through Italy during war, the citizens of Boys and Girls Towns are today more likely to have illegally fled to Italy from countries across Eastern Europe, Africa, Asia, and the Middle East (Boys' Towns of Italy, Inc. 2005). In fact, today over half the children and youth served by Boys and Girls Towns are not Catholic, or even Christian, but Muslim (Moffett 2000). The young man to whom I was introduced wore an expression of anxious anticipation. Originally from Eastern Europe, he had been separated from his family for over a year. However, an uncle had been located and, on that afternoon, they would be reunited. Nothing else mattered.

Although increasingly diverse, contested, and often at risk, the family continues to have widespread normative acceptance as a core structure of society. Even among members of societies in which marriage is postponed, deferred, or, as in the case of gays and lesbians, not permitted, new family forms are emerging to ensure that adults and children across the lifespan are enmeshed in ongoing, cooperative, intimate systems, be they of friendship groups, reconstituted families, or even the traditional nuclear, conjugal couple with children. I have faith that individuals, society, and humanity can flourish in the presence of authentic, intimate bonds, even when those bonds are among global families.

Summary

In this final chapter, I have offered an examination of the family in an increasingly global society in the second decade beyond the United Nations' Year of the Family. Social policies which fall short on gender sensitivity have also fallen short of meaningful, assessable social change in the quality of life for families and their members. Meaningful social change is not only inextricably bound to issues of gender, but also to social action by organizations that span supranational, national, and even local and network to share resources. The greatest urgency for family impact-based social policy at a global level is in the areas of HIV/AIDS, immigration, transnational employment, violence against women and children, and global media and consumption.

Significant improvements in the quality of life for women and their families have been documented across institutional areas and across a wide range of countries, but women and their daughters remain the poorest on the planet. Shamefully, the United States falls toward the bottom of some indexes of family policy. Social development can be viewed through a variety of perspectives (e.g., women in development, gender and development), but, again, real enhancement of the lives of families depends on understanding how gender reveals the intersections among micro- and macrosocial forces.

The argument follows that family rights are human rights, as illustrated by the cases of the politics of human reproduction and the politics of abortion in particular. Transnational movements for the rights of families and their members include the work of organizations like the International Women's Rights Action Watch (IWRAW), the United Nations Commission on the Elimination of Discrimination Against Women (CEDAW), and the other declarations of the United Nations dealing with children and families.

Finally, while some scholars continue to emphasize the extent to which globalization is propelling families toward greater disparities between the "haves" and the "have nots," others emphasize that families remain critical and persistent keystones to society and members' well-being. In conclusion, although globalization offers a wide range of serious challenges to family structures, functions, and interactions, the evolving family remains a critical, persistent keystone to societal adjustment and individual intimacy and success.

The Global Human Rights of Families
By Marsha A. Freeman, Ph.D., J.D.

All human beings are born into a family. Families may have two members or two hundred. They may or may not receive the protection by their government and their community to which they are entitled according to the universal standards of the Universal Declaration of Human Rights. They may or may not provide adequate nurture and material support to bring children to productive adulthood. They may sacrifice everything to promote the welfare of individual family members whose accomplishments carry honor and wealth, and they may murder members in the name of family honor. Intact or broken, healthy or abusive, honored or rejected, the family is a primary element of human identity.

Late twentieth-century global developments have placed enormous pressure on families and communities. Pressure on communities and families is not unique in history, but this era's pressures are unique in the level of documentation and analysis focused on them and the resources available to deal with them if political will exists to do so. But governments and other institutions have risen to the occasion inconsistently and with varied results, frequently leaving families and their individual members less well off and less cohesive than they could be, essentially less protected than the plain language of the Universal Declaration of Human Rights indicates is their entitlement.

The United Nations declared the International Year of the Family (IYF) in 1994. Considerable rhetoric and some useful research and policy recommendations inevitably result from such United Nations declarations and events. Ten years later, in an IYF anniversary event, close examination of family trends in all regions of the world indicated that although families had changed in some significant ways, the fundamental, global issues that impeded their general health and the ability of individual family members to develop to their full potential remained largely unaddressed.

Ten years is not a long time in which to solve vast, fundamental problems, such as entrenched poverty, the negative impact of globalization on local livelihoods, the HIV/AIDS global epidemic, and patriarchal attitudes. But it is enough time to develop and start to implement intelligent responses. Some progress has in fact occurred, such as programs to lower the rate of new HIV/AIDS cases and to provide cheap and effective treatment, but only in a few countries. In many places, school enrollment rates, particularly for girls, are up, attributable to a significant push by donor countries and international agencies. The quality of that education and the real achievement levels, however, are not indicated by the general statistics. And achievement of the Millennium Development Goals, adopted by the United Nations in 2000 as a set of reachable targets to reduce poverty, improve health, and increase gender equality by 2015, is well behind schedule as of 2007.

Policy discussions relating to the family and development generally lack one element that is critical to consistent and sustainable improvement in their well-being: human rights. Both families and individuals within them have a right to protection by the state and by their community. Full realization of human rights would mean that governments and communities pay attention to the distribution of resources, the exercise of freedoms, and the balance of power inside and outside the family unit. To date, no government has a stellar record as to all of these issues; even the states with excellent social welfare and external human rights records have much to answer for with respect to their minority populations, disabled citizens, gender equality, and income distribution.

In short, although everyone celebrates the family, few take care of it.

What Is a Family? And Why Does It Matter?

One of the impediments to good family policy is an imperfect understanding and acceptance of the varied forms of family. Traditionally, "family" refers to persons who are related by blood, marriage, or adoption. This very broad definition can encompass the family formations that are recognized throughout the world: nuclear (two married parents and their children), extended (multiple generations, multiple wives, siblings, cousins of all degrees), and clan (extended families related to each other). In recent decades, the definition has been challenged to expand, with an increase in one-parent families, unmarried heterosexual partnerships, and, most recently, acknowledged same-sex partnerships.

The distinction between family and household is frequently, and unfortunately, blurred in policy discussions. Households may include persons who are not related, but who are considered *de facto* family for purposes of child and elder care and resource sharing. Extended families may share resources and child and elder care, but not be in the same household. Blood and marital relations may be legally unrecognized, as in countries in which women cannot transmit their citizenship to children or spouses, or in which the concept of illegitimacy is preserved by statute or by legally recognized custom. Development economics usually focuses on households rather than on families, discounting cross-household extended family dynamics that have a major impact on income and resource allocations. And development economists have only recently begun to seriously examine intrafamily status and power issues that affect individual and, ultimately, family well-being.

Family or household definitions govern the allocation of public resources and the recognition of rights. In some countries, children of local mothers and foreign fathers, who therefore are deemed not to be citizens, do not have a right to education or health care. "Illegitimate" children may be denied property use or inheritance. In countries in which nuclear families are the norm, grandparents may lose access to the grandchildren in a divorce. In extended-family settings in which children belong to the paternal line, mothers may lose access if they are forced to leave a marriage because of abuse or dowry issues. Children of a same-sex unmarried couple may be denied access to one of the adults in a separation if the nonparent has not legally adopted the child. State support for an elder may be denied if children have stepped in to help financially. Conversely, state support for elders may not exist at all in countries in which family support of elders has always been the norm, even where the extended family is shrinking because of employment or conflict-based migration and decreasing fertility rates. Governments therefore face an enormous challenge to provide for resource allocation and rights recognition on the basis of actual household and family organization, rather than on artificially and traditionally defined household or family models. Few have met all the challenges satisfactorily.

Economic and Social Organization

Families provide social and psychological space for the nurturing of children. They also function as an economic unit, frequently with prescribed economic roles; a political unit, from the family dynasties in democracies to the clan- or ethnicity-based governance of many less developed countries; and a social unit, enforcing norms of behavior and alliance on both micro- and macrolevels. At its best, a family provides positive support to its members, encouraging expression of ideas and freedom to develop personal potential. At its worst, a family oppresses its individual members in the name of cultural identity and family cohesion—an excuse for abuse—and conditions social and material support on submission to that abuse.

Members of very poor families, of course, rarely have the choices of personal development and escape from abuse, even with the best of caring relationships. Children are kept home from school to do household or farm chores, forced to work from a very young age, and may be sold into labor or prostitution in another town or across a border. Valuing children for their own potential, no matter how much parents may wish to do so, is an unaffordable luxury. Abused women cannot escape because they have no way to support themselves and their children outside the family structure. Class exploitation is common; a family's value to the larger society may be only as cheap labor. Families may be broken up by the necessity of migrating to work, leaving children in the care of a single parent or of other family members. Many women left to care for families when men migrate for work have few skills and no individual legal capacity to handle finances or property or to make decisions about the children. When migrant parents return, the family relationships are upended again, as children and other relatives will have evolved in maturity and roles while the workers are away.

Families in less difficult circumstances may also be stressed by conditions of work, as where childcare is not supported by the state and family leave policies are narrow. Employment discrimination makes life difficult for many people; even where legal protection is clear, *de facto* discrimination remains, with a major impact on female workers and families whose members are disabled or are racial, ethnic, or religious minorities.

A human rights approach to policy on family income security and access to basic needs would go much farther than the usual rhetoric to truly protect families. Protection of workers from arbitrary treatment and harmful working conditions, a living wage, a safety net for workers in the informal economy, universal primary health care and education, and financial support for persons who cannot work because of age or disability are fundamental human rights for which all governments should provide. Equal access to these basic social and economic goods is critical to family well-being and is required under international law and many national laws. International law, as stated in the International Covenant on Economic, Social and Cultural Rights, requires rich countries to assist poor countries in providing for these basic needs. However, governments are far from guaranteeing these rights universally, and even where rights exist in law and policy, implementation frequently falls short. Consider, for example, the difference between law and reality in the United States with respect to K–12 education, worker rights, and discrimination.

A family is expected to provide for its members' social as well as economic support. In many cultures, individuals are identified first and foremost by their family name and history. Even where family identity is not central, individuals frequently use family as a significant marker for placing themselves and others in a social space. Certainly a child's socialization, which starts with family roles and expectations, is critical to his or her success as an individual and as a member of the larger society. Marriage, educational opportunity, and employment status are deeply affected in all cultures by family ties and identity.

Expanding on the role of families as social space, families and clans have enormous importance as political entities in a number of countries. The headlines tell us that in Iraq, Afghanistan, and Somalia, where institutions are in disarray or have failed, clans are the key political authority. In the Occupied Territories in 2007, politically opposed members of a powerful clan stated that they would settle Fatah–Hamas issues among themselves, within the clan, since the public authorities were so inept. In more well-organized states, clans and families may have a particular political heritage and community standing, such that individuals in public life are understood to represent their background as much as they stand for individual positions.

Globalization certainly has had an impact on family size, identity, and ability to provide adequately for family members. Economic migration, pressures on local markets, and shifts in donor priorities have made for physical dislocation and disappointed expectations. But globalization also has brought more information to more people, resulting in lower fertility and challenges to oppressive customs such as forced marriage and female genital mutilation, as well as opportunities for women and men to escape the economic dead end of poor villages. People with new information and new opportunities will challenge roles and customs that seem to keep their lives static or disadvantaged—they will challenge the social space. The social space can expand, or it can resist and either explode or fossilize. Governments and citizens must consider using the energy and opportunities of a changing world to provide greater opportunities for family members and to reexamine oppressive family constructs that keep individuals from making choices to develop their own potential, which ultimately contributes to the well-being of the entire family.

Human Rights and the Family

The family is the natural and fundamental group unit of society and is entitled to protection by society and the State (Universal Declaration of Human Rights, Article 16.3).

. . . recognition of the inherent dignity and of the equal and inalienable rights of all members of the human family is the foundation of freedom, justice and peace in the world (Universal Declaration of Human Rights, preamble).

Families and societies cannot be sustainably successful unless they are built on an ethical infrastructure that accounts for the well-being of all their members. The Universal Declaration of Human Rights (UDHR), adopted in 1948 by the member states of the United Nations, outlines that infrastructure. In the nearly 60 years since its adoption, the UDHR and the human rights treaties that derive from its language have been universally accepted, although not totally without reservation, as the standard to which all governments must adhere in developing domestic and, to a certain extent, foreign policy. The failure of individual governments and societies to live up to that standard entirely does not derogate from the standards themselves, but indicates the limitations of human nature and political will. Without the standard of the UDHR and the processes of human rights monitoring, governments would be free to deal arbitrarily and cruelly with their citizens and to undermine their material welfare, without any accountability to their citizenry or to the global community. Although a country cannot be put in jail, a country can be made to change by the sheer force of international public opinion coupled with advocacy by domestic constituencies empowered by knowing their rights.

Even though corruption, torture, wealth inequality, discrimination, lack of free expression, and sheer incompetence undermine the enjoyment of human rights in many countries, the international trend since the inception of the UDHR has been toward increased openness and some level of government accountability. Frequently, this change is the result of activism by a relatively small number of people who risk their safety and their lives to press for change. Even where change advocacy does not carry a risk of physical harm, their actions frequently places advocates at risk of ostracism and social or economic damage. Taking on human rights issues that directly affect the family and its internal dynamic can be particularly risky because they strike at the heart of identity and intimate power relations.

As the basic unit of society, the family also can be the basic site of oppression. Violence against family members, usually the women and the children and sometimes the elders, is globally endemic. Women experience denial of opportunities for education, employment, healthcare and healthy spacing of children, property rights, adequate nutrition, and freedom of expression inside the household and in public. Children are beaten, sold into slavery, denied education, sexually exploited by teachers and other adults in their personal circle, and instructed to remain silent at all costs and never to argue with an adult. The scale of these issues is indicated by the adoption of international human rights treaties to deal specifically with discrimination against women (1979) and with the rights of children (1989), when it became clear that their human rights were not adequately articulated and protected under the general treaties, the International Covenant on Civil and Political Rights and the International Covenant on Economic, Social and Cultural Rights.

Dealing with the rights of women and of children is particularly difficult because culture is frequently invoked as an excuse for denial of their rights. Physical and economic oppression of women and the beating of children are defended as necessary for culturally appropriate socialization. The response to that excuse—and it is not a defense, it is merely an excuse—is that as a matter of fundamental human rights, stated in the Convention on the Elimination of All Forms of Discrimination against Women (Article 5), governments are under an obligation to eliminate cultural customs and stereotypes that support inequality and discrimination. Essentially, there is no cultural defense for the violation of human rights.

Family members cannot possibly contribute fully to their own family's well-being or to the well-being of their community if they are kept enslaved by ignorance, individual poverty, and violence. A family, community, or national regime that is organized on the basis of oppression robs itself, as tremendous political and personal energy and material resources go into maintaining power and privilege, while individuals are prevented from making their full economic and intellectual contribution to society.

Conclusion

Families of all descriptions and sizes are the fundamental social, economic, and political units in which individuals are shaped and on which societies are built. They are universal and indispensable. Not only are governments obligated to protect families, doing so is in their interest. The definition of family for policy and legal purposes should be as expansive as it needs to be to recognize individuals' commitments to care for each other, nurture children, and build community.

Family protection requires mobilization of resources to provide both for basic needs, such as primary education, primary health, food security, and housing, and for opportunities for intellectual and physical growth. Countries with more resources have a greater responsibility in this respect. Rich countries have a global responsibility to assist poor countries in establishing sufficient family support to help their families develop economically and socially. And all countries involved in the processes of globalization, which means *all countries*, have a responsibility to deal positively with the impact of global markets and cultural change on their families.

Healthy families are the basis of healthy societies that can function well economically and politically. If internal exploitation and violence in the family are accepted as the norm, the larger culture will be exploitive and, in some way, violent, with a forced cohesion that can be quite fragile. Protecting the family means protecting the individuals within it, and thereby protecting all of society throughout the globe.

Marsha A. Freeman, Ph.D., J.D., is Senior Fellow, Law School Institutes, University of Minnesota, Minneapolis, and Director of the International Women's Rights Action Watch at the University of Minnesota Human Rights Center.

Critical Thinking Questions:

1. Thinking globally, what are the most critical issues facing families today?

2. In what ways has world development policy compromised family well-being? What is the potential of gender-sensitive policies to improve family well-being?

3. Is globalization leading the world toward a "postfamily" condition? Why or why not?

4. In the essay at the end of this chapter, Marsha Freeman, Director of International Women's Rights Action Watch at the University of Minnesota Human Rights Center, argues, "Not only are governments obligated to protect families, it is in their interest to do so." Based on what you have learned about *global families*, what should governments and supranational bodies do to protect families? Why is doing so in the best interests of society?

REFERENCES

Abdi, C. M. 2006. *Diasporic Lives and Threatened Identities: Gender Struggles of Somalis in America*. Ph.D. dissertation, Department of Sociology, University of Sussex, Brighton, UK.

———. 2007. "Convergence of Civil War and the Religious Right: Re-Imaging Somali Women." *Signs: Journal of Women in Culture and Society* 33(1): 183–207.

Abel, E. K. and M. K. Nelson. 1990. *Circles of Care: Work and Identity in Women's Lives*. New York: State University of New York Press.

Achebe, N. 2004. "The Road to Italy: Nigerian Sex Workers at Home and Abroad." *Journal of Women's History* 15(4):178–185.

Adam, B. D. 1995. *The Rise of a Gay and Lesbian Movement*. Rev. ed. New York: Twayne.

Adam, B. D., J. W. Duyvendak, and A. Krouwel. 1999a. *The Global Emergence of Gay and Lesbian Politics: National Imprints of a Worldwide Movement*. Philadelphia, PA: Temple University Press.

———. 1999b. "Introduction." Pp. 1–11 in *The Global Emergence of Gay and Lesbian Politics: National Imprints of a Worldwide Movement*, edited by B. D. Adam, J. W. Duyvendak, and A. Krouwel. Philadelphia, PA: Temple University Press.

Adams, B. N. 2004. "Families and Family Study in International Perspective." *Journal of Marriage and the Family* 66(5):1076–1088.

Adams, B. N. and J. Trost, eds. 2005. *Handbook of World Families*. 3rd ed. Thousand Oaks, CA: Sage.

Addams, J. 1910. *Twenty Years at Hull House*. New York: Macmillan.

d'Addio, A. C. and M. M. d'Ercole. 2005. *Trends and Determinants of Fertility Rates in OECD Countries: The Role of Policies*. Organization of Economic Cooperation and Development. Working Paper 27. Retrieved December 20, 2006 (http://www.oecd.org/dataoecd/7/33/353047511.pdf).

Adorno, T. 1991. *The Culture Industry: Selected Essays on Mass Culture*. Edited by J. M. Bernstein. London: Routledge.

Afshar, H. and C. Dennis. 1992. *Women and Adjustment Policies in the Third World*. New York: St. Martin's.

Aghajanian, A. and A. L. Moghadas. 1998. "Correlates and Consequences of Divorce in an Iranian City." *Journal of Divorce and Remarriage* 28(304): 53–71.

Al-Ali, N. 2002. "Loss of Status or New Opportunities? Gender Relations and Transnational Ties among Bosnia Refugees." Pp. 83–102 in *The Transnational Family: New European Frontiers and Global Networks*, edited by D. F. Bryceson and U. Vuorela. Oxford, UK: Berg.

Albrow, M. 1997. "The Impact of Globalization on Sociological Concepts: Community, Culture and Milieu." Pp. 20–36 in *Living the Global City: Globalization as Local Process*, edited by J. Eade. London: Routledge.

Allen, J. and D. Massey, eds. 1995. *Geographical Worlds*. Oxford, UK: Oxford University Press.

Allen, K. R. 1989. *Single Women/Family Ties: Life Histories of Older Women*. Newbury Park, CA: Sage.

Alvi, S., M. D. Schwartz, W. DeKeserdy, and J. Bachaus. 2002. "Victimization and Attitudes Toward Wife Abuse of Impoverished Minority Women." Presented at the annual meeting of the American Society of Criminology, November, Chicago.

Andall, J. 2004. "Acli-Colf and Immigration: Gender, Class, and Ethnicity." *Polis* 18(1): 77–106.

Anderson, B. 2000. *Doing the Dirty Work? The Global Politics of Domestic Labor*. London: Zed.

Anderson, B. and J. O'Connell Davidson. 2002. *Trafficking–A Demand Led Problem?* Stockholm: Save the Children.

Andrews, E. L. 2006. "Global Trends May Hinder Effort to Curb U.S. Inflation." *New*

York Times. Retrieved September 8, 2006 (http://www.nytimes.com).

Angrist, J. D. and J. H. Johnson, IV. 2000. "Effects of Work-Related Absences on Families: Evidence from the Gulf War." *Industrial and Labor Relations Review* 54(1): 41–58.

Ansell, N. 2005. *Children, Youth, and Development.* London, UK: Routledge.

Anthias, F. and G. Lazaridis. 2000. "Introduction: Women on the Move in Southern Europe." Pp. 1–13 in *Gender and Migration in Southern Europe: Women on the Move,* edited by F. Anthias and G. Lazaridis. Oxford, UK: Berg.

Appadurai, A. 1996. *Modernity at Large: Cultural Dimensions of Globalization.* Minneapolis: University of Minnesota Press.

Apple, R. 1987. *Mothers and Medicine: A Social History of Infant Feeding, 1890–1950.* Madison: University of Wisconsin Press.

Aries, P. 1960. *L'enfant et la Vie Familiale sous l'Ancien Regime.* Paris: Librairie Plon.

Askin, K. D. 2001. "Comfort Women—Shifting Shame and Stigma from Victims to Victimizers." *International Criminal Law Review* 1(1/2):5–32.

Assay, S. M. 2003. "Family Strengths in Postcommunist Transition: Romania and the Former East Germany." *Journal of Family and Consumer Science* 95(1): 26–32.

Australian Government. 2006a. "European Discovery and the Colonization of Australia." Retrieved December 10, 2006 (http://www.cultureandrecreation.gov.au/articles/australianhistory/).

———. 2006b. "Linking Thinking—Self-Directed Learning in the Digital Age." Retrieved December 14, 2006 (http://www.dest.gov.au/sectors/training_skills/publications_resources/summaries_brochures/ linking_thinking.htm).

Baber, K. M. and K. R. Allen. 1992. *Women and Families: Feminist Reconstructions.* New York: Guilford.

Baca, M. E. 2006. "Immigrant Children's Roles Open to Interpretation: Kids Acting as Translators Isn't New, but the Long-Term Impact for Them and Their Parents is Mixed at Best." *Minneapolis* (MN) *Star Tribune,* July 23, p. E1.

Bachrach, C. 2001. "Comment: The Puzzling Persistence of Postmodern Fertility Preferences." Pp. 332–338 in *Global Fertility Transition,* edited by R. A. Bulato and J. B. Casterline. New York: Population Council.

Bakan, A. and D. Stasiuli, eds. 1997. *Not One of the Family: Foreign Domestic Workers in Canada.* Toronto: University of Toronto Press.

Bales, K. 1999. *Disposable People: New Slavery in the Global Economy.* Berkeley: University of California Press.

Balfour, M. C., R. F. Evans, F. W. Notestein, and I. B. Taeuber. 1950. *Public Health and Demography in the Far East: Report of a Survey Trip, September 13–December 13, 1948.* New York: Rockefeller Foundation.

Barber, B. R. 1995. *Jihad vs. McWorld: Terrorism's Challenge to Democracy.* New York: Random House.

Barkawi, T. 2006. *Globalization and War.* Lanham, MA: Rowman and Littlefield.

Barker, D. K. and S. F. Feiner. 2004. *Liberating Economics: Feminist Perspectives on Families, Work, and Globalization.* Ann Arbor: University of Michigan Press.

Barot, R. 2002. "Religion, Migration and Wealth Creation in the Swaminarayan Movement." Pp. 197–213 in *The Transnational Family: New European Frontiers and Global Networks,* edited by D. F. Bryceson and U. Vuorela. Oxford, UK: Berg.

Barrett, M. and M. McIntosh. 1991. *The Anti-Social Family.* 2nd ed. London: Verso.

Baudrillard, J. 1988. *Jean Baudrillard: Selected Writings.* Stanford, CA: Stanford University Press.

———. 1989. *America.* London: Verso.

———. 1990. *Fatal Strategies.* New York: Semiotext(e).

Bauman, Z. 1992. *Intimations of Postmodernity.* London: Routledge.

———. 1998. *Globalization: The Human Consequences.* New York: Columbia University Press.

———. 2001. *The Individualized Society.* Cambridge, UK: Polity.

———. 2003. *Liquid Love: On the Frailty of Human Bonds.* Cambridge, UK: Blackwell.

———. 2004. *Wasted Lives: Modernity and Its Outcastes.* Cambridge, UK: Blackwell.

———. 2007. *Liquid Times: Living in an Age of Uncertainty.* Cambridge, UK: Polity.

BBC News. 2006. "Dutch Government Backs Burqa Ban." Retrieved November 17, 2006 (http://news.bbc.co.uk/2/hi/europe/6159046.stm).

Beck, U. 1992. *Risk Society: Towards a New Modernity*. Translated by M. Ritter. Newbury Park, CA: Sage.

———. 1998. *Democracy without Enemies*. Cambridge, UK: Polity.

———. 2000. *The Brave New World of Work*. Translated by P. Camiller. Cambridge, UK: Polity.

———. 2001. "Living Your Own Life in a Runaway World: Individualisation, Globalisation, and Politics." Pp. 164–174 in *Global Capitalism*, edited by W. Hutton and A. Giddens. New York: New Press.

Beck, U. and E. Beck-Gernsheim. 2002. *Individualization: Institutionalized Individualism and Its Social and Political Consequences*. Newbury Park, CA: Sage.

———. 2004. "Families in a Runaway World." Pp. 499–514 in *The Blackwell Companion to the Sociology of Families*, edited by J. Scott, J. K. Treas, and M. Richards. Cambridge, UK: Cambridge University Press.

Beck-Gernsheim, E. 2001. "Household-Migrant Women and Marriage-Migrant Women in a Globalizing World." Pp. 61–80 in *Women and Social Transformation*, edited by E. Beck-Gernsheim, J. Butler, and L. Puigvert. Oxford, UK: Berg.

Beck-Gernsheim, E., J. Butler, and L. Puigvert. Translated by J. Vaida. 2001. *Women and Social Transformation*. New York: Peter Lang.

Berger, P. and B. L. Berger. 1983. *The War Over the Family: Capturing the Middle Ground*. London, UK: Hutchinson.

Bergmann, M. S. and M. E. Jucovy, eds. 1982/1990. *Generations of the Holocaust*. New York: Columbia University Press.

Bernardotti, A., V. Capecchi, and P. Pinto. 1994. "L'Osservatorio delle Immigrazioni del Comune di Bologna: Un Servizio per chi Vuole Documentarsi e conoscere." *Osservatorio* 0(November): 2–3. As translated by and quoted in Orsini-Jones and Gattullo (2000).

Bhagwati, J. N. 2004. *In Defense of Globalization*. New York: Oxford University Press.

Billington, R., J. Hockey, and S. Strawbridge. 1998. *Exploring Self and Society*. Basingstoke, UK: Macmillan.

Bilsen, K. and H. de Witte. 2001. "Waarom Worden Individuen Actief Binnen een Extreem-Rechtse Organisatie? Integratie van de Beschikbare Literatuur in een Hypothetische Kader ter Verklaring van Extreem-Rechts Militantisme." *Tijdschrift voor Sociologie* 22(1):37–62.

Binnie, J. 2004. *The Globalization of Sexuality*. Thousand Oaks, CA: Sage.

Blank, J. 2003. "Sex Trafficking: An Exploratory Study Interviewing Traffickers." Master of Arts thesis, Department of Criminology, Middlesex University, London.

Blank, R. M. 1993. "What Should Mainstream Economists Learn from Feminist Theory?" Pp. 133–143 in *Beyond Economic Man: Feminist Theory and Economics*, edited by M. A. Ferber and J. A. Nelson. Chicago, IL: University of Chicago Press.

Bliss, K. E. 2004. "A Right to Live as Gente Decente: Sex Work, Family Life, and Collective Identity in Early Twentieth Century Mexico." *Journal of Women's History* 15(4): 164–169.

Blumberg, R. L. 1988. "Gender Stratification, Economic Development, and the African Food Crisis: Paradigm and Praxis in Nigeria." Pp. 115–137 in *Social Structures and Human Lives*, edited by M. W. Riley, Vol. 1, American Sociological Association Presidential Series: *Social Change and the Life Course*. Newbury Park, CA: Sage.

Bodnar, J. 1987. *The Transplanted: A History of Immigrants in Urban America*. Bloomington: Indiana University Press.

Bogenscheider, K. 2000. "Has Family Policy Come of Age? A Decade Review of the State of U.S. Family Policy in the 1990s." *Journal of Marriage and the Family* 62(4): 1136–1159.

Booth, A., A. C. Crouter, and N. Landale, eds. 1997. *Immigration and the Family: Research and Policy on U.S. Immigrants*. Mahwah, NJ: Lawrence Erlbaum Associates.

Bose, C. E. 2006a. "Immigration 'Reform': Gender, Migration, Citizenship and SWS." *Gender & Society* 20(5):569–575.

————. 2006b. "Puerto Rico, Globalization, and Gender Issues." *SWS Network News* XXIII(1):4–5.

Bosrock, R. M. 2006. "Globalization Can Change World for Better." *Minneapolis (MN) Star Tribune*, December 25, p. D8.

Boss, P. 2006. *Loss, Trauma, and Resilience: Clinical Work with Ambiguous Loss*. New York: Norton Professional Books.

Boulding, E. 1983. "Familia Faber: The Family as Maker of the Future." *Journal of Marriage and the Family* 45(2): 257–266.

Bourdieu, P. 1998. *Practical Reason: On the Theory of Action*. Cambridge, UK: Polity.

Boyer, R. and D. Drache, eds. 1996. *States Against Markets: The Limits of Globalization*. London, UK: Routledge.

Boys' Towns of Italy, Inc. 2005. Retrieved January 10, 2007 (http://www.citrag.it/ boystown/index.htm).

Brajsa-Zganec, A. 2005. "The Long-Term Effects of War Experiences on Children's Depression in the Republic of Croatia." *Child Abuse and Neglect* 29(1):31–43.

Brantley, C. 2003. "Colonial Africa: Transforming Families for Their Own Benefit (and Ours)." Pp. 139–155 in *Families in a New World: Gender, Politics and State Development in a Global Context*, edited by L. Haney and L. Pollard. New York: Routledge.

Briggs, L. 2003. "Familiar Territory: Prostitution, Empires, and the Question of U.S. Imperialism in Puerto Rico, 1849-1916." Pp. 40–63 in *Families in a New World: Gender, Politics and State Development in a Global Context*, edited by L. Haney and L. Pollard. New York: Routledge.

Browning, D. S. 2003. *Marriage and Modernization: How Globalization Threatens Marriage and What to Do About It*. Grand Rapids, MI: William B. Erdmans.

Brownmiller, S. 1975. *Against Our Will: Men, Women, and Rape*. New York: Simon and Schuster.

Bryceson, D. F. and U. Vuorela. 2002. "Transnational Families in the Twenty-First Century." Pp. 3–30 in *The Transnational Family: New Frontiers and Global Networks*, edited by D. F. Bryceson and U. Vuorela. Oxford, UK: Berg.

Bubloz, M. M. and M. S. Sontag. 1993. "Human Ecology Theory." Pp. 419–448 in *Sourcebook of Family Theories and Methods: A Contextual Approach*, edited by P. G. Boss, W. J. Doherty, R. LaRossa, W. R. Schumm, and S. K. Steinmetz. New York: Plenum.

Bulato, R. A. 2001. "Introduction." Pp. 1–14 in *Global Fertility Transition*, edited by R. A. Bulato and J. B. Casterline. New York: Population Council.

Bureau of International Information Programs. 2003. "World AIDS Day 2003 Marks a 'Turning Point' in Pandemic, Powell Says." Retrieved December 3, 2006 (http://usinfo.state.gov).

Butron, M. A. G. 2001. "The Effects of Free-Market Globalization on Women's Lives. Pp. 43–50 in *Globalization and Its Victims*, edited by J. Sobrino and F. Wilfred. London: SCM–Canterbury.

Caldwell, J. C. 2001. "The Globalization of Fertility Behavior." Pp. 93–115 in *Global Fertility Transition*, edited by R. A. Bulato and J. B. Casterline. New York: Population Council.

————. 2004. "Social Upheaval and Fertility Decline." *Journal of Family History* 29(4): 382–406.

Castells, M. 2000. *The Rise of the Network Society*. 2nd ed. Oxford, UK: Blackwell.

————. 2004. *The Power of Identity*. 2nd ed. Malden, MA: Blackwell.

Center for Women Policy Studies. 2006. *News*, Winter.

Central Intelligence Agency (CIA). 2006. "The World Factbook." Retrieved December 12, 2006 (http://cia.gov/cia/publications/factbook/geos/as.html#People).

Chang, G. 2000. *Disposable Domestics: Immigrant Women Workers in the Global Economy*. Cambridge, MA: South End.

Chang, I. 1997. *The Rape of Nanking: The Forgotten Holocaust of WWII*. New York: Basic.

Chant, S. 1997. *Women Headed Households: Diversity and Dynamics in the Developing World*. New York: St. Martin's.

Chaplin, D. 1978. "Domestic Service and Industrialization." *Comparative Studies in Sociology* 1:97–127.

Chart, S. 2000. "Men in Crisis? Reflections on Masculinities, Work and Family in North-West Costa Rica." *European Journal of Development Research* 12(2): 350–358.

Chase-Dunn, C. K. 1998. *Global Formation: Structures of the World Economy*. Updated edition. Lanham, MD: Rowman and Littlefield.

Chee, M. W. L. 2005. *Taiwanese American Transnational Families: Women and Kin Work*. London, UK: Taylor and Francis.

Chell-Robinson, V. 2000. "Female Migrants in Italy: Coping in a Country of New Immigration." Pp. 103–123 in *Gender and Migration in Southern Europe: Women on the Move*, edited by F. Anthias and G. Lazaridis. Oxford, UK: Berg.

Christensen, H. T., ed. 1964. *Handbook of Marriage and the Family*. Chicago: Rand McNally.

Chung, C. S. 1995. "Korean Women Drafted for Military Sexual Slavery by Japan." Pp. 11–32 in *True Stories of the Korean Comfort Women*, edited by K. Howard. London: Cassell.

———. 1997. "The Origin and Development of the Military Sexual Slavery Problem in Imperial Japan." *Positions* 5(1):219–253.

Clarke-Stewart, A. 1993. *Daycare*. Rev. ed. Cambridge, MA: Harvard University Press.

Coale, A. J. 1973. "The Demographic Transition." Pp. 53–72 in *International Population Conference, Liège, 1973*. Vol. 1. Liège: IUSSP. As cited in Caldwell 2001.

Cochrane, A. and K. Pain. 2000. "A Globalizing Society?" Pp. 5–46 in *A Globalizing World? Culture, Economics, Politics*, edited by D. Held. London: Routledge.

Cohen, R. 1997. *Global Diasporas: An Introduction*. Seattle: University of Washington Press.

———. 2000. "Mom is a Stranger: The Negative Impact of Immigration Policies on the Family Life of Filipina Domestic Workers." *Canadian Ethnic Studies* 32(3): 76–88.

Cohen, S. K. 2006. "The Experience of the Jewish Family in the Nazi Ghetto: Kovno—A Study." *Journal of Family History* 31(3): 267–288.

College of Saint Benedict/Saint John's University Faculty and Staff Profiles. 2006. *Ron*

Bosrock. Retrieved December 27, 2006 (http://www.csbsju.edu/profiles/faculty/bosrock_r.htm).

Collins, P. H. 1990. *Black Feminist Thought: Knowledge, Consciousness, and the Politics of Empowerment*. Boston: Unwin Hyman.

Comunian, A. L. 2005. "The Italian Family: Past and Present." Pp. 225–241 in *Families in Global Perspective*, edited by L. Jaipul, L. Roopnarine, and U. P. Gielen. Boston: Pearson.

Congregation of the Sisters of St. Joseph of Carondelet St. Paul. 2003 *Constitution and Acts of Chapter*. Retrieved January 15, 2007 (http://www.csjstpaul.org).

Constable, N. 2002. "Filipina Workers in Hong Kong Homes: Household Rules and Relations." Pp. 115–141 in *Global Women: Nannies, Maids, and Sex Workers in the New Economy*, edited by B. Ehrenreich and A. R. Hochschild. New York: Metropolitan/Owl of Henry Holt.

Coontz, S. 1992. *The Way We Never Were: Americans and the Nostalgia Trap*. New York: Basic Books.

———. 1997. *The Way We Really Are: Coming to Terms with America's Changing Families*. New York: Basic Books.

———. 2005. *Marriage, A History: From Obedience to Intimacy or How Love Conquered Marriage*. New York: Penguin.

Coser, L. 1973. "Servants: The Obsolescence of an Occupational Role." *Social Forces* 52(1): 31–40.

Cowan, R. S. 1983. *More Work for Mother: The Ironies of Household Technology from the Open Hearth to the Microwave*. New York: Basic Books.

Crowley, M., D. T. Lichter, and Z. Qian. 2006. "Beyond Gateway Cities: Economic Restructuring and Poverty among Mexican Immigrant Families and Children." *Family Relations* 55(3): 345–360.

Cruz-Malavé, A. and M. F. Manalansan, IV. 2002. "Dissident Sexualities/Alternative Globalism." Pp. 1–10 in *Queer Globalizations: Citizenship and the Afterlife of Colonialism*, edited by A. Cruz-Malavé and M. F. Manalansan, IV. New York: New York University Press.

Dalla, R. L, and A. Christensen. 2005. "Latino Immigrants Describe Residence in Rural

Midwestern Meatpacking Communities: A Longitudinal Assessment of Social and Economic Change." *Hispanic Journal of Behavioral Sciences* 27(1): 23–42.

Dalla, R. L., F. Villarruel, S. C. Cramer, and G. Gonzalez-Kruger. 2004. "Examining Strengths and Challenges of Rapid Rural Immigration." *Great Plains Research* 14: 231–251.

Davidson, J. O. 2006. *Children in the Global Sex Trade*. Cambridge, UK: Polity.

Denemark, D. 2005. "Mass Media and Media Power in Australia." Pp. 220–239 in *Australian Social Attitudes: The First Report*, edited by S. Wilson, G. Meagher, R. Gibson, D. Denemark, and M. Western. Sydney: University of New South Wales Press.

Diekmann, A. and H. Engelhardt. 1999. "The Social Inheritance of Divorce: Effects of Parent's Family Type in Postwar Germany." *American Sociological Review* 64(6): 783–793.

Dill, B. T. 1994. *Across the Boundaries of Race and Class: An Exploration of the Relationship Between Work and Family among Black Female Domestic Servants*. New York: Garland.

"Dolls No More American Whore." 2002. *Newsweek no*, (March 25), p. 5. Retrieved September 11, 2006 (http:// plinks.ebscohost.com).

Doole, C. 2000. "Australia Attacked over Aborigine Treatment." Retrieved December 5, 2006 (http://news.bbc.co. uk/2/hi/ asiapacific/845400.stm).

Dorow, S. K. 2006. *Transnational Adoption: A Cultural Economy of Race, Gender, and Kinship*. New York: New York University Press.

Dreby, J. 2006. "Honor and Virtue: Mexican Parenting in the Transnational Context." *Gender & Society* 20(1):32–59.

Durkheim, E. 1897/1951. *Suicide*. Translated by J. A. Spaulding and G. Simpson. New York: The Free Press.

Duyvendak, J. W. 1995. "From Revolution to Involution: The Disappearance of the Gay Movement in France." *Journal of Homosexuality* 29(4):369–385.

Economic and Social Commission for Asia and the Pacific (ESCAP). 1998. *Asia and the Pacific into the Twenty-First Century:* *Prospects for Social Development*. Kuala Lumpur: ESCAP.

Edelman, M. W. 2006. *The Global Women's Action Network for Children*. Child Watch™ Column. Retrieved December 26, 2006 (http://www.childrensdefense. org/site /News2? page= NewsArticle& id-7010).

Edgar, D. 1999. "Families as the Crucible of Competence in a Changing Social Ecology." Pp. 109–129 in *Learning to Cope: Developing as a Person in Complex Societies*, edited by E. Frydenberg. Oxford, UK: Oxford University Press.

———. 2004. "Globalization and Western Bias in Family Sociology." Pp. 3–16 in *The Blackwell Companion to the Sociology of Families*, edited by J. Scott, J. K. Treas, and M. Richards. Cambridge, UK: Cambridge University Press.

Ehrenreich, B. and A. R. Hochschild. 2002. *Global Women: Nannies, Maids, and Sex Workers in the New Economy*. New York: Metropolitan/Owl of Henry Holt.

Ehrlich, P. R. 1968. *The Population Bomb*. New York: Ballantine Books.

Eisenstein, Z. 2004. *Against Empire: Feminism, Racism, and the West*. London: Zed.

Elder, G. 1974. *Children of the Great Depression*. Chicago: University of Chicago Press.

Elder, G. and E. C. Clipp. 1988. "War Experience and Social Ties: Influences Across Forty Years in Men's Lives." Pp. 306–327 in *Social Structures and Human Lives*, edited by M. W. Riley. Newbury Park, CA: Sage.

Ender, M. G. 2000. "Beyond Adolescence: The Experiences of Adult Children of Military Parents." Pp. 241–255 in *The Military Family: A Practice Guide for Human Service Providers*, edited by J. Martin, L. Rosen, and L. Sparacino. Westport, CT: Praeger.

———. ed. 2002. *Military Brats and Other Global Nomads: Growing Up in Organization Families*. Westport, CT: Praeger.

——— 2006. "Voices from the Backseat: Growing Up in Military Families." Pp. 138–166 in *Military Life: The Psychology of Serving in Peace and Combat*, Vol. 3, *The Military Family*. Westport, CT: Praeger.

England, P. 1993. "The Separative Self: Androcentric Bias in Neoclassical Arguments." Pp. 23–36 in *Beyond Economic Man: Feminist Theory and Economics*, edited by M. A. Ferber and J. A. Nelson. Chicago: University of Chicago Press.

Epstein, C. F. 2007. "Great Divides: The Cultural, Cognitive, and Social Bases of the Global Subordination of Women." 2006 Presidential Address. *American Sociological Review* 72(1):1–22.

Esser, R. 2003. "'Language No Obstacle': War Brides in the German Press, 1945-49." *Women's History Review* 12(4):577–603.

Euronet. 1997. *Building a Europe with and for Children*. Brussels: International Save the Children Alliance.

European Commission. 2006. *Gender Equality*. Retrieved August 8, 2006 (http://ec.europa.eu/employment_soci/gender_equality/gender_mainstreaming/ gender_ove).

Evans, A. and E. Gray. 2005. "What Makes an Australian Family?" Pp. 12–29 in Australian Social Attitudes: The First Report, edited by S. Wilson, G. Meagher, R. Gibson, D. Denemark, and M. Western. Sydney: University of New South Wales Press.

Fairlie, R. W., R. A. London, R. Rosner, and M. Pastor. 2006. "Crossing the Divide: Immigrant Youth and Digital Disparity in California." Center for Justice, Tolerance, and Community, University of California, Santa Cruz. Retrieved December 8, 2006 (http://www.cjtc.ucsc.edu/docs/digital.pdf).

Faramarz, S. 2005. "Plight of Women Adds to France's Immigrant Woes." *Minneapolis (MN) Star Tribune* (Associated Press), November 18, p. A20.

Farber, B. 1971. *Kinship and Class: A Midwestern Study*. New York: Basic Books.

Farwell, N. 2004. "War Rape: New Conceptualizations and Responses." *Affilia* 19(4): 389–403.

Featherstone, M. 1990. "Global Culture: An Introduction." *Theory, Culture and Society* 7:1–14.

———. 1991. *Consumer Culture and Postmodernism*. London: Sage.

Ferber, M. A. and J. A. Nelson, eds. 1993a. *Beyond Economic Man: Feminist Theory and Economics*. Chicago: University of Chicago Press.

———. 1993b. "Introduction: The Social Construction of Economics and the Social Construction of Gender." Pp. 1–22 in *Beyond Economic Man: Feminist Theory and Economics*, edited by M. A. Ferber and J. A. Nelson. Chicago: University of Chicago Press.

Field, N. 1997. "War and Apology: Japan, Asia, the Fiftieth, and After." *Positions* 5(1):1–49.

Fifty Years Is Enough: U.S. Network for Global Economic Justice. 2006. Retrieved July 11, 2006 (http://www.50years.org).

Fischer, A. K. and L. Srole. 1978. "Antecedents and Consequences of Residential Mobility: The Midtown Manhattan Longitudinal Study." Presented at the annual meetings of the International Sociological Association, August, Uppsala, Sweden.

Flusty, S. 2004. *De-Coca-Colonization: Making the Globe from the Inside Out*. New York: Routledge.

Folbre, N. 1993. "Socialism, Feminist and Scientific." Pp. 94–110 in *Beyond Economic Man: Feminist Theory and Economics*, edited by M. A. Ferber and J. A. Nelson. Chicago, IL: University of Chicago Press.

Foner, N. 1997. "The Immigrant Family: Cultural Legacies and Cultural Changes." *International Migration Review* 31(4): 961–974.

———. 2000. *From Ellis Island to JFK: New York's Two Great Waves of Immigration*. New Haven, CT: Yale University Press.

Footrankoon, O. 2000. "Lived Experiences of Thai War Brides in Mixed Thai-American Families in the United States." Ph. D. dissertation, Department of History, University of Minnesota, Minneapolis, MN.

"France Relaxes 35-Hour Week Rule." 2005. *BBC News*. Retrieved January 19, 2006 (http://news.bbc.co.uk/1/hi/world/europe/4373167.stm).

Francome, C. 2004. *Abortion in the USA and the UK*. Burlington, VT: Ashgate.

Frankel, G. and C. Whitlock. 2005. "London Probe Extends Abroad." *Washington Post*, July 16, 2005. Retrieved July 21, 2005 (http://www. washingtonpost. com).

Freeman, J. M. and N. D. Hũu. 2003. *Voices from the Camps: Vietnamese Children Seeking Asylum*. Seattle: University of Washington Press.

Furlong, A. and F. Cartmel. 1997. *Young People and Social Change: Individualization and Risk in Late Modern Society*. Buckingham, UK: Open University Press.

Gabilondo, J. 2002. "Like Blood for Chocolate, Like Queers for Vampires." Pp. 236–363 in *Queer Globalizations: Citizenship and the Afterlife of Colonialism*, edited by A. Cruz-Malavé and M. F. Manalansan, IV. New York: New York University Press.

Gamburd, M. 2000. *The Kitchen Spoon's Handle: Transnationalism and Sri Lankan Migrant Housemaids*. Ithaca, NY: Cornell University Press.

Gdadebo, P., A. R. Rayman-Read, and S. J. Heymann. 2003. "Biological and Social Risks Entwined: The Case of AIDS in Africa." Pp. 31–51 in *Global Inequalities at Work: Work's Impact on the Health of Individuals, Families, and Societies*, edited by S. J. Heymann. New York: Oxford University Press.

Genovese, E. D. 1974. *Roll, Jordan, Roll: The World the Slaves Made*. New York: Pantheon.

George, S. 1999. *The Lugano Report: On Preserving Capitalism in the Twenty-First Century*. Sterling, VA: Pluto.

"Germany Beefs Up Benefits to Bolster the Nation's Birth Rate." 2006. *Minneapolis (MN) Star Tribune*, January 4, 2007, p. A16.

Gerner, M. E. and F. L. Perry, Jr. 2002. "Gender Differences in Cultural Acceptance and Career Orientation among Internationally Mobile and Noninternationally Mobile Adolescents." Pp. 165–192 in *Military Brats and Other Global Nomads: Growing Up in Organization Families*, edited by M. G. Ender. Westport, CT: Praeger.

Giddens, A. 1991. *Modernity and Self-Identity: Self and Society in the Modern Age*. Cambridge, UK: Polity.

———. 1992. *The Transformation of Intimacy: Sexuality, Love, and Eroticism in Modern Societies*. Cambridge, UK: Polity.

———. 2000. *Runaway World: How Globalization is Reshaping Our Lives*. New York: Routledge.

———. 2001. "The Global Revolution in Family and Personal Life." Pp. 17–23 in *Family in Transition*, 11th ed., edited by A. S. Skolnick and J. H. Skolnick. Boston: Allyn and Bacon.

Giddens, A., M. Duneier, and R. P. Appelbaum. 2006. *Essentials of Sociology*. New York: W. W. Norton.

Giele, J. Z. 2004. "Women and Men as Agents of Change in Their Own Lives." Pp. 299–317 in *Changing Life Patterns in Western Industrial Societies*, Vol. 8 of *Advances in Life Course Research*, edited by J. Z. Giele and E. Holst. Oxford, UK: Elsevier.

Giele, J. Z. and E. Holst. 2004. "New Life Patterns and Changing Gender Roles." Pp. 3–22 in *Changing Life Patterns in Western Industrial Societies*, Vol. 8 of *Advances in Life Course Research*, edited by J. Z. Giele and E. Holst. Oxford, UK: Elsevier.

Gielen, U. P. 1993. "Gender Roles in Traditional Tibetan Cultures." Pp. 413–437 in *International Handbook on Gender Roles*, edited by L. L. Adler. Westport, CT: Greenwood.

Gil, A. G., W. A. Vega, and J. M. Dimas. 1994. "Acculturative Stress and Personal Adjustment among Hispanic Adolescent Boys." *Journal of Community Psychology* 22(1):43–54.

Glele-Ahanhanzo, M. 2002. "Racism, Racial Discrimination, Xenophobia and All Forms of Discrimination." *Economic and Social Council Report*, February 12, 2002. Retrieved December 19, 2006 (http://www.unhchr.ch/Huridocda/Huridocda.nsf/0/d7d491c643c20b21c1256b84005a41d0?Opendocument).

Glenn, E. N. 1986. *Issei, Nisei, War Bride: Three Generations of Japanese American Women in Domestic Service*. Philadelphia, PA: Temple University Press.

"Global AIDS Epidemic Continues to grow." 2006. Retrieved February 18, 2007 (http://www.who.int/hiv/mediacentre/news62/en/index.html).

Global Alliance Against Traffic in Women. 2001. *Human Rights and Trafficking in Persons: A Handbook*. Bangkok: Indochina Publishing.

Goldman, M. 2005. *Imperial Nature: The World Bank and Struggles for Social Justice in the Age of Globalization*. New Haven, CT: Yale University Press.

Gonzales, N. A., J. Deardorff, D. Formoso, A. Barr, and M. Barrerra, Jr. 2006. "Family Mediators of the Relation Between Acculturation and Adolescent Mental Health." *Family Relations* 55(3):318–330.

Gonzales, N. A., G. P. Knight, A. Morgan-Saenz, and A. Sirolli. 2002. "Acculturation and the Mental Health of Latino Youth: An Integration and Critique of the Literature. Pp. 45–74 in *Latino Children and Families in the United States: Current Research and Future Directions*, edited by J. Contreras, A. Neal-Barnett, and K. Kerns. Westport, CT: Praeger.

Goode, W. J. 1963. *World Revolution and Family Patterns*. New York: Free Press.

Goodkind, D. 1997. "The Vietnamese Double Marriage Squeeze." *International Migration Review* 1(117):108–127.

Gornick, J. D. and M. K. Meyers. 2004. "Welfare Regimes in Relation to Paid Work and Care." Pp. 45–67 in *Changing Life Patterns in Western Industrial Societies*, Vol. 8 of *Advances in Life Course Research*, edited by J. Z. Giele and E. Holst. New York: Elsevier.

Granot, H. 1995. "Impact of the Gulf War on Marriage and Divorce in Israel." *International Journal of Sociology of the Family* 25(2):39–46.

Greenhouse, S. and Leonhardt, D. 2006. "Real Wages Fail to Match a Rise in Productivity." *New York Times*. Retrieved September 7, 2006 (http:// www.nytimes. com).

Greenstein, T. N. 2006. "Domestic (In) Justice: National Context, Family Satisfaction, and Fairness in the Division of Household Labor." Paper presented at the annual meeting of the American Sociological Association, August 2006, Montréal, Canada.

Greider, W. 1997. *One World, Ready or Not: The Manic Logic of Global Capitalism*. New York: Simon Schuster.

Grochowski, J. R. 2000. "Families as 'Strategic Living Communities'." Paper presented at the annual meeting of the American Academy of Health Behavior, September 2006, Santa Fe, NM.

Gupta, S. 1999. "The Effects of Transitions in Marital Status on Men's Performance of Housework." *Journal of Marriage and the Family* 61(3):700–711.

Haas, L. and C. P. Hwang. 2007. "Gender and Organizational Culture: Correlates of Companies' Responsiveness to Fathers in Sweden." *Gender & Society* 21(1): 52–79.

Haksun, K. 1995. "Bitter Memories I am Loath to Recall." Pp. 32–40 in *True Stories of the Korean Comfort Women*, edited by K. Howard. London: Cassell.

Hampton, K. N. and B. Wellman. 2004. "Long Distance Community in the Network Society: Contact and Support Beyond Netville." Pp. 94–107 in *The Family Experience: A Reader in Cultural Diversity*, 4th ed., edited by M. Hutter. Boston, MA: Pearson.

Hamwi, M. 2006. "Sending Babies Abroad." *Newsweek* (November 13), p. 17.

Hancock, Linda. 2002. "The Care Crunch: Changing Work, Families and Welfare in Australia." *Critical Social Policy* 22(1): 119–140.

Haney, L. 2003. "Welfare Reform with a Familial Face: Reconstituting State and Domestic Relations in Post-Socialist Eastern Europe." Pp. 159–178 in *Families of a New World: Gender, Politics and State Development in a Global Context*, edited by L. Haney and L. Pollard. New York: Routledge.

Haney, L. and L. Pollard, eds. 2003a. *Families of a New World: Gender, Politics, and State Development in a Global Context*. New York: Routledge.

———. 2003b. "In a Family Way: Theorizing State and Familial Relations." Pp. 1–14 in *Families in a New World: Gender, Politics and State Development in a Global Context*, edited by L. Haney and L. Pollard. New York: Routledge.

Hardt, M. and A. Negri. 2000. *Empire*. Cambridge, MA: Harvard University Press.

———. 2004. *Multitude, War, and Democracy in the Age of Empire*. New York: Penguin.

Hareven, T. K. 1977. "Family Time and Historical Time." *Daedalus* 97(2):385–396.

———. 1982. *Family Time and Industrial Time: The Relationship Between the Family and Work in a New England Industrial Community*. Cambridge, UK: Cambridge University Press.

———. 2000. *Families, History, and Social Change: Life-Course and Cross-Cultural Perspectives*. Boulder, CO: Westview.

Hawkesworth, M. E. 2006. *Globalization and Feminist Activism*. Lanham, MA: Rowman and Littlefield.

Heaven, C. and M. Tubridy. 2006. "Global Youth Culture and Youth Identity." Pp. 151–160 in International Youth Parliament, *Highly Affected, Rarely Considered*. Retrieved December 12, 2006 (http://iyp.oxfamorg/documents/Chapter%2011%20Global%20Youth%20Culture%20&%Youth%20Identity.pdf).

Held, D., H. McGrew, D. Goldblatt, and J. Perraton. 1999. *Global Transformations: Politics, Economics, and Culture*. Cambridge, UK: Polity.

Herbert, W. 1996. *Foreign Workers and Law Enforcement in Japan*. London: Kegan Paul International.

Herman, E. and R. McChesney. 1997. *The Global Media: The New Missionaries of Corporate Capitalism*. London: Cassell.

Heymann, J. 2006. *Forgotten Families: Ending the Growing Crisis Confronting Children and Working Parents in the Global Economy*. Oxford, UK: Oxford University Press.

Hicks, G. 1995. *The Comfort Women: Japan's Brutal Regime of Enforced Prostitution in the Second World War*. New York: W. W. Norton.

Hightower, K. and H. Scherer. 2007. *Help! I'm a Military Spouse—I Want a Life Too!: How to Craft a Life for YOU as You Move with the Military*, 2nd ed. Dulles, VA: Potomac.

Hill, R. and R. H. Rodgers. 1964. "The Developmental Approach." Pp. 171–211 in *Handbook of Marriage and the Family*, edited by H. T. Christensen. Chicago: Rand McNally.

Hirst, P. and G. Thompson. 1992. "The Problem of 'Globalization': International Economic Relations, National Economic Management, and the Formation of Trading Blocs." *Economy and Society* 21(4): 357–396.

Hochschild, A. R. 1989. *The Second Shift: Working Parents and the Revolution at Home*. New York: Viking.

———. 1997. *The Time Bind: When Work Become Home and Home Becomes Work*. New York: Metropolitan.

———. 2000a. "Global Care Chains and Emotional Surplus Value." Pp. 130–146 in *On the Edge: Living with Global Capitalism*, edited by W. Hutton and A. Giddens. London: Jonathan Cape.

———. 2000b. "The Nanny Chain." *American Prospect* 11(4). Retrieved October 6, 2006 (http://www.prospect. org).

Hondagneu-Sotelo, P. 2001. *Doméstica: Immigrant Workers Cleaning and Caring in the Shadows of Affluence*. Berkeley: University of California Press.

Hondagneu-Sotelo, P. and E. Avila. 1997. "'I'm Here, but I'm There': The Meanings of Latina Transnational Motherhood." *Gender & Society* 5(2):548–571.

Hook, J. 2006. "Care in Context: Men's Unpaid Work in 20 Countries, 1965-2003." *American Sociological Review* 71(4):639–660.

Hopfensperger, J. 2006. "A Freeze in the Nursing Pipeline." *Minneapolis (MN) Star Tribune*, December 2, pp. A1, A21.

Hosek, J. 2002. *Married to the Military: The Employment Earnings of Military Wives Compared with Those of Civilian Wives*. Santa Monica, CA: Rand.

Hovey, J. D. and C. A. King. 1996. "Acculturative Stress, Depressions, and Suicidal Ideation among Immigrant and Second-Generation Latino Adolescents." *Journal of the American Academy of Child and Adolescent Psychology* 35(9):1183–1192.

"How to Survive Double Deployment." 2003. *USAA Magazine* (March):20–21.

Howard, K., ed. 1995. *True Stories of the Korean Comfort Women*. London: Cassell.

Huang, S. and B. S. A. Yeoh. 1996. "Ties That Bind: State Policy and Migrant Female Domestic Helpers in Singapore." *Geoforum* 27:479–493.

Huebner, A. J. and J. A. Mancini. 2005. *Adjustments Among Adolescents in Military Families When a Parent is Deployed*. Final report to the Military Family Research Institute and Department of Defense Quality of Life Office. South Bend, IN: Purdue University.

Hughes, D. M. 2001a. "Globalization, Information Technology, and Sexual Exploitation of Women and Children." *Rain and Thunder—A Radical Feminist Journal of Discussion and Activism* 13(Winter):1–3.

———. 2001b. "The 'Natasha' Trade: Transntional Sex Trafficking." *National Institute of Justice Journal* 246(January): 8–15.

Human Rights Watch. 2001. *Refugees, Asylum Seekers, and Internally Displaced Persons*

World Report 2001. Retrieved December 20, 2006 (http:// www.hrw.org/wr2k1/ special/ refugees2. html).

Human Rights Watch. 2006. "Occupied Palestinian Territories: Authorities Must Address Violence against Women and Girls: Inadequate Laws Deny Victims Justice." Retrieved November 9, 2006 (http://hrw .org/english/docs/ 2006/11/07/palab14496 .htm).

Huntington, S. P. 1996. *The Clash of Civilizations and the Remaking of World Order*. New York: Simon and Schuster.

Hutter, M. 1981. *The Changing Family: Comparative Perspectives*. New York: Wiley.

———. 1986-1987. "Immigrant Families in the City." *The Gallatin Review* 6:60–69.

Hutton, W. and A. Giddens, eds. 2001. *On the Edge: Living with Global Capitalism*. London: Vintage.

Hylmö, A. 2002. "'Other' Expatriate Adolescents: A Postmodern Approach to Understanding Expatriate Adolescents Among Non-U.S. Children." Pp. 193–210 in *Military Brats and Other Global Nomads: Growing Up in Organization Families*, edited by M. G. Ender. Westport, CT: Praeger.

Immigrant Law Center. 2003. *Non-Citizen Women and Children: A Vulnerable Population*. St. Paul, MN: Immigrant Law Center.

Inclan, J. 2003. "Class, Culture, and Gender Contradictions in Couples Therapy with Immigrant Families." Pp. 333–348 in *Feminist Family Therapy: Empowerment and Social Location*, edited by L. B. Silverstein and T. J. Goodrich. Washington, D.C.: American Psychological Association.

Inglis, C. 2004. "Australia's Continuing Transformation." Retrieved October 26, 2006 (http://www.migrationinformation.org/ Feature/display.cfm?ID=242).

Ingoldsby, B. B. and S. Smith. 2006. *Families in Global and Multicultural Perspective*, 2nd ed. Thousand Oaks, CA: Sage.

Ingoldsby, B. B., S. Smith, and J. E. Miller. 2004. *Exploring Family Theories*. Los Angeles, CA: Roxbury.

International Organization for Migration. 2006. Retrieved November 17, 2006 (http://www. iom.int/jahia/jsp/index.jsp).

International Women's Rights Action Watch. 2004. *Equality and Women's Economic, Social, and Cultural Rights: A Guide to Implementation and Monitoring Under the International Covenant on Economics, Social and Cultural Rights*. Minneapolis, MN: International Women's Rights Action Watch.

Itzin, C. 1992. "Social Construction of Sexual Inequality." Pp. 57–75 in *Pornography, Women, Violence, and Civil Liberties: A Radical New View*, edited by C. Itzin. Oxford: Oxford University.

Iwao, S. 2001. "Japan's Battle of the Sexes: The Search for Common Ground." Pp. 114–118 in *Family in Transition*, 11th ed., edited by A. S. Skolnick and J. H. Skolnick. Boston: Allyn and Bacon.

Izuhara, M. and H. Shibata. 2002. "Breaking the Generational Contract? Japanese Migration and Old-Age Care in Britain." Pp. 155–169 in *The Transnational Family: New European Frontiers and Global Networks*, edited by D. F. Bryceson and U. Vuorela. Oxford, UK: Berg.

Jackson, R. M. 2001. "Destined for Equality." Pp. 81–88 in *Family in Transition*, 11th ed., edited by A. S. Skolnick and J. H. Skolnick. Boston: Allyn and Bacon.

James, P. 2006. "Review of *Are Australians Open to Globalisation?* by I. Marsh, G. Meagher, and S. Wilson." Pp. 240–257 in *Australian Social Attitudes: The First Report*," edited by S. Wilson, G. Meagher, R. Gibson, D. Denemark, and M. Western. Retrieved December 15, 2006 (http://www.lib.latrobe .edu.au/AHR/archive/Issue-April-2006/ james).

Jasso, G. 1997. "Migration and the Dynamics of Family Phenomena." Pp. 63–77 in *Immigration and the Family: Research and Policy on U.S. Immigrants*, edited by A. Booth, A. C. Crouter, and N. Landale. Mahwah, NJ: Lawrence Erlbaum Associates.

Jelin, E. 2004. "The Family in Argentina: Modernity, Economic Crisis, and Politics." Pp. 391–413 in *Handbook of World Families*, edited by B. N. Adams and J. Trost. Thousand Oaks, CA: Sage.

Jennings, A. L. 1993. "Public or Private? Institutional Economics and Feminism." Pp.

111–130 in *Beyond Economic Man: Feminist Theory and Economics*, edited by M. A. Ferber and J. A. Nelson. Chicago, IL: University of Chicago Press.

Johnson, M. M. 1989. "Feminism and the Theories of Talcott Parsons." Pp. 101–118 in *Feminism and Sociological Theory*, edited by R. A Wallace. Newbury Park, CA: Sage.

Joseph, M. 2002. "Family Affairs: The Discourse of Global/Localizations." Pp. 71–99 in *Queer Globalizations: Citizenship and the Afterlife of Colonialism*, edited by A. Cruz-Malavé and M. F. Manalansan, IV. New York: New York University Press.

Journal of Marriage and the Family. 2004. Special Issue: International Perspectives on Families and Social Change 66(5).

Kallis, A. A. 2005. "From the Editor: Remembering (the Shoah) and Forgetting (the Itsembambor)." *Journal of Genocide Research* 7(1):5–29.

Kamerman, S. B. and A. J. Kahn. 1997. *Family Change and Family Policies in Great Britain, Canada, New Zealand, and the United States*. New York: Oxford University Press.

Kandido-Jaksic, M. 1999. "Ethnically-Mixed Marriages and Social Distance Towards Members of Some Ex-Yugoslav Nations." *Sociologija* 41(2):103–124.

Karner, T. X. 1998. "Professional Care Giving: Homecare Workers as Fictive Kin. *Journal of Aging Studies* 12(1): 69–83.

Karraker [Wilkes], M. W. 1975. "Occupation and Anomia in the Rural South: 1960–1970." Master's thesis, Department of Rural Sociology, North Carolina State University, Raleigh, NC.

———. 2004. "The Stranger and Marginality, Sociation and Social Processes: Concepts for Globalizing Knowledge Around Issues of Transnational Immigration." Presented at the International Education Seminar on Immigration in Western Europe, June, Berlin, Marseilles, Paris.

———. 2006. "Competition, Conflict, Accommodation, and Assimilation: Applications of Robert Park's Social Processes to International Migration." Presented at the annual meeting of the British Sociological Society, April, Harrogate, UK.

Karraker, M. W. and J. R. Grochowski. 2006. *Families with Futures: A Survey of Family Studies for the Twenty-First Century*. Mahwah, NJ: Lawrence Erlbaum Associates.

Katragadda, C. P. and R. Tidwell. 1998. "Rural Hispanic Adolescents at Risk for Depressive Symptoms." *Journal of Applied Social Psychology* 28(20): 1916–1930.

Kellerman, N. P. F. 2001. "Perceived Parenting Rearing Behavior in Children of Holocaust Survivors." *Israel Journal of Psychiatry* 38(1):58–68.

Kilbride, P. and J. Kilbride. 1990. *Changing Family Life in East Africa: Women and Children at Risk*. University Park: Pennsylvania State University Press.

Kingston, B. and L. Byron. 2006. "A Brief History of Australian Women." Retrieved November 28, 2006 (http://www.eurekacouncil .com.au/ Australian-History Heritage/a_brief_history_of_australian_wo.htm).

Kirk, D. 1996. "Demographic Transition Theory." *Population Studies* 50(3): 361–387.

Kraut, R., M. Paterson, V. Lundmark, S. Kiesler, T. Mukopadhyay, and W. Schlerlis. 1998. "Internet Paradox: A Social Technology That Reduces Social Involvement and Psychological Well-Being?" *American Psychologist* 53(9):1017–1031.

Krell, R., P. Suedfeld, and E. Soriano. 2004. "Child Holocaust Survivors as Parents: A Transgenerational Perspective." *American Journal of Orthopsychiatry* 74(4): 402–508.

Krohn, I. R. 1998. "Holocaust Scatters Family in '30s, Reunion Gathers It Back Together." Retrieved December 31, 2006 (http://www .jewishsf.com/content/2-0-/module/ displaystory/storyid/9960/ edition_id/190/).

Kroska, A. 2004. "Divisions of Domestic Work: Revising and Expanding the Theoretical Explanations." *Journal of Family Issues* 25(7):900–932.

Kŭmju, H. 1995. "I Want to Live Without Being Treated with Contempt." Pp. 70–79 in *True Stories of the Korean Comfort Women*, edited by K. Howard. London: Cassell.

Kunovich, R. M. and C. Deitelbaum. 2004. "Ethnic Conflict, Group Polarization, and Gender Attitudes in Croatia." *Journal of Marriage and the Family* 66(5):1089–1107.

LaFraniere, S. 2006. "Sex Abuse of Girls is Stubborn Scourge of Africa." *The New York Times* (December 1). Retrieved December 1, 2006 (http://www.nytimes.com/2006/12/01/world/africa/01madagascar.html?ei+5070&en+dld65).

Laliberte, D., B. Laplante, and V. Piche. 2003. "The Impact of Forced Migration on Marital Life in Chad." *European Journal of Population/Revue Européenne de Demographie* 19(4): 413–435.

Land, H. 2004. "Children, Families, States, and Changing Citizenship." Pp. 54–68 in *The Blackwell Companion to the Sociology of Families*, edited by J. Scott, J. Treas, and M. Richards. Malden, MA: Blackwell.

Landale, N. S. 1997. "Immigration and the Family: An Overview." Pp. 281–291 in *Immigration and the Family: Research and Policy on U.S. Immigrants*, edited by A. Booth, A. C. Crouter, and N. Landale. Mahwah, NJ: Lawrence Erlbaum Associates.

Larney, B. E. 1994. "Children of World War II in Germany: A Lifecourse Analysis." Ph.D. dissertation, Department of Sociology, Arizona State University, Phoenix, AZ.

Lash, S. and C. Lury. 2006. *Global Culture Industry*. Oxford, UK: Blackwell.

Lawson, H. A. 2001a. "Globalization, Flows of Culture and People, and New-Century Frameworks for Family-Centered Policies, Practices, and Development." Pp. 338–376 in *Family-Centered Policies and Practices: International Implications*, edited by K. Briar-Lawson, H. A. Lawson, and C. B. Hennan, with A. R. Jones. New York: Columbia University Press.

———. 2001b. "Introducing Globalization's Challenges and Opportunities and Analyzing Economic Globalization and Liberalization." Pp. 293–337 in *Family-Centered Policies and Practices*, edited by K. Briar-Lawson, H. A. Lawson, and C. B. Hennon, with A. R. Jones. New York: Columbia University Press.

Leeder, E. J. 2004. *The Family in Global Perspective: A Gendered Journey*. Thousand Oaks, CA: Sage.

Legarde, E., M. S. van der Loeff, C. Enel, B. Holmgren, R. Dray-Spira, G. Pison, J. P. Piau, V. Delaunay, S. M'Boup, I. Ndoye, M. Pellicer, H. Whittle, and P. Aaby. 2003. "Mobility and the Spread of Human Immunodeficiency Virus into Rural Areas of West Africa." *International Journal of Epidemiology* 32:744–752.

Lemberger, J., ed. 1995. *A Global Perspective on Working with Holocaust Survivors and the Second Generation*. Jerusalem: JDC–Brookdale Institute of Gerontology and Human Development.

Lemert, C. and A. Elliott. 2006. *Deadly Worlds: The Emotional Costs of Globalization*. Lanham, MA: Rowman and Littlefield.

Lengermann, P. M. and G. Niebrugge. 2007a. "Contemporary Feminist Theories." Pp. 185–249 in *Contemporary Sociological Theory and Its Classical Roots*, 2nd ed., edited by G. Ritzer. New York: McGraw Hill.

———. 2007b. "Feminism and Postmodern Social Theory." Pp. 247–249 in *Contemporary Sociological Theory and Its Classical Roots*, 2nd ed., edited by G. Ritzer. New York: McGraw Hill.

Leung, H-C and K-M Lee. 2005. "Immigration Controls, Life-course Coordination, and Livelihood Strategies: A Study of Families Living across the Mainland–Hong Kong Border." *Journal of Family and Economic Issues* 26(4): 487–507.

Levine, P. 2004. "'A Multitude of Unchaste Women': Prostitution in the British Empire." *Journal of Women's History* 15(4):159–163.

Lipovetsky, G. and S. Charles. 2005. *Hypermodern Times: Themes for the 21st Century*. Translated by A. Brown. Cambridge, UK: Polity.

Litt, J. 2000. *Medicalized Motherhood: Perspectives from the Lives of African-American and Jewish Women*. New Brunswick, NJ: Rutgers University Press.

Liu, D. 2007. "When Do National Movements Adopt or Reject International Agenda? A Comparative Analysis of the Chinese and Indian Women's Movements." *American Sociological Review* 71(6): 921–942.

Longino, H. E. 1993. "Economics for Whom?" Pp. 158–168 in *Beyond Economic Man: Feminist Theory and Economics*, edited by M. A. Ferber and J. A. Nelson. Chicago: University of Chicago Press.

Lopata, H. Z. 1971. *Occupation Housewife*. Westport, CT: Greenwood.

Lorber, J. 2005. "Women's Worlds 2005 Seoul, South Korea." *SWS Network News* XXII(3):5–8.

Lorentzen, L. A. and J. Turpin, eds. 1998. *The Women and War Reader*. New York: New York University Press.

MacAskill, E. 2007. "UN Clashes with Iraq on Civilian Death Toll." *Guardian Unlimited*, January 17, 2007. Retrieved January 31, 2007 (http://www.guardian.co.uk/international/story /0,,1991876,00.html).

MacKay, H. 2000. "The Globalization of Culture?" Pp. 47–84 in *A Globalizing World: Culture, Economics, Politics*, edited by D. Held. London: Routledge.

Mandle, J. 2006. *Global Justice: An Introduction*. Cambridge, UK: Polity.

Marchand, M. H. and A. S. Runyan, eds. 2000. *Gender and Global Restructuring: Sightings, Sites, and Resistances*. London: Routledge.

Marling, W. H. 2006. *How "American" is Globalization?* Baltimore, MD: Johns Hopkins University Press.

Marsh, I., G. Meagher, and S. Wilson. 2005. "Are Australians Open to Globalisation?" Pp. 240–257 in *Australian Social Attitudes: The First Report*, edited by S. Wilson, G. Meagher, R. Gibson, D. Denemark, and M. Western. Sydney: University of New South Wales Press.

Martinez, C. R., Jr. 2006. "Effects of Differential Family Acculturation on Latino Adolescent Substance Use." *Family Relations* 55(3): 306–317.

Marty, M. E. and R. S. Appleby. 1991. *Fundamentalism Observed,* Vol. I of *The Fundamentalism Project*. Chicago: University of Chicago Press.

Massey, D. 1994. *Space, Place, and Gender*. Minneapolis: University of Minnesota Press.

Mattelart, A. 1994. *Mapping World Communication: War, Progress, Culture*. Translated by S. Emanuel and J. A. Cohen. Minneapolis: University of Minnesota Press.

Mayer, K. U. 1988. "German Survivors of World War II: The Impact on the Life Course of the Collective Experience of Birth Cohorts." Pp. 229–246 in *Social Structures and Human Lives*, edited by M. W. Riley. Newbury Park, CA: Sage.

McCluskey, K. C., ed. 1994. *Notes from a Traveling Childhood. Reading for Internationally Mobile Parents*. Washington, D.C.: Foreign Service Youth Foundation.

McCorry, P. 1984. "The Lost Rosary; or, Our Irish Girls, Their Trials, Temptations, and Triumphs." Pp. 153–159 in *The Exiles of Erin: Nineteenth-Century Irish-American Fiction*, edited by C. Fanning. Notre Dame, IN: University of Notre Dame Press.

McCubbin, H. I., B. B. Dahl, P. J. Metres, Jr., E. J. Hunter, and J. A. Plag (eds.). 1974. *Family Separation and Reunion: Families of Prisoners of War and Servicemen Missing in Action*. San Diego: Center for Prisoner of War Studies, Naval Health Research Center.

McGregor, J. H. S. 2006. *Venice from the Ground Up*. Cambridge, MA: Belknap Press of Harvard University Press.

McLuhan, M. 1964. *Understanding Media*. New York: McGraw-Hill.

McMahon, K. and J. Stanger. 2002. *Speaking Out: Three Narratives of Women Trafficked to the United States*. Los Angeles: Coalition to Abolish Slavery and Trafficking.

Meissner., D. M., R. D. Hormats, A. G. Walker, and S. Ogata. 1993. *International Migration Challenges in a New Era: Policy Perspectives and Priorities for Europe, Japan, North America, and the International Community*. New York: Trilateral Commission.

Mendoza, K. R. 2003. "Freeing the 'Slaves of Destiny': The Lolas of the Filipino Comfort Women Movement." *Cultural Dynamics* 15(3):247–266.

Merry, S. E. 2005. *Human Rights and Gender Violence: Translating International Law into Local Justice*. Chicago: University of Chicago Press.

Merton, R. K. 1968. *Social Theory and Social Structure*, enl. ed. New York: Free Press.

Meyer, M. H., ed. 2000. *Care Work: Gender, Labor and the Welfare State*. New York: Routledge.

Mies, M. 1994. "Gender and Global Capitalism." Pp. 107–122 in *Capitalism and Development*, edited by L. Sklair. New York: Routledge.

Miles, S. 2000. *Youth Lifestyles in a Changing World*. Buckingham, UK: Open University Press.

Miller, C. R. and E. W. Butler. 1966. "Anomia and Eunomia: A Methodological Evaluation of Leo Srole's Anomia Scale." *American Sociological Review* 31(3):400–406.

Miller, D. 1997. *Capitalism: An Ethnographic Approach*. Oxford, UK: Berg.

Min, P. G. 2003. "Korean 'Comfort Women': The Intersection of Colonial Power, Gender, and Class." *Gender & Society* 17(6): 938–957.

Minnesota Advocates for Human Rights. 1995. *The Energy of a Nation: Immigrants in America*. Minneapolis: Minnesota Advocates for Human Rights.

———. 2004. *The Government Response to Domestic Violence Against Refugee and Immigrant Women in the Minneapolis/St. Paul Metropolitan Area: A Human Rights Report*. Minneapolis: Minnesota Advocates for Human Rights.

Minnesota Advocates for Human Rights Women's Program. 2006. *Women's Rights*. Retrieved July 18, 2006 (http:// www.mnadvocates.org/Women_s _Program.html).

Miyoshi, M. 1993. "A Borderless World? From Colonialism to Transnationalism and the Decline of the Nation-State." *Critical Inquiry* 19(Summer):726–751.

Mizruchi, E. H. 1960. "Social Structure and Anomia in a Small City." *American Sociological Review* 25(5):645–654.

Moffett, P. S., CFC. 2000. Personal communication from Moffett, then President, Boys' and Girls' Towns of Italy, Inc., June, Città dei Ragazzi, Rome, Italy.

Mohanty, C., A. Russo, and L. Torres. 1991. *Third World Women and the Politics of Feminism*. Bloomington: Indiana University Press.

Moore, M. 2006. "As Europe Grows Grayer, France Devises a Baby Boom." *Washington Post*, October 18, p. A01. Retrieved January 17, 2007 (http:// www.washingtonpost .com/wpdyn/content/article/2006/10/17/AR 2006101701652.html).

Moreno, J. C. 2002. "Entering into the Realm of 'the Other': A Few Suggestions for Crossing Boundaries of Human Difference." Presented at the annual meeting of the *Minnesota Council of Family Relations*, December, St. Paul.

Morley, D. 1986. *Family Television: Cultural Power and Domestic Leisure*. London: Comedia.

Morley, D. and K. Robins. 1995. *Spaces of Identity: Global Media, Electronic Landscapes, and Cultural Boundaries*. London: Routledge.

Moses, A. 2004. *Genocide and Settler Society: Frontier Violence and Stolen Indigenous Children in Australian History*, Vol. 6. NY: Berghahn.

Moya, F-N. 2006. "Fighting Poverty by Another Name." *Mail and Guardian*, July 28–August 3, p. 22.

Murdock, G. P. 1949. *Social Structure*. New York: Macmillan.

———. 1982. *Outline of Cultural Materials*. New Haven, CT: Human Relations Area Files.

Muroi, H. and N. Sasaki. 1997. "Tourism and Prostitution in Japan." Pp. 180–219 in *Gender, Work, and Tourism*, edited by M. T. Sinclair. London: Routledge.

Nairn, T. and P. James. 2005. *Global Matrix: Nationalism, Globalism and State-Terrorism*. London: Pluto.

Naples, N. A. and M. Desai, eds. 2002. *Women's Activism and Globalization: Linking Local Struggles and Transnational Politics*. London: Routledge.

Nashef, Y. 1992. *The Psychological Impact of the Intifada on Palestinian Children Living in Refugee Camps in the West Bank, as Reflected in their Dreams, Drawings and Behavior*. Frankfurt am Main: Peter Lang.

Nayak, A. 2003. *Race, Place, and Globalization: Youth Cultures in a Changing World*. Oxford, UK: Berg.

Nederveen Pieterse, J. 2004. *Globalization and Culture: Global Mélange*. Lanham, MD: Rowman and Littlefield.

Nozaki, Y. 2001. "Feminism, Nationalism, and the Japanese Textbook Controversy over 'Comfort Women'." Pp. 170–189 in *Feminism and Antiracism: International Struggles for Justice*, edited by F. W Twine and K. M. Blee. New York: New York University Press.

Oakley, A. 1974. *The Sociology of Housework*. New York: Pantheon.

Obama, B. 2006. *The Audacity of Hope: Thoughts on Reclaiming the American Dream*. New York: Crown.

Ode, K. 2007. "Foreign Adoptions Decline as Rules Shift." *Minneapolis* (MN) *Star Tribune*, January 14, pp. A1, A13.

Ohmae, K. 1995. *The End of the Nation State.* New York: Free Press.

Oishi, N. 2005. *Women in Motion: Globalization, State Policies, and Labor Migration in Asia.* Stanford, CA: Stanford University Press.

Okpun, Y. 1995. "Taken Away at Twelve." Pp. 95–103 in *True Stories of the Korean Comfort Women,* edited by K. Howard. London: Cassell.

Ollenburger, J. C. and H. A. Moore. 1998. *A Sociology of Women: The Intersection of Patriarchy, Capitalism, and Colonization,* 2nd ed. Upper Saddle River, NJ: Prentice Hall.

Ong, A. 1999. *Flexible Citizenship: The Cultural Logics of Transnationality.* Durham, NC: Duke University Press.

Orecklin, M. 2002. "Puppet Politics." *Time* (September 30). Retrieved September 11, 2006 (http://www.time.com/time/magazine/article/0,9171,1003371-3,00. html).

Organization for Economic Co-operation and Development (OECD). 2002. *Babies and Bosses: Reconciling Work and Family Life,* Vol. I of *Australia, Denmark and the Netherlands.* Paris: OECD.

———. 2006. *About OECD.* Retrieved December 20, 2006 (http://www.oecd.org/about/).

Orsini-Jones, M. and F. Gattullo. 2000. "Migrant Women in Italy: National Trends and Local Perspectives." Pp. 125–144 in *Gender and Migration in Southern Europe: Women on the Move,* edited by F. Anthias and G. Lazaridis. Oxford, UK: Berg.

Park, R. E. 1950. *Race and Culture.* New York: The Free Press.

———. 1952. *Human Communities.* New York: The Free Press.

Parra-Cardona, J. R., L. A. Bulock, D. R. Imig, F. A. Villaruel, and S. J. Gold. 2006. "'Trabajando Duro Todos Los Días': Learning from the Life Experiences of Mexican-Origin Migrant Families." *Family Relations* 59(3):361–375.

Parreñas, R. S. 2000. "Migrant Filipina Domestic Workers and the International Division of Reproductive Labor." *Gender & Society* 14(4):560–580.

———. 2001. *Servants of Globalization: Women, Migration, and Domestic Work.* Stanford, CA: Stanford University Press.

———. 2002. "The Care Crisis in the Philippines: Children and Transnational Families

in the New Global Economy." Pp. 39–54 in *Global Women: Nannies, Maids, and Sex Workers in the New Economy,* edited by B. Ehrenreich and A. R. Hochschild. New York: Metropolitan/Owl of Henry Holt.

Parsons, T. 1966. *Societies: Evolutionary and Comparative Perspectives.* Englewood Cliffs, NJ: Prentice-Hall.

Pavalko, E. K. and G. H. Elder, Jr. 1990. "World War II and Divorce: A Life-Course Perspective." *American Journal of Sociology* 95(5):1213–1234.

Pearce, R. L. D. 2002. "Children's International Relocation and the Developmental Process." Pp. 145–165 in *Military Brats and Other Global Nomads: Growing Up in Organization Families,* edited by M. G. Ender. Westport, CT: Praeger.

Peskin, H. 1981. "Observations on the First International Conference on Children of Holocaust Survivors." *Family Process* 20(4):391–394.

Picard, A. 2006. "Gathering Opens with Focus on AIDS Prevention." *The Globe and Mail,* August 14, pp. A1, A11.

P'ilgi, M. 1995. "I So Much Wanted to Study." Pp. 80–87 in *True Stories of the Korean Comfort Women,* edited by K. Howard. London: Cassell.

Piper, N. 2000. "Globalization, Gender, and Migration: The Case of International Marriage in Japan." Pp. 205–225 in *Towards a Gendered Political Economy,* edited by J. Cook, J. Roberts, and G. Waylen. London: Macmillan.

———. 2001. "Transnational Women's Activism in Japan and Korea: The Unresolved Issue of Military Sexual Slavery." *Global Networks* 1(2): 155–170.

———. 2003. "Bridging Gender, Migration, and Governance: Theoretical Possibilities in the Asian Context." *Asian and Pacific Migration Journal* 12(1–2): 21–48.

Pitts, J. R. 1964. "The Structural-Functional Approach." Pp. 51–124 in *Handbook of Marriage and the Family,* edited by H. T. Christensen. Chicago: Rand McNally.

Pollard, L. 2003. "The Promise of Things to Come: The Image of the Modern Family in State-Building, Colonial Occupation, and Revolution in Egypt, 1805-1922."

Pp. 17–39 in *Families in a New World: Gender, Politics and State Development in a Global Context*, edited by L. Haney and L. Pollard. New York: Routledge.

"Pope Extols Virtues of Traditional Families in a Changing Spain." 2006. *Minneapolis (MN) Star Tribune*, July 11, p. A9.

Pope John Paul II. 1981. *Familiaris Consortio: The Role of the Christian Family in the Modern World*. Vatican translation. Boston: Pauline Books and Media.

Portes, A. and M. Zhou. 1993. "The New Second Generation: Segmented Assimilation and its Variants." *Annals of the American Association of Political and Social Science* 530 (November): 74–96.

Project on Global Working Families. 2002. *Public Policy Index for Over 100 Nations*. Retrieved December 20, 2006 (http://www.hsph.harvard.edu/globalworkingfamilies/PPIndex.htm).

———. 2006. Work, Family, and HIV. Retrieved December 20, 2006 (http://www.hsph.harvard.edu/global/workingfamilies/HIV.htm).

Purewal, N. K. 2001. "New Roots for Rights: Women's Responses to Population and Development Policies." Pp. 96–117 in *Women Resist Globalization*, edited by S. Rowbotham and S. Linkogle. London: New York.

Purkayastha, B. 2005. *Negotiating Ethnicity: South Asian Americans Traverse a Transnational World*. New Brunswick, NJ: Rutgers University Press.

Putnam, R., with L. M. Feldstein and D. Cohen. 2001. *Bowling Alone: The Collapse and Revival of American Community*. New York: Simon and Schuster.

Quester, G. H. 1990. "The Psychological Effects of Bombing on Civilian Populations: Wars of the Past." Pp. 201–214 in *Psychological Dimensions of War*, edited by B. Glad. Newbury Park, CA: Sage.

Quotations Page. 2007. Retrieved January 15, 2007 (http://www.quotationspage.com/search.php3?Search=the+future+belongs&start search=Search&Author=Eleanor+Roosevel&C=coles&C=poorc&C=lindsly&C=net&C=devils&C= contrib).

Ray, L. 2006. *Globalization and Everyday Life*. New York: Routledge.

Rheingold, H. 1993. *The Virtual Community*. Reading, MA: Addison-Wesley.

Richmond, A. 1994. *Global Apartheid: Refugees, Racism, and the New World Order*. Toronto: Oxford University Press.

Rippi, S. 2003. "Kompensation oder Konflikt? Zur Erklarung Negativer Einstellungen zur Zuwanderung." Instit Soziologie, Universität Chemnitz.

Ritzer, G. 1993. *The McDonaldization of Society: An Investigation into the Changing Character of Contemporary Social Life*. Newbury Park, CA: Pine Forge.

———. 1995. *Expressing America: A Critique of the Increasingly Global Credit Card Society*. Thousand Oaks, CA: Pine Forge.

———. 1996. *The McDonaldization of Society*. Rev. ed. Thousand Oaks, CA: Pine Forge.

———. 2004a. *The Globalization of Nothing*. Thousand Oaks, CA: Pine Forge.

———. 2004b. *The McDonalization of Society*. Rev. New Century edition. Thousand Oaks, CA: Pine Forge.

———. 2005a. *Enchantment in a Disenchanted World: Revolutionizing the Means of Consumption*, 2nd ed. Thousand Oaks, CA: Pine Forge.

———. 2005b. "The 'New' Means of Consumption: A Postmodern Analysis." Pp. 280–298 in *Illuminating Social Life: Classical and Contemporary Theory Revisited*, 3rd ed., edited by P. Kivisto. Thousand Oaks, CA: Pine Forge.

———. 2007. *Contemporary Sociological Theory and its Classical Roots*, 2nd ed. New York: McGraw Hill.

Robertson, R. 1990. "Mapping the Global Condition: Globalization as the Central Concept." *Theory, Culture, and Society* 7(1):15–30.

———. 1995. "Glocalization: Time-Space and Homogeneity-Heterogeneity." Pp. 25–44 in *Global Modernities*, edited by M. Featherstone, S. Lash, and R. Robertson. Thousand Oaks, CA: Sage.

Robila, M., ed. 2004. *Families in Eastern Europe*. New York: Elsevier.

Roeder, V. D. and A. V. Millard. 2000. "Gender and Employment among Latino Migrant Farmworkers in Michigan." Working Paper No. 52. Michigan State University, Julian

Samora Research Institute, Ann Arbor, MI. Retrieved January 16, 2007 (http://www.jsri.msu.edu/RandS/research/wps/wp52abs.html).

Romero, M. 1992. *Maid in the U.S.A.* New York: Routledge.

Roopnarine, J. L. and U. P. Gielen, 2005. "Families in Global Perspective: An Introduction." Pp. 3–13 in *Families in Global Perspectives*, edited by J. L. Roopnarine and U. P. Gielen. Boston, MA: Pearson.

Roopnarine, J. L. and M. Shin. 2003. "Caribbean Immigrants from English-Speaking Countries: Socio-Historical Forces, Migratory Patterns, and Psychological Issues in Family Functioning." Pp. 123–142 in *Migration, Immigration, and Emigration in International Perspectives*, edited by L. L. Adler and U. P. Gielen. Westport, CT: Greenwood.

Rosen, E. I. 2002. *Making Sweatshops: The Globalization of the U.S. Apparel Industry.* Berkeley: University of California Press.

Rosenau, J. N. 1997. *Along the Domestic Frontier: Exploring Governance in a Turbulent World.* Cambridge, UK: Cambridge University Press.

———. 2003. *Distant Proximities: Dynamics beyond Globalization.* Princeton, NJ: Princeton University Press.

Rosenthal, G. 2000. "Social Transformation in the Context of Familial Experience: Biographical Consequences of a Denied Past in the Soviet Union." Pp. 115–138 in *Biographies and the Division of Europe*, edited by R. Breckner, D. Kalekin-Fischman, and I. Miethe. Opladen: Leske and Budrich.

———. 2002a. "Introduction. Family History: Life Stories." *History of the Family: An International Quarterly* 7(2):175–182.

———. 2002b. "Veiling and Denying the Past: The Dialogue in Families of Holocaust Survivors and Families of Nazi Perpetrators." *History of the Family: An International Quarterly* 7(2):225–238.

Rosero-Bixby, L. 2001. Comment: Population Programs and Fertility. Pp. 205–209 in *Global Fertility Transition*, edited by R. A. Bulato and J. B. Casterline. New York: Population Council.

Rostow, W. W. 1961. *The Stages of Economic Growth.* Cambridge, UK: Cambridge University Press.

Rothenberg, D. 1998. *With These Hands: The Hidden World of Migrant Farm-Workers Today.* New York: Harcourt Brace.

Rotheram-Borus, M. J. 1989. "Ethnic Differences in Adolescents' Identity Status and Associated Behavioral Problems." *Journal of Adolescence* 12(4):361–374.

Rowbotham, S. 1992. *Women in Movement: Feminism and Social Action.* London: Routledge.

Ruff-O'Herne, J. 1994. *Fifty Years of Silence.* Sydney: ETT Imprint.

Ruger, W., S. E. Wilson, and S. L. Waddoups. 2002. "Warfare and Welfare: Military Service, Combat, and Marital Dissolution." *Armed Forces and Society* 29(1): 85–107.

Rumbaut, R. G. 1997. "Ties That Bind: Immigration and Immigrant Families in the United States." Pp. 3–46 in *Immigration and the Family: Research and Policy on U.S. Immigrants*, edited by A. Booth, A. C. Crouter, and N. Landale. Mahwah, NJ: Lawrence Erlbaum Associates.

Safa, H. I. 2002. "Women and Globalization: Lessons from the Dominican Republic." Pp. 141–156 in *The Spaces of Neoliberalism: Land, Place and Family in Latin America*, edited by J. Chase. Bloomfield, CT: Kumarian.

Said, E. W. 1978. *Orientalism.* New York: Pantheon.

Salzinger, L. 2003. *Gender in Production: Making Workers in Mexico's Global Factories.* Berkeley, CA: University of California Press.

Sand, H. A., RGS. 2004. Personal communication from Sand, member of the Sisters of the Good Shepherd (Buon Pastore) community, January 5, Rome, Italy.

Sangok, Y. 1995. "I Came Home but Lost My Family." Pp. 124–133 in *True Stories of the Korean Comfort Women*, edited by K. Howard. London: Cassell.

Sanminiatelli, M. 2007. "Italy Accuses 2,000 of Human Trafficking." Retrieved January 26, 2007 (http://www.sun-sentinel.com/news/nationworld/sfl-atrafficking25jan25,0,6590825.story?coll=sfla-news-nationworld).

Sarker, S. and E. N. De. 2002. *Trans-Status Subjects: Gender in the Globalization of South and Southeast Asia.* Durham, NC: Duke University Press.

Sassen, S. 2002. "Global Cities and Survival Circuits." Pp. 254–274 in *Global Women:*

Nannies, Maids, and Sex Workers in the New Economy, edited by B. Ehrenreich and A. R. Hochschild. New York: Metropolitan/Owl of Henry Holt.

Saxena, P. C., A. Kulczycki, and R. Jurdi. 2004. "Nuptiality Transitions and Marriage Squeeze in Lebanon: Consequences of Sixteen Years of Civil War." *Journal of Comparative Family Issues* 35(2): 251–258.

"Scarred by History: The Rape of Nanjing." 2005. Retrieved December 31, 2006 (http://news.bbc.co.uk/2/hi/asiapacific/223038.stm).

Schiller, N. G., L. Basch, and C. Blanc-Szanton. 1992a. "Towards a Definition of Transnationalism: Introductory Remarks and Research Questions." Pp. ix-xiv in *Towards a Transnational Perspective on Migration: Race, Class, Ethnicity, and Nationalism Reconsidered*, edited by N. G. Schiller, L. Basch, and C. Blanc-Szanton. Annals of the New York Academy of Sciences 645 (July 6). New York: The New York Academy of Sciences.

———. 1992b. "Transnationalism: A New Analytic Framework for Understanding Migration." Pp. 1–24 in *Towards a Transnational Perspective on Migration: Race, Class, Ethnicity, and Nationalism Reconsidered*, edited by N. G. Schiller, L. Basch, and C. Blanc-Szanton. Annals of the New York Academy of Sciences 645 (July 6). New York: The New York Academy of Sciences.

Schmickle, S. 2006. "Old Habits vs. New Hungers." *Minneapolis* (MN) *Star Tribune*, July 11, pp. A1, A7.

Schmitt, J. and J. Wadsworth. 2006. "Changing Patterns in the Relative Economic Performance of Immigrants to Great Britain and the United States, 1980." Center for Economic Performance Working Paper 1422, April. Retrieved August 24, 2006 (http://www.cepr.net/publications/immigration_2006_04.htm).

Schwartzberg, B. 2004. "'Lots of Them Did That': Desertion, Bigamy, and Marital Fidelity in Late-Nineteenth-Century America." *Journal of Social History* 37(3):573–600.

Scott. D. 2000. "Embracing What Works: Building Communities That Strengthen Families." *Children Australia* 25(2): 4–9.

Scott, J., J. Treas, and M. Richards, eds. 2004. *The Blackwell Companion to the Sociology of Families*. Oxford, UK: Blackwell.

Seager, J. 2003. *The Penguin Atlas of Women in the World*. New York: Penguin.

Seccombe, K. 2006. *Families in Poverty*. Boston: Allyn and Bacon.

Segal, S. J. 2003. *Under the Banyan Tree: A Population Scientist's Odyssey*. New York: Oxford University Press.

Shah, A. 2007. "New Kid on the Block." *Minneapolis* (MN) *Star Tribune*, January 7, pp. E1, E3.

Shaw, A. 2004. "Immigrant Families in the UK." Pp. 270–285 in *The Blackwell Companion to the Sociology of Families*, edited by J. Scott, J. Treas, and M. Richards. Oxford, UK: Blackwell.

Shea, N. 1954. *The Army Wife*, 3rd Rev. ed. New York: Harper and Brothers.

Sheng, X. 2004. "Chinese Families." Pp. 99–128 in *Handbook of World Families*, edited by B. N. Adams and J. Trost. Thousand Oaks, CA: Sage.

Sick, R. 2007. Personal Communications, January 16 and 17.

Sigle-Rushton, W. and C. Kenney. 2004. "Public Policy and Families." Pp. 457–477 in *The Blackwell Companion to the Sociology of Families*, edited by J. Scott, J. Treas, and M. Richards. Malden, MA: Blackwell.

Silverstein, L. B. and C. F. Auerbach. 2005. "(Post)modern Families." Pp. 33–47 in *Families in Global Perspectives*, edited by J. L. Roopnarine and U. P. Gielen. Boston, MA: Allyn and Bacon.

Simonen, M. 2006. United Nations and Women's Rights. *ASA Footnotes*, 34(6):4.

Singh, J. P. 2004. "The Contemporary Indian Family." Pp. 129–166 in *Handbook of World Families*, edited by B. N. Adams and J. Trost. Thousand Oaks, CA: Sage.

Sirjamaki, J. 1964. "The Institutional Approach." Pp. 33–50 in *Handbook of Marriage and the Family*, edited by H. T. Christensen. Chicago: Rand McNally.

Sklair, L. 2002. *Globalization: Capitalism and Its Alternatives*. Oxford, UK: Oxford University Press.

Skolnick, A. S. and J. H. Skolnick. 2001. *Family in Transition,* 11th ed. Boston: Allyn and Bacon.

Slouka, M. 1995. *War of the Worlds: Cyberspace and the High-Tech Assault on Reality*. New York: Basic Books.

Smith, A. D. 1990. "Towards a Global Culture?" *Theory, Culture, & Society* 7:171–191.

Smith, M. 2005. "Item 6: Racism, Racial Discrimination, Xenophobia and All Forms of Discrimination." Presented at the Sixty-First Session of the Commission on Human Rights, March 21, 2005, Geneva. Retrieved December 20, 2006 (http://www.dfat.gov.au/hr/comm_ hr/chr61_item6.html).

Smyth, L. 2005. *Abortion and Nation: The Politics of Reproduction in Contemporary Ireland*. Burlington, VT: Ashgate.

Snyder, A. 2006. "Fostering Transnational Dialogue: Lessons Learned from Women Peace Activists." *Globalization* 3(1):31–47.

Soh, C. S. 2000a. "From Imperial Gifts to Sex Slaves: Theorizing Symbolic Pepresentations of the 'Comfort Women'." *Social Science Japan Journal* 3(1):59–76.

———. 2000b. "Human Rights and the 'Comfort Women'." *Peace Review* 12(1): 123–129.

———. 2004. "Aspiring to Craft Modern Gendered Selves: 'Comfort Women' and Chongsindair in Late Colonial Korea." *Critical Asian Studies* 36(2):175–198.

Solow, R. M.. 1993. "Feminist Theory, Women's Experience, and Economics." Pp. 153–157 in *Beyond Economic Man: Feminist Theory and Economics*, edited by M. A. Ferber and J. A. Nelson. Chicago: University of Chicago Press.

Sørenson, A. 2004. "Economic Relations Between Women and Men: New Realities and the Re-Interpretation of Dependence." Pp. 281–297 in *Changing Life Patterns in Western Industrial Societies*, Vol. 8, *Advances in Life Course Research*, edited by J. Z. Giele and E. Holst. New York: Elsevier.

Sparr, P., ed. 1994. *Mortgaging Women's Lives: Feminist Critiques of Structural Adjustment*. London: Zed Books.

Spybey, T. 1996. *Globalization and World Society*. Cambridge, UK: Polity.

Srole, L. 1956. "Social Integration and Certain Corollaries: An Exploratory Study." *American Sociological Review* 21(6):709–716.

Stack, C. B. 1974. *All Our Kin: Strategies for Survival in a Black Community*. New York: Harper and Row.

Standing, G. 2001. "Care Work: Overcoming Insecurity and Neglect." Pp. 15–31 in *Care Work: The Quest for Security*, edited by M. Daly. Geneva: International Labour Organization.

Stanger, J. E. 2005. "Children of *Holocaust* Survivors: A Life-History Study." Ph.D. dissertation, Department of Humanistic Studies, State University of New York, Albany, New York.

Stein, G. 1937/1973. *Everybody's Autobiography*. New York: Vintage.

Stevenson, B. 1991. "Distress and Discord in Virginia Slave Families." Pp. 103–124 in *In Joy and in Sorrow: Women, Family, and Marriage in the Victorian South*, edited by C. Bleser. New York: Oxford University Press.

Stewart, F. 1991. "The Many Faces of Development." *World Development* 19(12): 1847–1864.

Strasser, S. 1982. *Never Done: A History of American Housework*. New York: Pantheon.

Strassman, D. 1993. "Not a Free Market: The Rhetoric of Disciplinary Authority in Economics." Pp. 54–68 in *Beyond Economic Man: Feminist Theory and Economics*, edited by M. A. Ferber and J. A. Nelson. Chicago: University of Chicago Press.

Stryker, S. 1964. "The Interactional and Situational Approaches." Pp. 125–170 in *Handbook of Marriage and the Family*, edited by H. T. Christenson. Chicago: Rand McNally.

Sunok, Y. 1995. "It Makes Me Sad That I Can't Have Children." Pp. 115–123 in *True Stories of the Korean Comfort Women*, edited by K. Howard. London: Cassell.

T'aesŏn, K. 1995. "Death and Crisis." Pp. 151–157 in *True Stories of the Korean Comfort Women*, edited by K. Howard. London: Cassell.

Tambe, A. 2005. "The Elusive Ingénue: A Transnational Feminist Analysis of European Prostitution in Colonial Bombay." *Gender & Society* 19(2): 160–179.

Thomas, W. I. and F. Znaniecki. 1927. *The Polish Peasant in Europe and America*. New York: Knopf.

Tilly, L. A. and J. W. Scott. 1990. *Women, Work and Family*. New York: Routledge.

Timera, M. 2002. "Righteous or Rebellious? Social Trajectory of Sahelian Youth in

France." Pp. 147–154 in *The Transnational Family: New European Frontiers and Global Networks*, edited by D. F. Bryceson and U. Vuorela. Oxford, UK: Berg.

Tomlinson, J. 1999. *Globalization and Culture*. Chicago: University of Chicago Press.

Toro-Morn, M. I. 1995. "Gender, Class, Family, and Migration: Puerto Rican Women in Chicago." *Gender & Society* 9(6):712–726.

"Trafficking in Persons Report 2006." 2006. *Stop Trafficking! Anti-Human Trafficking Newsletter*, 4(7).

Tremblay, G. 1992. "Is Quebec Culture Doomed to Become American?" *Canadian Journal of Communication* 17. Retrieved September 11, 2006 (http://www.cjc-online.ca/viewarticle .php?id=86&layout=html).

Tung, C. 2000. "The Cost of Caring: The Social Reproductive Labor of Filipina Live-In Home Health Caregivers." *Frontiers: A Journal of Women's Studies* 21(1/2):61–82.

Turpin, J. and L. A. Lorentzen, eds. 1996. *The Gendered New World Order: Militarism, Development, and the Environment*. New York: Routledge.

UNESCO. 1999. *Statistical Yearbook, 1999 (updated 2005)*. Montréal, Quebec, Canada: United Nations Educational, Scientific and Cultural Organization, Institute for Statistics. Retrieved July 3, 2006 (http://www.uis.unesco .org/TEMPLATE/html/CultAndCom/Table_ IV _S_3.html).

———. 2003. *Proceedings of the International Symposium on Culture Statistics, Montréal, 21 to 23 October 2002*. Montréal, Quebec, Canada: United Nations Educational, Scientific and Cultural Organization, Institute for Statistics. Retrieved July 7, 2006 (http:// www.uis.unesco.org/ev_en .php?ID=5509_ 201& ID2=DO_TOPIC).

———. 2005. *International Flows of Selected Cultural Goods and Services, 1994–2003: Defining and Capturing the Flows of Global Cultural Trade*. Montreal, Quebec, Canada: United Nations Educational, Scientific and Cultural Organization, Institute for Statistics. Retrieved July 3, 2006 (http:// www .uis.unesco.org/ev_en.php?ID=6383_201& ID2=DO_TOPIC).

UNICEF. 2000. *Protocol to Prevent, Suppress and Punish Trafficking in Persons, Especially Women and Children, Supplementing the United Nations Convention Against Transnational Organized Crime*. New York: United Nations.

———. 2004. *Trafficking in Human Beings, Especially Women and Children in Africa*. Florence, Italy: Innocenti Insight.

United Nations. 1948. Universal Declaration of Human Rights. Retrieved November 19, 2006 (http://www.un.org/Overview/rights .htm).

———. 1997. *Working Towards a More Gender Equitable Macro-Economic Agenda*. Report of a conference held in Rajendrapur, Bangladesh, November 26–28. Geneva, Switzerland: United Nations Research Institute for Social Development.

———. 1998. *International Day of Families, 15 May 1998*. Retrieved November 19, 2006 (http://www.un.org/esa/socdev/family/IntObs/ IDF/Backgrounders/Backg98.htm).

———. 1998/1999 (updated). *United Nations Workshop on Technology and Families Report*. New York: United Nations Retrieved December 18, 2006 (http://www .un.org/esa/socdev/family/Meetings/FamTech/ FamTec.htm).

———. 1999a. *Assessing the Status of Women: A Guide to Reporting Under the Convention on the Elimination of All Forms of Discrimination Against Women*. New York: United Nations Division for the Advancement of Women, Department of Social and Economic Affairs.

———. 1999b. *Globalization with a Human Face*. Retrieved June 1, 2006 (http://hdr .undp.org/reports/global/ 1999/en/).

———. 2003. *Families in the Process of Development*. New York: United Nations Division for Social Policy and Development. Retrieved November 21, 2005 (http://www .un.org/esa/socdev/family).

———. 2005a. *The Role of Information and Communication Technologies in Global Development: Analysis and Policy Recommendations*. New York: United Nations External Publications Office.

———. 2005b. UN Millennium Development Goals. New York: United Nations Department of Public Information. Retrieved July 25, 2006 (http:// www.un .org/millenniumgoals/).

————. 2005c. *World Population Prospects: The 2004 Revision.* New York: United Nations Population Division. Retrieved July 7, 2006 (http://esa.un.org/unpp/ p2k0data.asp).

United Nations Programme on the Family. 2003a. *Families in the Process of Development: Major Trends Affecting Families World-Wide.* Retrieved June 1, 2006 (http://www.un.org/esa/socdev/family/majortrends .htm).

————. 2003b. *International Observances on the Family.* Retrieved June 1, 2006 (http://www.un.org/esa/socdev/family/ majortrends.htm).

Upton, R. 2003. "'Women Have No Tribe': Connecting Carework, Gender, and Migration in an Era of HIV/AIDS in Botswana." *Gender & Society* 17(2): 314–322.

U.S. Census Bureau. 2006. *Statistical Abstract of the United States: 2006.* Table 6: Immigrants Admitted by Class of Admissions: 1990 to 2004. Washington, D.C.: United States Government Printing Office.

U.S. Holocaust Memorial Museum. 2006a. "Beyond Every Name a Story: Miriam [Rot] Eshel. Part I—Introduction." Retrieved December 31, 2006 (http:// www.ushmm .org/wlc/en/).

————. 2006b. "Beyond Every Name a Story: Miriam [Rot] Eshel. Part II—After the Holocaust." Retrieved December 31, 2006 (http://www. ushmm.org/wlc/en/).

————. 2006c. "Beyond Every Name a Story: Miriam [Rot] Eshel. Whence Your Strength?" Retrieved December 31, 2006 (http://www .ushmm.org/ wlc/en/).

————. 2006d. "Burundi Overview." Retrieved December 31, 2006 from U.S.(http://www .ushmm.org/conscience/alert/burundi/ contents/ 01-overview/).

————. 2006e. "Chechnya Overview." Retrieved December 31, 2006 from U.S. (http:// www.ushmm.org/conscience/alert/chechnya/ contents/01-overview/).

————. 2006f. "Children." Retrieved December 31, 2006 (http://www.ushmm.org/wlc/article .php?lang=en& ModuleId=10005142).

————. 2006g. "D.R. Congo Overview." Retrieved December 31, 2006 (http:// www .ushmm.org/conscience/alert/congo/contents/ 01-overview/).

————. 2006h. "The Holocaust." Retrieved December 31, 2006 (http://www. ushmm .org/wlc/article/php?lang=en& ModuleId+ 10005143).

————. 2006i. "Rwanda Overview." Retrieved December 31, 2006 (http://www.ushmm .org/conscience/alert/rwanda/contents/ 01-overview/).

————. 2006j. "Sudan: Darfur Overview." Retrieved December 31, 2006 (http:// www .ushmm.org/conscience/alert/darfur/ contents/01-overview/).

————. 2006k. "What is Genocide?" Retrieved December 31, 2006 (http:// www.ushmm .org/conscience/history/what/).

Vanek, J. 1974. "Time Spent in Housework." *Scientific American* 231(November): 116–120.

Vélez-Ibáñez, C. G. 2004. "Regions of Refuge in the United States: Issues, Problems, and Concerns for the Future of Mexican-Origin Populations in the United States." *Human Organization* 63(1):1–20.

Veseth, M. 2005. *Globaloney: Unraveling the Myths of Globalization.* Lanham, MA: Rowman and Littlefield.

Vincent, S. 2000. "Flexible Families: Capitalist Development and Crisis in Rural Peru." *Journal of Comparative Family Studies* 31(2):155–170.

Wainwright, M. 2006. "Tribunal Dismisses Case of Muslim Woman Ordered Not to Teach in Veil." *Manchester Guardian* (October 20). Retrieved November 17, 2006 (http:// education.guardian.co.uk/schools/story/ 0,,1927251,00.html).

Wallerstein, I. 1990. "Culture as the Ideological Battleground of the Modern World-System." *Theory, Culture & Society* 7:31–55.

————. 1996. *Historical Capitalism with Capitalist Civilization.* New York: W. W. Norton.

Walsh, D. 2006. "The Third Parent: What Do We Know? And What Do We Need to Know About the Role Popular Media Plays in Family Process?" Plenary address presented at the annual meeting of the National Council on Family Relations, November, Minneapolis, MN.

"War Crimes Court." 2007. *Minneapolis* (MN) *Star Tribune*, January 29, p. A15.

Ward, K. 1990. "Introduction and Overview." Pp. 1–24 in *Women Workers and Global*

Restructuring, edited by K. Ward. Ithaca, NY: Industrial and Labor Relations Press of Cornell University.

Waters, M. 1994. "Ethnic and Racial Identities Among Second-Generation Black Immigrants in New York City." *International Immigration Review* 28(4):795–820.

West, E. 2004. *Chains of Love: Slave Couples in Antebellum South Carolina.* Urbana: University of Illinois Press.

White, J. M. 2005. *Advancing Family Theories.* Thousand Oaks, CA: Sage.

White, J. M. and D. M. Klein. 2002. *Family Theories: An Introduction.* Thousand Oaks, CA: Sage.

White, L. 2004. "True Confessions." *Journal of Women's History* 15(4): 142–144.

Williams, R. M. 1993. "Race, Deconstruction, and the Emergent Agenda of Feminist Economic Theory." Pp. 144–152 in *Beyond Economic Man: Feminist Theory and Economics*, edited by M. A. Ferber and J. A. Nelson. Chicago, IL: University of Chicago Press.

Williams, T. K. 1991. "Marriage Between Japanese Women and U.S. Servicemen Since World War II." *Amerasia Journal* 17(1): 135–154.

Wilson, S., G. Meagher, R. Gibson, D. Denemark, and M. Western. 2005. *Australian Social Attitudes: The First Report.* Sydney: University of New South Wales.

Wolton, D. 1998. *Au dela de l'Internet.* (Over the Internet.) Paris: La Decouverte.

World Bank. 1992. *Population and the World Bank: Implications from Eight Case Studies.* Washington, D.C.: World Bank. As cited in Purewal, 2001.

World Health Organization. 2003. "HIV/AIDS." Retrieved June 1, 2006 (http://www.who.int/ceh/risks/otherisks/en/index2.html).

Wrigley, J. 1995. *Other People's Children: An Intimate Account of the Dilemmas Facing Middle-Class Parents and the Women They Hire to Raise Their Children.* New York: Basic Books.

Yang, H. 1997. "Revisiting the Issue of Korean 'Military Comfort Women': The Question of Truth and Positionality." *Positions* 5(1): 1–71.

Yi, Z. 2002. "A Demographic Analysis of Family Households in China, 1982–1995." *Journal of Comparative Family Studies* 33(1):15–34.

Yongnyŏ, Y. 1995. "I Thought I Would Die." Pp. 143–150 in *True Stories of the Korean Comfort Women*, edited by K. Howard. London: Cassell.

Yŏngsuk, Y. 1995. "I Will No Longer Harbor Resentment." Pp. 50–57 in *True Stories of the Korean Comfort Women*, edited by K. Howard. London: Cassell.

Youngsu, Y. 1995. "Return My Youth to Me." Pp. 88–94 in *True Stories of the Korean Comfort Women*, edited by K. Howard. London: Cassell.

Zimmerman, M. K., J. S. Litt, and C. E. Bose. 2006a. *Global Dimensions of Gender and Carework.* Stanford, CA: Stanford University Press.

———. 2006b. "Globalization and Multiple Crises of Care." Pp. 9–29 in *Global Dimensions of Gender and Carework*, by M. K. Zimmerman, J. S. Litt, and C. E. Bose. Stanford, CA: Stanford University Press.

INDEX